# VIGILANTES AND LYNCH MOBS

Lisa Arellano

# VIGILANTES AND LYNCH MOBS

## Narratives of Community and Nation

TEMPLE UNIVERSITY PRESS
PHILADELPHIA

TEMPLE UNIVERSITY PRESS
Philadelphia, Pennsylvania 19122
*www.temple.edu/tempress*

Library of Congress Cataloging-in-Publication Data

Arellano, Lisa, 1968–
   Vigilantes and lynch mobs : narratives of community and nation / Lisa Arellano.
      p. cm.
   Originally presented as the author's dissertation at Stanford University.
   Includes bibliographical references and index.
      ISBN 978-1-4399-0844-0 (cloth : alk. paper) — ISBN 978-1-4399-0845-7 (pbk. : alk. paper) —
   ISBN 978-1-4399-0846-4 (e-book)   1. Lynching—United States.   2. Vigilantes—United States.
   I. Title.
   HV6457.A74 2012
      364.1'34—dc23

                                                                              2012003235

♾ The paper used in this publication meets the requirements of the American National Standard for
Information Sciences—Permanence of Paper for Printed Library Materials, ANSI Z39.48-1992

Printed in the United States of America

2 4 6 8 9 7 5 3 1

*For Carleen*

# Contents

# Acknowledgments

When we are lucky, interdisciplinarity finds us at improbable but spectacular intellectual crossings; the graduate program in Modern Thought and Literature at Stanford University, where this book was first a dissertation, enabled a number of such intersections. My dissertation committee of Hans (Sepp) Gumbrecht, Richard White, and Arnold Rampersad was one, and I am grateful for the role each of them played in this project's development. In particular, I thank Sepp for the essay that drew me to his door and for the myriad ways he fulfilled his role as my advisor thereafter. I thank Richard White for recognizing what I wanted to do in this project and for helping me figure out how it might actually be done. I consider myself to be singularly lucky to have had the chance to work with him.

Before anyone could help me finish, my earliest graduate mentors at San Francisco State University helped me to begin—Sandra Luft, Arturo Arias, and Mary Scott enabled, in all respects, my choice to be a scholar. My initial work at Stanford was significantly influenced by Yvonne Yarbro-Bejarano, Janet Halley, and Estelle Freedman. I owe a particular intellectual debt of gratitude to Michael Thompson—when I wandered into his class during my first year of graduate school, I thought of myself as a theorist; by the time the semester was over, I really wanted to be a historian. I spent my final two years at Stanford at the Center for Comparative Studies in Race and Ethnicity and in the Program in Feminist Studies. Paula Moya's mentorship and friendship during this period taught me all of the best things I know about how to survive in this profession. I also taught my first courses during those years, and

I am quite convinced that it was the joy of working in those classrooms that motivated me to finish graduate school so that I could make teaching my life's work. Elizabeth Tallent, Monica Moore, and Margaret Tompkins also played significant roles in my time at Stanford and contributed materially to my ability to move on.

Throughout my time in graduate school, I was surrounded by incredibly talented people. To this day, I have an abiding respect for them as scholars and individuals. In writing groups, readings groups, classrooms, and hallways, my graduate school peers helped me to become a better intellectual in every sense of the word. I thank, in particular, Yael Ben-Zvi, Raúl Coronado, Celine Parreñas Shimizu, and Mishuana Goeman. Ardel Thomas read, and reread, drafts and chapters, asking only that I pay the favor forward; I continue to try. Alicia Chavez and Shelley Lee welcomed me into their graduate history world and became my friends and the best sort of intellectual playmates. Nicole Fleetwood and Kyla Wazana Thompkins remain colleagues I admire and friends I value—they have helped me materially to finish this book, and they also enable me to feel real joy in the friendships that this work brings with it. And most of all, of course, I thank Bakirathi Mani. I can scarcely remember a moment of this process when she was not standing next to me, and that has much to do with why it has been such a magnificent ride.

As I tally my debts for this project, one of the greatest is to my current institutional home, Colby College. Because this book has been so closely tied to my quest for tenure, its completion has been propelled by certain professional anxieties and expectations. And while that may not have been altogether pleasant in the happening, I find myself now oddly grateful to the institution and culture that demanded that I finish. Colby also provided significant support for this project through a pre-tenure leave, start-up research funding, and two summers' worth of divisional grants. More significantly, I have benefited from work in writing groups with Margaret McFadden, Emma Garcia, Laura Saltz, and Chandra Bhimull. I have also worked with four remarkable research assistants: Liz Doran, Heather Pratt, Hali Castleman, and Jessica Villella. Last, I benefited from the help of a former Colby colleague, Jason Opal, and the mentorship of Marc Stein. Both of these individuals offered substantive and crucial feedback during my final round of work with the manuscript and helped me materially in the process of publication.

Before and after any of this, I have a personal support team of remarkable quality—my families of origin and choice cheered me off to and through graduate school, sustained me through the distance and challenges of a first job, and remain generous in their willingness to celebrate and console as circumstances require. Joan Bristol went through all of this first and then was unendingly generous is doing everything she could to help me along in my own journey. And because I cannot thank Colleen and Terry (or Michael and Danny) enough, I will simply remind them that they are at the center of my heart and my happiness.

Over the years it has taken me to complete this book, my sister has served as both incomparably able tech support and cheerleader—she has resolved my pagination dilemmas and frustration with equal good cheer. My mother not only kept me company on a number of the early archive trips; she enthusiastically became the best research assistant imaginable. This "job" once included copying an out-of-print book for me—a task that required feeding dimes into an antiquated Xerox machine in the basement of a library. I found her late one afternoon painstakingly filling in the missing letters along the margin where the machine had failed to copy the book. I needed her company on those trips, and it turned out I needed those words and letters along the margin; I am profoundly grateful for both.

And, finally, I thank my partner, Carleen Mandolfo. Confronted by her belief in me, I could not help but finish. Now that this book is done, my dedication of the project to her marks, most of all, my excitement about what comes next.

# Introduction

*History, Memory, and Narrative*

I magine a lifeless body hanging from a noose. This body is a marker not of what Michel Foucault calls the state's power over life and death but, rather, of the power of unsanctioned citizens to "execute" a fellow citizen in the name of justice and order.[1] This is, in other words, a *lynched* body. This book begins with this body and its simultaneous occurrence in two radically different contemporary American contexts. Each of the subsequent chapters in this book seeks to illuminate some aspect of how we have come to understand the significance and meaning of this body through narrative.

The first occurrence is in an image belonging to *Without Sanctuary*—a collection of 101 such images documenting sixty-five different lynchings.[2] This monumental project (exhibit, website, and book) is centrally concerned with lynching in the Jim Crow South and the significance of this history with respect to the broader history of racial violence in the United States. The body in the image is that of a southern black man whom we necessarily read as the victim of a larger social system of white racial exclusion, hatred, and denigration. This body represents the most familiar aspect of lynching in the American past and is met with rage and horror; the story of southern racial lynching, while no longer necessarily surprising, has appropriately not ceased to be shocking. *Without Sanctuary* documents the murderous and bloodthirsty violence lynch mobs enacted on (predominantly) black southern men.

The second body belongs to a civic celebration in Helena, Montana—the Vigilante Parade.[3] It is not a photographed body like those in *Without Sanctuary*; it is a real body—a teenager suspended from a harness and rope in order to *appear* lifeless. This body is on a float that is in a parade honoring legends of local history and narratives of a heroic frontier past. This is a western white male body made meaningful in this context as the by-product of frontier lawlessness and heroic vigilantism. The body in the parade produces little response at all. Vigilantes and those they targeted are staid images in this context of frontier nostalgia—neither shocking nor surprising. Any recreation of the "Wild West" predictably includes some saloon gals, bonneted ladies, and representations of the rough-and-tumble "hang 'em high" crowd.

The topic and tone of *Without Sanctuary* are familiar. The vast majority of lynching scholarship in the past two decades has focused on lynching in the southern states and on the legacy of this devastating racial violence.[4] In fact, the treatment of lynching as the exemplar of racial inequality and violence is over a century old. Beginning with Ida B. Wells,[5] writers have worked to create a context of meaning for the lynching images in *Without Sanctuary*. While quite different, the Vigilante Parade in Montana has a long-standing context as well. In this case the background is also over a century old, though it originates in the nineteenth-century fascination with the American frontier. Though significantly smaller, there is also a body of scholarship focused on frontier vigilantism and on lynching within the larger context of frontier mythology.[6]

In many obvious respects the exhibit and the parade are different. *Without Sanctuary* images depict real lynchings; the bodies in the photographs and postcards in the collection are real historical bodies that endured, in many cases, unimaginable torture and, in all cases, public death. The bodies in the parade are merely simulations—markers of real historical bodies but simulations nonetheless. *Without Sanctuary* is a multimedia, professionally curated collection of artifacts that has drawn a global viewership; the Vigilante Parade is a small-town civic festival produced by high school students for an audience of grade school children and their parents. One is a story primarily concerned with race; the other is not. But while the particulars of each of these present-day engagements with the past are quite different, the bodies depicted in each represent the same violent practice of lynching. In *Regarding the Pain of Others*, Susan Sontag addresses the function of images of suffering, including those contained in the *Without Sanctuary* collection.[7] Most relevant here is Sontag's important distinction between the illusion of "collective memory" and the imperative for "collective instruction."[8] Sontag writes, "Ideologies create substantiating archives of images, representative images, which encapsulate common thoughts, feelings."[9] The *Without Sanctuary* images function as Sontag describes, as both image archive and as marker of what Sontag calls a "stipulation" to understand the past contained within the images as significant and specifically meaningful. But this is no less true of the bodies in the

Vigilante Parade. All of these bodies come from the same public historical present, and yet they present—and represent—entirely different stories about the American past.[10] This book seeks to explain this simultaneous difference and sameness through a focus on lynching stories—the narratives that made, and in some sense continue to make, these violent practices legible and meaningful in particular ways.

Traditionally, multiregional work on lynching has attempted to explain how one potentially legitimate practice (frontier vigilantism) evolved into another, wholly illegitimate one (southern lynching).[11] More recently, scholars have begun to question this regional and temporal bifurcation and to challenge the favorable regard historians have held for vigilantes outside of the post-Reconstruction South. Ken Gonzalez-Day relinks the two fractured histories by foregrounding the centrality of race in western lynching;[12] Christopher Waldrep organizes his broad etymological study around the word, or concept, of lynching itself;[13] and Michael Pfeifer analyzes lynching, or what he calls "rough justice," as an evolving conflict between community-based and often ritualized retribution and an emerging, state-sponsored criminal justice system.[14] Like each of these scholars I seek to challenge the conventional bifurcation of lynching history by period and region. There are moments in my own work on vigilantism and lynching violence when I draw on these scholars' arguments about collective meaning making, racial violence, and disputes over the role of an emerging state. My primary focus, however, is on a unique narrative form and the ways that it functioned to constitute particular practices *as lynching*. My work is most closely aligned with Waldrep's project in that we are both attentive to the ways in which the meaning, or legitimacy, of lynching was the subject of cultural debate, and we both identify a formal narrative associated with vigilante self-legitimation. But my focus in this project is both more narrow (insofar as I am principally interested in the narratives used by vigilantes themselves, whereas Waldrep works with a much broader range of textual sources) and slightly broader (insofar as I focus on the formal aspects of narratives from an earlier period than Waldrep, who concentrates on the San Francisco vigilantes from the 1850s).[15] Further, whereas Waldrep masterfully draws on a range of narrative practices, from journalism to political rhetoric, I am specifically interested in the *formal* narrative construction that (I argue) was adjacent, if not simultaneous to, violence and that was essential to making the violence meaningful.

I understand my entry into the growing conversation about lynching and vigilantism as one that focuses on neither people nor practices but on the unique way in which narratives function materially to constitute both. So while in some sense this is a book about lynching and vigilantism, I don't claim to offer a definitive account of either; rather, I hope to provide an extended and archivally grounded account of the unique and real function of narrative formation and particularly how a set of narrative formations function(ed) to legitimate and or delegitimize forms of violence. The specific narrative form I attend to in this project is arguably historically unique—the archival sources I work with suggest as much. At the same time, I hope to uncover a larger set of conceptual connections that enable us to better understand how central narrative forms are in constituting and legitimating violence and in enabling the violent enforcement of social categories.

I begin by focusing on the ways that vigilantes in the early nineteenth century relied on narratives of justification to make their violent practices recognizable and legitimate to themselves and those around them. I demonstrate the ways that the self-aggrandizing and sometimes inaccurate stories vigilantes told about themselves came to dominate histories of frontier localities and of the larger regional West. I explain the ways that vigilante narratives have been used to illustrate our most idealized democratic aspirations and our darkest, most exclusionary impulses. This is a book about the power of stories—about the ways that narratives make and unmake both our past and our present. This introductory chapter lays out the ways that this project engages with narrative. The next section focuses on three lynching stories by Mark Twain—two drawn from *Roughing It* and one from "The United States of Lyncherdom." These accounts introduce many of the formal characteristics of lynching stories more generally, including the defining force of region on these narratives.

## The Stories We Are Told

In 1870, Mark Twain was in the midst of writing *Roughing It*, a semiautobiographical account of his travels in the West. Consistent with expectations of the popular genre of western adventure writing, Twain wanted to include a desperado, a larger-than-life frontier "bad guy." Luckily, Twain had met such a character a decade earlier during his travels on the Overland Express—the infamous desperado J. A. Slade. By many accounts (including Twain's), Slade was a striking character—famous for carrying in his vest pocket the ear of a man he once murdered. At the same time, Slade was a "conundrum" for Twain—for despite his chilling reputation, Twain had met Slade one day at breakfast during his travels and couldn't reconcile Slade the man with Slade the legend:

> He was so friendly and so gentle-spoken that I warmed to him in spite
> of his awful history. It was hardly possible to realize that this pleasant

person was the pitiless scourge of the outlaws, the raw-head-bloody-bones the nursing mothers of the mountains terrified their children with.[16]

The conundrum of Slade must have grown even more intriguing for Twain when word reached him that Slade had been lynched in a Montana mining community. Had Slade been, to borrow one of Twain's own descriptive phrases, a "humanized fragment of the original devil," or had he been a misunderstood man who fell victim to a murderous mob?[17] Like all lynching stories, Twain's story about Slade in *Roughing It* turns on these very questions.

To write his account, Twain set about researching Slade, writing to his brother and traveling companion, Orion Clemmens: "Torture your memory & write down in minute detail every fact & exploit in the desperado Slade's life that we heard on the Overland—& also describe his appearance & conversation as we saw him at Rocky Ridge station at breakfast."[18] Orion's response could hardly have set Twain's mind at ease. He wrote:

> I don't know how he came to leave that road, but he went to Montana, where he was ~~worked up into~~ hanged by a vigilance committee. I believe his offence was belonging to a gang of horse thieves and robbers, with some particular murder laid to his charge. On the scaffold he was unmanned by terror and begged piteously for his life.[19]

Not satisfied with his own, or his brother's, recollections, Twain wrote as well to Hezekiah Hosmer, a Montana territorial judge and resident of the town where Slade was lynched: "Four or five years ago a righteous Vigilance Committee in your city hanged a casual acquaintance of mine named Slade. . . . Now I am writing a book . . . and . . . I thought I would rescue my late friend Slade from oblivion & set a sympathetic public to weeping for him."[20] Specifically, Twain wanted Hosmer to send him local newspapers from the day Slade was killed. The principal source of Twain's information on Slade, however, ended up being Thomas Dimsdale's *The Vigilantes of Montana or Popular Justice in the Rocky Mountains: Being a Correct and Impartial Narrative of the Chase, Trial, Capture, and Execution of Henry Plummer's Road Agent Band*.[21] Twain never resolved the conundrum of Slade. His two chapters on Slade's lynching in *Roughing It* offer contradictory accounts of the famous desperado and of his lynching at the hands of the Montana vigilantes.

Twain first offers a story of the legendary outlaw in chapter 10, wherein he acknowledges that Slade will serve in the text as an exemplary prototype: "In order that the Eastern reader may have a clear conception of what a Rocky

Mountain desperado is, in his highest state of development, I will reduce all this mass of overland gossip to one straightforward narrative, and present it in the following shape."[22] Twain's story of Slade, true to his promise to metonymize the legend of the outlaw, includes Slade's time as a station agent, trainmaster, Indian fighter, and "matchless marksman." The story details many of the worst rumors about Slade's violent exploits, including his propensity for cutting off his enemies' ears and his fatal willingness to cheat at gunfights. The colorful account wraps up with Twain's surprise over the genteel Slade's appearance at a breakfast table in the passage cited above. Overall, the story serves to offer eastern readers not only a vivid idea of what a frontier desperado might be like, as Twain claims, but a larger impression of frontier lawlessness and violence. In fact, Twain's description of the Rocky Mountain region where Slade worked as a station agent is as colorful and fanciful as Slade's own reputation:

> It was the very paradise of outlaws and desperadoes. There was absolutely no semblance of law there. Violence was the rule. Force was the only recognized authority. The commonest misunderstandings were settled on the spot with the revolver or the knife. Murders were done in open day, and with sparkling frequency, and nobody thought of inquiring into them.[23]

As a lynching narrative, Twain's story of Slade is familiar both through reference to a hyperbolically dangerous outlaw individual *and* through a narration of a hyperbolically lawless and deadly frontier environment. Ultimately, it is a story about the extraordinary criminality of a region told through the extraordinary criminality of one man.

But lynching narratives are never as simple as Twain's first chapter suggests; the next chapter, also focused on Slade, is both more troubling and more complicated. This second account is not exclusively Twain's; the chapter is taken verbatim from Dimsdale's account—a book Twain describes as a "bloodthirstily interesting little Montana book"—and is distinguished only by Twain's judicious italicization.[24] This second Slade, the one described by Dimsdale, is principally defined by his utter inability to hold liquor, as opposed to more legend-making desperado behavior. In fact, Dimsdale specifically says "[Slade] was never accused, or even suspected, of either murder or robbery, committed in this Territory." Dimsdale further notes that "J. A. Slade was himself . . . a Vigilante; he openly boasted of it, and said he knew all that they knew."[25] Of course, this was an unfortunate misjudgment on Slade's behalf, for what he *didn't* know was that the vigilance committee in Alder Gulch had grown weary of his drunken exploits and that many of the miners in the community had lost tolerance for his behavior. Slade was locally infamous for drunken pranks: "On many occasions he would ride his horse into stores, break up bars, toss the scales out of doors and use most insulting language to parties present."[26] On Slade's last night of drunken carousing, "he and his companions had made the town a perfect Hell." He had ridden into one town store and, upon being asked to leave, had threatened to kill the owner. He had concluded his antics by leading his horse into a saloon and, "buying a bottle of wine, . . . tried to make the animal drink it."[27] As these behaviors were "not considered an uncommon performance," it is easy enough to see why the local store owners and saloon keepers had had more than enough of the drunken Slade and his gang of ruffian pals. On the fatal night, one of the vigilantes attempted to arrest Slade, presenting him with the vigilantes' self-authorized warrant, but he "became uncontrollably furious, and seizing the writ, he tore it up, threw it on the ground and stomped on it."[28]

Twain's second story about Slade is complicated precisely because it turns on this detail of tearing the vigilantes' writ (as recounted by Dimsdale and emphasized by Twain's later italicization). Slade's blatant disregard for the sheriff's authority, according to Dimsdale, left him

> the master of the situation and the conqueror of the courts, law and law-makers. This was a declaration of war, and was so accepted. The Vigilance Committee now felt that the question of social order and preponderance of the law of the law-abiding citizens had then and there to be decided.[29]

In other words, Slade did not become a target of the vigilance committee because he had committed one of the crimes for which vigilantes claimed to target men—robbery or murder—and he did not become a target because he had destroyed local stores, threatened local saloon keepers, or been wildly drunk and disorderly as a point of common practice. He became a target of the vigilantes, the committee of which he himself was a member, because he threatened the capacity of the vigilantes to assume power in, and over, their community. Slade's flagrant (and ultimately deadly) disregard for the vigilantes' authority was further expressed after he was approached by one committee member and ordered to go home.

> Still being intoxicated . . . [Slade] seemed to have forgotten the warning that he had received and became again uproarious, shouting the name of a well-known courtesan in company with those of two men who he

considered heads of the [vigilante] committee, as a sort of challenge; perhaps, however, as a simple act of bravado.[30]

It really didn't matter what Slade's intentions were by this point—for simple bravado or not, he had made the deadly mistake of challenging the self-asserted authority of the vigilantes. The question of authority was particularly complicated in this mining community. There was a state-sanctioned system of law and order, replete with officers, but the local vigilance committee didn't *like* the state-sanctioned system. In fact, they were convinced that many of the officers were members of the criminal gang they sought to control. Slade's disregard for the vigilantes' authority was singularly dangerous in the context of this committee's tenuous but, in their minds, crucial power in the community. In the end, Slade was hanged by his friends and vigilante compatriots because he was defiant.

These two chapters in Twain's *Roughing It* highlight a few different things about the way lynching narratives work. The first chapter, notably, focuses on Slade as a criminal and is mostly shaped by the idea that a lynching story is primarily a story about the criminal being lynched. In this version, we are encouraged to believe that Slade, "the pitiless scourge of the outlaws, the raw-head-bloody-bones the nursing mothers of the mountains terrified their children with," deserves the fate that befalls him. The second story, however, is more about the vigilance committee and suggests that a lynching story primarily expresses the social investments of those doing the lynching. We are left wondering about Slade's actual guilt and/or the legitimacy of his "execution" because Twain's second account reveals that the local vigilantes had a deadly investment in maintaining their control in a community.

Twain's specific conundrum concerning Slade was that the man seemed to embody such oppositional characteristics. He was, Twain wrote, a "bloody, desperate, kindly-mannered, urbane gentleman, who never hesitated to warn his most ruffianly enemies that he would kill them."[31] But the conundrum he leaves us with about Slade is more interesting. Are lynching stories about criminality, or are lynching stories about the social investments of vigilantes? To a great extent, these two questions have traditionally divided lynching narratives into two distinct strands: the field of western history favoring the former and studies of southern lynching focusing on the latter. Because the two fields have long asked very different questions, until quite recently scholarship on lynching and vigilantism has evolved along two parallel and relatively unrelated lines. Twain gives us back-to-back but quite different accounts of the same lynching, which demonstrates the degree to which narrative produces what we know, or think we know, about lynching in the past.

The question of which of Twain's accounts is more accurate becomes secondary in this context. As revealed through even brief excerpts of Twain's correspondence, and by his use of the hardly neutral account written by Dimsdale, stories about Slade and his lynching were largely produced by rumor and hearsay.

What we know and think about lynching in the past has a great deal to do with what we think and know about lynching in the present. The vigilantes who lynched Slade are the same vigilantes celebrated by the high school students in the present-day Vigilante Parade in Helena, Montana. Within the context of Twain's first story about Slade, the parade makes a certain kind of sense, acting as a celebration of long-dead city fathers who faced down ear-collecting local outlaws on behalf of their upright fellow citizens and families. But a celebration of the vigilantes in the second story seems rather different; *these* vigilantes hanged one of their friends because he wouldn't accede to their self-sanctioned rule over the community. Granted, Slade may have been obnoxious and unruly, but the disproportionate reaction of the vigilantes makes them a more questionable object of historical celebration.

Twain set out to write the account in *Roughing It* to "rescue [his] late friend Slade from oblivion & set a sympathetic public to weeping for him." But in 1901, Twain set out to write about lynching with very different motivations and changed ideas about the function of the lynching narrative. In his essay "The United States of Lyncherdom" he wrote:

> A much-talked-of lynching will infallibly produce other lynchings here and there and yonder, and . . . in time these will breed a mania, a fashion; a fashion which will spread wide and wider, year by year, covering state after state, as with an advancing disease.[32]

By the time he wrote the essay, the memorial aspirations of his stories about Slade in *Roughing It* had been replaced by a much keener understanding of the extent to which a lynching story—particularly a lynching story that advances the act of lynching as heroic—will invite, encourage, and legitimate other acts of lynching violence. And by the time of this essay, lynching was no longer for Twain the practice of "a righteous vigilance committee," as it had been when he had researched Slade's lynching. Even the ambiguities associated with the two contradictory accounts in *Roughing It* had been replaced by Twain's fervent belief that lynching is an act of cowardice and a source of shame. The essay opens with his anguish about the association of his home state, Missouri, with the practice of lynching. He writes, "And so, Missouri has fallen, that great state! Certain of her children have joined the lynchers, and the smirch is upon the rest of us."[33] This characterization of lynching as shameful is markedly different from Twain's earlier work on the subject in *Roughing It* and introduces part of what is regionally distinct about narratives about southern lynching.[34]

The first difference, of course, is the kind of generality with which the essay opens. Slade, in *Roughing It*, is the metonym for frontier lawlessness and desperado lore more broadly. In the later essay, Twain uses a recent lynching in Pierce City, Missouri, to illustrate the shame and cowardice of lynching itself.[35] Consistent with the general differences between frontier and southern lynching stories, this reflects the degree to which the essay focuses, throughout, on the perverse motivations of those who lynched rather than on the crimes or misdeeds of those who were lynched. If the second account of Slade in *Roughing It* raises the possibility that vigilante practice might be related to the social and cultural motivations of lynchers, this possibility is absolute in Twain's assessment of the South. Twain goes on to argue that people participate in, or fail to stop, lynchings primarily because they are unable to demonstrate the courage or independence to do otherwise.

"The United States of Lyncherdom" not only is interesting because of Twain's vehement condemnation of lynching; the essay also reveals the ways that lynching stories are shaped by regionally distinct figures and myths. In *Roughing It*, Slade was Twain's stand-in for a specifically regional figure—the western desperado or outlaw. The lynching events at the center of "The United States of Lyncherdom" rely on a regionally specific idea as well, though Twain seems unaware of his own reliance on mythical figures. In brief, Twain describes "the tragedy" as follows:

> On a Sunday afternoon a young white woman who had started alone from church was found murdered. . . . Although it was a region of churches and schools the people rose, lynched three negroes—two of them very aged ones—burned out five negro households, and drove thirty negro families into the woods. . . . [A] thousand provocations are no defense. The Pierce City people had bitter provocation—indeed, as revealed by certain of the particulars, the bitterest of all provocations— but no matter.[36]

Twain's account here is a familiar story: A vulnerable southern white woman is sexually assaulted by one or more black men, and an outraged community reacts swiftly and violently to the crime. He refers to this "bitterest provocation" again later in the essay, asking, "Why has lynching, with various barbaric accompaniments, become a favorite regulator in cases of 'the unusual crime' in several parts of the country?"[37]

Twain's assertions notwithstanding, neither the coroner's jury report nor the undertaker in Pierce City documented any evidence of sexual assault—there was no "unusual crime" or "bitterest provocation" associated with the death of the young Gazelle Wild.[38] But even at the time of the murder, rumors of rape circulated in conjunction with Wild's death. One of the men lynched for the crime, Will Godley, had been convicted of a prior rape but released from prison after serving only two years of a ten-year sentence. Circulating cultural hysteria about black rapists may have been amplified by perceptions of an anemic response to Godley's past crime.[39] Indeed, so sure were community members about Godley's status as a "miscreant" rapist that two other young white women stepped forward after Godley's arrest to accuse him of attempting to rape them as well—charges that were most likely manufactured in response to rising community outrage.[40] But in terms of narrative significance, it is important to note that while Twain was centrally concerned with decrying both this lynching and lynching more generally, in his attempts to do so, he participated in the very cultural mythology that legitimated and defined the lynching in Pierce City and southern lynching more broadly for the better part of four decades.

In *Revolt against Chivalry: Jessie Daniel Ames and the Women's Campaign against Lynching*, Jacquelyn Dowd Hall looks closely at the southern rape myth in her chapter "A Strange and Bitter Fruit." Her reading of this narrative leads to her frequently cited assertion that "rape and rumors of rape became a kind of acceptable folk pornography in the Bible Belt."[41] Of course, as Hall points out near the end of her chapter, "Despite its tenacity, this southern 'rape complex' was never founded on objective reality. Of the known victims of lynch mobs in the period 1882–1946, only 23 percent were accused of rape or of attempted rape."[42] Ida B. Wells first drew attention to the mythological quality of "the unusual crime" as the cause of southern lynching. In 1892, her editorial pamphlet *Southern Horrors: Lynch Law in All Its Phases* presented a detailed critique of the allegory, arguing persuasively that one of its central functions was to draw attention away from white men's sexual assaults on black women. She stated the case against southern lynchers even more powerfully two years later in *A Red Record*:

> To justify their own barbarism they assume a chivalry which they do not possess. True chivalry respects all womanhood, and no one who reads the record, as it is written in the faces of the million mulattos in the South, will for a minute conceive that the southern white man had a very chivalrous regard for the honor due the women of his own race or respect for the womanhood which circumstances placed in his power.[43]

While Twain's antilynching editorial was moving and persuasive, it was also part and parcel of a narrative formula that harmed, rather than helped, southern black people. Twain was correct when he wrote that "a much-talked-of lynching will infallibly produce other lynchings" and that this talk "will breed a mania, a fashion." Indeed, this was precisely what stories about black men sexually assaulting white women did—produce a mania in which hundreds of black men were brutally murdered within a culture that legitimated these killings according to a largely imaginary, but deeply persuasive, story. But Twain's own accounts were deeply imbedded within and structured by the regionalized narrative frames that enabled and legitimated vigilantes and their lynching practices.

These Twain texts on lynching introduce many of the key features of lynching stories. Some lynching stories, such as the first account of Slade, are focused on the depravity of particular criminals or crime. Almost without fail, these are the kinds of lynching stories told by lynchers or vigilantes. Some lynching stories, such as the second account about Slade, raise the possibility that lynching violence is best understood as an expression of social control or power. This type of story reaches its fullest expression in narratives about lynching in the South, such as Twain's "United States of Lyncherdom" essay. This essay also, however, introduces a third type of lynching story—one wherein lynching is understood as shameful and as a practice of the morally inferior and hateful. Chapter 4 focuses on the ways that this narrative formulation emerged in the writings of antilynching activists, first and most notably Ida B. Wells. All of these stories have regional undertones and themes—so much so that regional expectations about frontier desperadoes and sexual assaults sometimes have as much to do with any given lynching story as real events do.

These Twain texts also draw our attention to one final, and useful, idea about lynching stories. These are all intensely literary accounts of real historical events; accordingly, the texts preclude any easy distinction between their historical and literary aspects. This enables the texts to stand in for something methodologically essential to this project—the idea that historical writing is inevitably, stubbornly, and exquisitely narrative. Neither entirely historical nor literary in any easy sense, *Roughing It* and "The United States of Lyncherdom" effectively introduce the complex narrative space that lynching stories often occupy.

## The Narrative of History versus the History of Narrative

The relationship between narrative and history has been much analyzed, discussed, and debated, so there is no need to rehearse in full these conversations here.[44] Instead, and in order to orient my inquiry with respect to these long-standing debates, I briefly touch on the particularly well-known and widely circulated treatment of the issues of narrative and history found in Hayden White's work.[45] In *Figural Realism*," White states:

> We must begin . . . with the undeniable historical fact that distinctively historical discourses typically produce narrative interpretations of their subject matter. The translation of these discourses into a written form produces a distinctive object, the historiographical text, which in turn can serve as the subject of a philosophical or critical reflection. Whence the distinctions, conventional in modern historical theory, between past reality, which is the historian's object of study; historiography, which is the historian's discourse about this object; and philosophy of history, which is the study of the possible relations obtaining between this object and this discourse.[46]

White's argument contains two ideas that I consider methodologically axiomatic for my work in this book. The first is the premise that historical writing is narrative and therefore comprehensible within models of narrative analysis. The second is the understanding that acknowledging the narrative conditions of historical writing does not equate to denying the reality of past events themselves. As White states in the book, "We must not confuse facts with events. Events happen, whereas facts are constituted by linguistic descriptions."[47] In other words, a narrative understanding of historical writing does not amount to linguistic determinism or relativism. In fact, an engagement with history's narrative processes enables us to see more, rather than less, about the past. By unraveling the layers of narrative constitution succeeding and surrounding an event, we come closer to understanding the event itself. In the most extreme (and arguably erroneous) interpretations, White and his successors seem to be suggesting that the world of the past is merely a discursive construction. White, of course, has always been careful to distinguish what we might understand as a wholly fictional event and an event that actually occurred. White's argument was never that events happen only as they are narrated; rather, he taught us the extraordinarily important lesson that we need to attend to the formulaic (or literary) character of historical writing to understand something about our relationship to past events and the ways that we characterize and narrate these events.

But White's remarkable lesson may best be applied as a general one. We should, of course, be mindful of the ways that our narrative compulsions, conventions, and constraints produce a particular kind of visible (or readable) past, but mindfulness of our narrative proclivities wouldn't necessarily offer a complete or adequate understanding of the relationship between any particular set of historical events and any particular set of historical writings or narratives. Michel-Rolph Trouillot provides an important and illuminating observation in this regard. In *Silencing the Past: Power and the Production of History*, he writes, "Constructivism's dilemma is that *while it can point to the hundreds of stories that illustrate its general claim that narratives are produced, it cannot give a full account of the production of any single narrative*."[48] One important difference between White and Trouillot here concerns the relative placement of the general and the specific or, to be more disciplinarily specific, the literary and the historical. White draws us toward a literary analysis of historical narratives, whereas Trouillot suggests a historical analysis of (possibly literary) historical narratives. The first approach enables us to think about the forms and formulas present in narratives about the past; the second reveals the ways these forms and formulas have changed or remained the same over time.

This book's methodology draws on White's and Trouillot's theories about narrative as the basis of a methodology that is stubbornly as literary as it is historical and as attentive to form as it is to archives.[49] It is certainly the case that vigilante narratives are characterized by particular formulaic, literary conventions. In fact, the repetition of these conventions is precisely what defines certain narratives *as* vigilante narratives. In this sense, these stories about the past are related to one another formally in ways that can best and most easily be understood as literary in the Hayden White sense. At the same time, however, these formulaic literary conventions have changed over time in crucial and defining ways. These changes are what make the narrative aspect of vigilantism *and its specific and particular history* so important, both to the practice and to the location of vigilantism within the larger U.S. culture. This aspect of vigilante narratives can be understood in the Trouillotian sense as demonstrating the evolution of a certain past-constructing set of narratives over time.

This project is engaged, throughout, in two related arguments. The first, which dominates in Chapters 1 and 2, concerns the real historical production and function of a set of narratives that vigilantes relied on to make their actions meaningful and legitimate. The second argument, which is central in Chapters 3 and 4, concerns the ways that different groups of people, over time, developed different investments in reifying, modifying, or undoing these vigilante narratives. Following White, the argument in this book is general—designed to advance our understanding of the ways that stories about the past are, at their core, *stories*. At the same time, this project follows Trouillot in paying close attention to the evolution of a particular genre of stories over time. At the intersection of White and Trouillot lies what Ann Fabian calls "the social history of a cultural form."[50] This project offers such a history of vigilante narrative by taking a literary mode of reading into archives—an approach centrally defined by an understanding of the constitutive function of text and narrative. The documents I work with represent the limit point of our ability to access what White calls "past events" and what are simultaneously "historical" in that, from their inception, they were self-conscious writings about past events. In my own, historiographical work with these texts, I focus on the relationships among the documents, their stories, and past events as well as the ways these documents have been incorporated into our topical, regional, and national histories.

## Archives, Documents, and Narratives

In the course of doing research for this project, I traveled to archives in Louisiana, Texas, Idaho, Montana, Wyoming, and California. As I sorted through extensive collections in these repositories, I encountered all manner of vigilante documentation, including meeting minutes, constitutions, equipment receipts, public proclamations, press accounts, and photographs. In spite of the unevenness of these archives and the disparity of these documents, I found myself reading one particular kind of source over and over again—one I now understand as "the official vigilante history." Simply put, these were narratives produced by vigilantes and/or their advocates shortly after the culmination of committee uprisings that were centrally designed to justify the violent practices of particular vigilance committees. But while these documents told stories that were ostensibly singular and unique, they all contained similar and recurring formulations such that they were virtually interchangeable.

In finding these odd and ubiquitous documents I discovered my primary sources. The occurrence of these sources in such disparate and unrelated local conditions enabled me to discover my argument. Hans Gumbrecht writes, "There is a moment in every historical investigation where the recurrence of certain types of materials and conclusions becomes empty—or, (to use a contrasting metaphor) a moment where our picture of the past reaches a level of saturation."[51] The recurrence of these narratives was decidedly both "empty," insofar as their very interchangeability belied the documents' claims to significance, and "saturating," insofar as their ubiquity revealed something significant about the nature of vigilantism itself. These narratives documented something significant about the history of lynching in part because that was their ostensible purpose; each offered an intriguing if not distorted glimpse into the past. But more intriguing was the fact that the narratives existed at all and, as it turned out, in predictable tandem with vigilante and lynching practices. The narratives' very interchangeability became, for me, the mark of their overall singularity and significance.

Having encountered these narratives in diverse regions and periods, I began to understand lynching itself as a set of violent practices made recognizable by a constellation of formulaic narrative practices. In other words, it is by virtue of *claiming* that a given act of violence is "enacted against a criminal" and is "a punishment" that a given act of violence becomes a lynching. Virtually every scholar who works on these topics confronts the challenge of defining "vigilantism" and "lynching" in a way that accounts for the wide variances in historical usage while being specific enough to function within the context of contemporary analysis and argument.[52] I address this challenge by foregrounding the narratives that define "vigilantes" as those who understood themselves and their actions in particular ways and "lynching" and the violence expressed as a result of this self-legitimation. The definition incorporates both fatal and nonfatal violence, as well as the violent practices of lynchers that may have had little or no relationship to real criminal events. It is a deliberately broad definition, and it incorporates events regardless of regional, temporal, or local cultural conditions or the race of any of the parties involved.

Chapters 1 and 2 engage in close readings of the archived vigilante narratives in order to argue that lynching in the frontier, and later in the South, can be traced through time and across region by examining a set of recurring narrative conventions used by lynchers to justify and legitimate their practices. Based on the "official vigilante histories" I have collected, I argue that vigilantes constituted and justified their violent practices through the adoption and adaptation of this general narrative of ideal vigilantism: *An ideal vigilance committee convened and acted in an organized and evenhanded manner in response to uncontrolled criminal conditions and was roundly supported and applauded by its community for doing so.* I understand this narrative claim to be comprised of five features: criminal conditions, state failure, the valorous vigilante, orderliness, and public popularity. I demonstrate that these narrative conventions had a historically peculiar relationship to actual lynching practices, neither wholly distorting nor entirely reflecting real lynching events. They also provide the framework through which I argue that lynching, when viewed through the perspective of those who lynched, remained largely the same throughout the nineteenth and twentieth centuries and transregionally.

In foregrounding narrative continuity across time and between regions, it becomes clear that frontier vigilantism and southern lynching were regional variants of the same violent practice. The bifurcation of these linked pasts is revealed to be an effect of later narrative accounts and treatments. Following my work with the vigilantes' archival documents, Chapter 3 focuses on the work of western collector, archivist, and historian Hubert Howe Bancroft. This chapter traces the ways in which Bancroft produced two massive volumes on vigilantism (*Popular Tribunals*, volumes 1 and 2) by drawing on the self-aggrandizing accounts of the vigilantes and by further shoring up the heroism of the two vigilance committees in San Francisco. The *Popular Tribunals* volumes are a representative part of both a longer series of books (the thirty-nine-volume *Works* series; see Appendix B) and Bancroft's larger project of collecting primary documents concerning the Pacific states (the materials that ultimately became the foundation of the Bancroft archive at Berkeley). Bancroft's document collection and *The Works* series demonstrate both the process whereby the practices and documents of vigilance committees were incorporated into a regional history and the significance of one man's capacity to produce a region and a past we now "know." Ultimately, Bancroft's desire to fix the significance of the regional West in a larger national history produced his explicit association of vigilante practice with an idealized national citizenship.

Chapter 4 focuses on Wells's antilynching pamphlets: *Southern Horrors* and *A Red Record*. I work closely with these pamphlets from the 1880s and 1890s to highlight the comparativist and multiregional strategy that Wells employed to rework the five features of the vigilante narrative. I argue that Wells's counternarrative—*mobs of white, sadistic racists gathered and enacted unspeakable violence on southern black men for the exclusive purpose of expressing their social power, and neither the state nor a cowardly public did anything to stop them*—effectively challenged the earlier, heroic narrative posited by vigilantes and indelibly altered the location of vigilantism within the American historical record. Wells's activist success demonstrates that vigilantism was not only constituted but ultimately undone through its unique relationship to narrative. Wells articulated an ideal national citizenship that directly countered the narrative established by Bancroft and the other pro-vigilante western historians.

To conclude, I return to *Without Sanctuary* and the Vigilante Parade, as well as a range of other present-day engagements with vigilante history. Since 2000, the wide circulation of James Allen's collection of lynching photographs, *Without Sanctuary*, has increasingly come to dominate public discourse about lynching history. During this same period, citizen border patrols in southern Arizona have organized to stem, in their own words, "the influx of criminal elements" from Sonora, Mexico. On the basis of a series of similarly discordant events, I argue that we must reintegrate the idealized vigilante, Bancroft's narrative, and Wells's narrative in order to create a context in which the relationships among these manifestations of vigilantism can be better understood. Unquestionably, Wells deserves enormous historical credit for launching a successful antilynching movement, but subsequent adoptions and adaptations of her narrative characterization of vigilantism have often lost sight of the nuance and complexity that were characteristic of her work. It was precisely because Wells understood the complicated and narratively constructed appeal of vigilantism that she was able to work effectively against it. Our understanding of America's long-standing and complicated relationship to vigilantism needs to be every bit as well developed.

In 1892, Frederick Douglass sent Ida B. Wells a letter thanking her for her courageous antilynching pamphlet, *Southern Horrors: Lynch Law in All Its Phases*. "Brave woman!" Douglass declared, "You have done your people and mine a service which can neither be weighed nor measured."[53] Indeed, Wells's narrative intervention into the practice of lynching in the United States was brave and arguably the inaugural moment of the second, and characteristically distinct, half of America's lynching past. Douglass trusted that Wells's careful study of southern lynching practices would generate "a scream of horror, shame and indignation"[54] when read by those unfamiliar with the violent events contained within the pages of her pamphlet. But of course, as Douglass acknowledged in the conclusion of the letter, the "southern horrors" of lynching were already well known to many. Known but both explicitly and implicitly condoned by the hundreds of participants and witnesses to southern lynchings. And thus, his rueful conclusion, "But alas! [E]ven crime has power to reproduce itself and create conditions favorable to its own existence."[55] At its broadest level, this book is about the history of lynching's power to create the conditions favorable to its own existence.

# 1

# From Street Brawls to Heroism

*The Official Vigilante Histories*

> The object of the writer in presenting this narrative to the
> public is twofold. His intention is, in the first place, to furnish
> a correct history of an organization administering justice
> without the sanction of constitutional law; and secondly, to
> prove not only the necessity for their action, but the equality of
> their proceedings.
>
> —Thomas Dimsdale, *The Vigilantes of Montana*

> When all is said and done, battles simply stamp the mark of
> history on nameless slaughters, while narrative makes the stuff
> of history from street brawls.
>
> —Michel Foucault, "Tales of Murder"

Early in his 1865 account of an 1864 vigilante movement in Montana, Thomas Dimsdale asserts, "It is probable that there never was a mining town of the same size that contained more desperadoes and lawless characters than did Bannack during the winter of 1862–63."[1] His assertion about the lawless conditions in this little mining settlement is followed by a corollary claim that the formation and actions of a vigilance committee were inevitable:

> Reviewing the long and bloody lists of crimes against persons and
> property, which last included several wholesale attempts at plunder of
> the stores in Virginia and Bannack, it was felt that the question was
> narrowed down to "kill or be killed." "Self-preservation is the first law
> of nature," and the mountaineers took the right side. We have to thank
> them for the peace and order which exist today in what are, by the
> concurrent testimony of all travelers, the best-regulated new mining
> camps in the West.[2]

Dimsdale elected to thank the vigilante miners by writing a "correct history" of the committee's proceedings; that is, by making their actions into, to borrow Michel Foucault's words from the epigraph, "the stuff of history."[3]

Dimsdale's assertion of unique criminal conditions aside, there is nothing singular about the crimes he describes, the vigilante response to this (perceived) lawlessness, or Dimsdale's account. From 1830 to 1890, vigilante committees in every region of the United States and its territories engaged in extra-juridical community regulation in response to real or perceived criminal conditions.[4] Dimsdale's account of the Montana committee is only one of a number of such narratives about these vigilante uprisings. On the basis of the prevalence of these narratives in archives along with their formal similarities, I have come to understand these narratives as belonging to a genre: the "official vigilante history." On the surface, and by self-description, these narratives are historical—designed to record events as they transpired—but they are also characterized by a conspicuous self-consciousness in each writers' stated and manifest intent to ensure that the vigilantes were regarded properly in a far-distant, imagined future.[5] The narratives all tell the same story in the same, highly stylized form: *An ideal vigilance committee convened and acted in an organized and evenhanded manner in response to uncontrolled criminal conditions and was roundly supported and applauded by its community for doing so.* This formula can be distilled into five basic elements: extraordinary criminal conditions, a failure of the state, a valorous vigilante response, orderliness, and public popularity. This chapter and the next look at each of these five features to understand both their individual function and the way that they worked together to produce the vigilante narrative of justification.

## The Voice of the People: Vigilantes, Regulators, and Popular Democracy

The vigilante histories are all characterized by a central tension between the local and the universal—a tension that is definitional of the paradoxical logic of vigilante narratives of justification. On the one hand, vigilantism could only be legitimated—either in practice or in written narratives—through reference to specific and extraordinary conditions. At the same time, the narratives were formally universal and drew on abstract, nearly mythical ideals of criminality and heroism, particularly as these mythical characteristics were made manifest in the context of an expanding nation and national identity. In this respect, vigilantism resonated with other eighteenth- and nineteenth-century forms of popular organizing that were simultaneously extra-governmental and rhetorically nationalistic.

Yet while other forms of popular organizing undoubtedly served to make vigilantism coherent, or even compelling, to its practitioners, there were also important differences between vigilantism and its closest analogues. For example, while vigilante organizations from Florida to California called themselves "regulators," vigilante and regulator movements were different in significant ways.[6] Regulator movements in the eighteenth century were largely associated with tax protest; well-known examples include the North Carolina Regulator movement (1766–1771), Shays's Rebellion (1786–1787), the Whiskey Rebellion (1790s), and Fries's Rebellion (1799–1800).[7] The South Carolina Regulators (1767–1769) were a notable exception in that they organized, like their nineteenth-century namesakes, to combat uncontrolled crime.[8] As Marjoleine Kars points out in her excellent study of the North Carolina Regulator Rebellion, the term "regulator" originated in England in 1655 and was used in the Piedmont counties to refer to activists who "pursued legal and extralegal means to put a stop to practices by local officials that they considered extortionate."[9] Though Kars correctly points out that "both 'Regulator' and 'Regulation' became widely used to denote popular insurgency in North America," protesting unfair taxes and attempting to control crime were not synonymous forms of insurgency.[10] The former was a protest of an *excess* of governmentality—made manifest through taxation; while the latter was defined by an allegation of *insufficient* governmentality—made manifest through a failure to properly control crime. Functionally, groups like the North Carolina Regulators engaged in extensive interaction with the government,[11] whereas vigilance committees largely conducted themselves either in the absence, or in open defiance, of state structures.

Over time, vigilantism and regulation did sometimes intersect in overlapping assertions of "corruption," a vague charge that might relate to excessive taxation, poor control of criminality, or any other "objectionable" practice. More significantly, vigilantism and regulation were animated by the widely held belief that citizens were not only entitled but obligated to act when faced with a flawed government; a belief that had clear roots in the revolutionary period and its incipient version of American national identity. Kars does an excellent job of linking insurrectionary impulses to Protestant doctrine and prerevolutionary religious practices that encouraged people to question and challenge authority spiritually. "In the increasingly millennial atmosphere of the 1760s, religious and secular dissent became progressively intertwined as people applied their religious beliefs to their understanding of legal and economic justice and used their experiences in dissenting charges to demand greater political participation."[12] And as Richard Maxwell Brown points out, the colonial period was characterized by a "pervasive antiauthoritarianism" that gave rise to "the concept of popular sovereignty by the majority" and that perfected "techniques of violence to enforce popular sovereignty."[13] In other words, violent insurgency was not only deeply imbedded in early U.S. nationalism but central to its constitution. Vigilantism throughout the eighteenth and nineteenth centuries continued to lay claim to these nominally national and nominally ideal origins making vigilantism and other forms of citizen organizing into what Peter Silver calls a "nationalizing experience."[14]

## Vigilante Narrative

I refer to Dimsdale's account, and the others I read in this chapter, as "official vigilante histories" because the narratives are so similar to one another in both form and function. These stories of "remarkable" and "unique" events appear with almost predictable frequency in archives from Louisiana to California. Reading these accounts is much like encountering a southern lynching narrative, although the "stock characters," or the "narrative tableaus," are constructed differently. Southern lynching narratives are populated by black male sexual predators, white female victims, and heroically avenging white men. Frontier lynching narratives, on the other hand, are populated by nefarious desperadoes, wholesome frontier folk, and heroically avenging vigilantes. As writers since Ida B. Wells in 1890 have established, it is essential to attend to the production of these formulaic elements to understand the ways that lynching violence was made meaningful.[15] This chapter takes up the first three of five formulaic elements of the frontier lynching narrative in order to understand both the makeup and the function of this narratively constructed lynching tableau. These first three elements are the triangular foundation of vigilante justification and established at the onset the necessity of the vigilance committee forming.

The production and circulation of these texts reveal one of the ways that the meaning of lynching itself was produced and circulated. Richard Maxwell Brown advances an argument much like this regarding Dimsdale's history, asserting, "*The Vigilantes of Montana* (1866), not only spread the fame of the Montana movement but was a veritable textbook on the vigilante method."[16] According to Brown, the Montana movement and Dimsdale's narrative can be attributed to the fact that "in 1851 and 1856, the restrained San Francisco vigilance committees restored to vigilantism an enormous prestige, which it retained through the remainder of the century."[17] While I agree with Brown's assertion regarding the "instructive" capacity of Dimsdale's text, I depart from his emphasis on the 1856 San Francisco committee. A number of the official histories I read in this chapter predate both San Francisco committees, indicating that the form and function of these narratives developed without the influence of these movements. Like Brown, I am interested in the *accrued* meaning and force of vigilante practice and narrative; however, I see this accrual taking place across a greater temporal and geographic range, encompassing movements throughout the nineteenth century and throughout the United States.

I am also centrally concerned with the extent to which narrative practices not only described but *constituted* certain violent practices as vigilantism and therefore as legitimate.[18] These narratives are not simply a retrospective glamorization of otherwise meaningless acts; rather, they are intrinsic to the acts themselves.[19] Without a narrative justification, vigilante practices hovered in a dangerously ambiguous space. Michel Foucault offers a useful theory about the link between violence and narrative that illuminates the critical function of these vigilante histories. His "Tales of Murder" essay focuses on the point at which violence and narrative converge.[20]

> Murder is the supreme event. It posits the relation between power and the people, stripped down to essentials: the command to kill, the prohibition against killing; to be killed, to be executed; voluntary sacrifice, punishment inflicted; memory, oblivion. . . . The narrative of murder settles into this dangerous area; it provides the communication between interdict and subjection, anonymity and heroism; through it infamy attains immortality.[21]

As Foucault asserts, violence and narratives of violence operate in the potentially ambiguous space defined by relationships of authority, power, and control. The practices of the vigilantes occurred in this intermediary space, simultaneously *il*legal in their defiance of state control over criminal proceedings and *extra*legal in their extension of the state's interests in community regulation. The vigilante historians sought to resolve the ambiguities of these violent practices through carefully formulated narrative justifications—by establishing that a death, for example, was an execution and not a murder.[22] In so doing, these narrators produced a historical record wherein the vigilantes seized the "right to kill" in the name of heroism, valor, and immortality. Recognizing the interchangeability of these narratives, and locating their formal qualities within Foucault's theory about who has the right to name, narrate, and legitimate violence, reveals the degree to which vigilantism required these justificatory narratives to both distinguish which particular violent practices were considered vigilantism and to make these practices appear necessary and legitimate.

## Local Conditions and the Making of Vigilantism

The accounts I read in this chapter represent, but do not exhaust, the genre of "official vigilante history." I am aware of a number of additional vigilante narratives containing similar formulaic repetitions.[23] The twelve narratives I focus on in this chapter cover a diverse regional and temporal span of seven vigilance committees (see Appendix A). The narratives also represent different possible relationships between vigilante violence and narrative. I have included narratives that show opposing sides of a warlike conflict between vigilance committees in Texas (known within vigilante vernacular as a "regulator/moderator" dispute). I also include three narratives that are contradictory accounts written about the same vigilante movement in Montana. The narratives I read in this chapter also represent a diversity of scale, ranging from an account about a lone-wolf vigilante in Illinois to a massive vigilance committee in California to an elaborate consortium of vigilance committees in Louisiana. The accounts themselves have differing pasts, ranging from the widely circulated description written by Thomas Dimsdale to obscure, barely archived narratives written by Amarin Paul and Levi Ashcraft. Regardless of ideological inclination, vigilance committee size, or narrative distribution, however, these vigilante histories are all formulaically interchangeable, each relying on and framed by the same essential narrative arc.

In reading these narratives, I am interested in foregrounding their formulaic aspects to draw out the relationship between vigilante violence and vigilante narrative. In many of these cases, it would be all but impossible to determine "what really happened," even though we know, with absolutely certainty, that *something* did. As Hayden White says, "Events happen, whereas facts are constituted by linguistic description."[24] I understand the "events" in these pasts to be the bodies—the punished, tortured, and dead bodies—that are the irrefutable truth at the core of any centrally violent history. But White is correct; the "facticity" of these bodies is ambiguous, which is why the vigilante historians were so intent on gaining a monopoly over the linguistic description of them.[25] My engagement with these movements here is deliberately condensed and abbreviated, designed to capture core events while avoiding, to the extent possible, characterizing these events in any particular way. I also want to highlight that these movements were simultaneously diverse in geographical and temporal origin while being remarkably similar to one another in other ways.

Three of these accounts narrate the Shelby County, Texas, "Regulator/ Moderator War" from 1840 to 1844. Shelby County is located on the far eastern border of Texas, adjacent to Louisiana. At the time of the conflict between the Shelby County Regulators and the Shelby County Moderators, Texas was an independent republic (Texas became a U.S. state in 1845).[26] "The great attraction of this region and the rest of early Texas was land—lots of land, in tracts of a size that settlers could not hope to acquire in the United States."[27] During the 1820s, in an effort to attract settlers to the area, the Mexican government offered stock and agricultural farmers vast tracks of land to draw them to the area.[28] When the Mexican territory became an independent republic in 1836, the new constitution protected the land rights of those already in Texas and granted further land allocations to men living in the newly designated republic. Shelby County's population was dominated by settlers from Tennessee and Alabama, primarily yeoman farmers of Anglo-European descent.[29] Settlement patterns in the area produced relatively little ethnic or linguistic diversity and, in comparison to the counties further south along the Gulf Coast, brought few large planters and slaves to the area.[30] Though localities with vigilante uprisings inevitably laid claim to criminal uprisings the assertion had a particular, and local, resonance in East Texas. Following the Louisiana Purchase, the U.S. and Spanish governments had negotiated a "neutral ground" between the Sabine River and the Calcasieu River and Arroyo Hondo Creek designed to lessen tensions between armies stationed at either country's border. By reputation, this "neutral zone," materially ungoverned for a period of time, encouraged criminals of all sorts to settle in the area.

Of the three accounts of the Shelby County vigilantes, Levi Ashcraft's slightly pro-moderator "Thrilling Scenes in Texas" was written first, in the early 1850s but was never published.[31] Eph Daggett's undated "Recollections of the War of the Moderators and Regulators" attempted to advance the Regulators' cause but was also never published.[32] John Middleton's *History of the Regulators and Moderators and the Shelby County War in 1841 and 1842 in the Republic of Texas* was published in 1883, and it was also intended to support the Regulator's cause.[33] The three authors were in Shelby County during the conflict and were all directly involved in the events. The Shelby County narratives differ from the others in this chapter insofar as they were written in support of *opposing* vigilante groups. Nonetheless, they are formulaically similar to the other vigilante histories, and because they are explicitly contradictory accounts of the same events, they reveal the degree to which the same formulaic elements are present in vigilante histories regardless of the ideological inclination of the narrative's author.

The Regulators and Moderators were typical vigilante practitioners to the extent that they convened and acted in the nominal interest of securing increased law and order for their criminally besieged community. But as the name "Shelby County War" suggests, these East Texas movements for law and order escalated out of control as the two vigilante organizations vied for dominion over their community. Initially targeting alleged horse thieves, counterfeiters, and the false land-certificate trade, Shelby County's two vigilante groups turned against each other, engaging in both legal and extralegal maneuvering and ultimately, all-out guerrilla warfare. In the course of the conflict, men were whipped, hanged, banished, and shot; although it is virtually impossible to determine how many of each as the accounts vary dramatically in their record of these events. The conflict ended when Sam Houston, then president of the Republic of Texas, sent in local militia groups and traveled to Shelby County to negotiate a treaty personally.[34]

There are also three narratives concerning the 1863–1864 vigilante uprising in Bannack/Virginia City, Montana (then the Idaho Territory). In the early 1860s, gold seekers flooded into the Idaho Territory in search of gold.[35] Mining communities developed quickly in the northwestern corner of the soon-to-be designated Montana Territory as successive waves of minors arrived from Colorado, Oregon, Washington, and California. As prospectors came from surrounding mining communities, miners' towns like Bannack and Alder Gulch developed virtually overnight—and were abandoned just as quickly as gold dwindled and word came of better prospects elsewhere.[36] The peak years of the rush were deep in the middle of the Civil War, and hostilities and factions played a significant role in the culture of the mining communities.[37] Moreover, the development of the Northern Rockies was embroiled in larger national processes of expansion that included treaty negotiations with local native populations and the development of rail transportation between the East and West.[38]

Among these narratives, *The Banditti of the Rocky Mountains and Vigilance Committee in Idaho* was written first, by an anonymous author, in 1865.[39] Thomas Dimsdale's *The Vigilantes of Montana*, which ran first in the *Montana Post*, was published later the same year and claimed heatedly to offer a corrective to the anonymous account. Nathaniel Langford's lengthy *Vigilante Days and Ways* was published in 1890 and added a wealth of personal recollections and anecdotes to the historical record.[40] The foreword to the 1996 edition of Langford's history suggests that Langford was one of the seventeen-member executive committee of the Alder Gulch vigilantes.[41] Unlike Shelby County, there was only one more or less unified vigilante movement in the Alder Gulch area. The three accounts are at odds then not because they support different vigilante groups but because the authors are supporting differing narrative accounts of the same vigilante committee. Allegedly, the Montana miners were faced with rampant stagecoach robberies, uncontrolled levels of interpersonal violence (including a proliferation of murders both associated and not associated with property crimes), and a well-organized gang of road agents led by Bannack's elected sheriff, Henry Plummer. The Montana committee hanged twenty-nine men in the period from December 1863 to February 1864, executed one man by shooting, and banished a number of others.[42]

Edward Bonney's *The Banditti of the Prairies or, The Murderer's Doom!! A Tale of the Mississippi Valley* was written in the late 1840s and published for the first time in 1850.[43] La Salle County is located in north central Illinois. Initially settled agriculturally in the 1830s by farmers moving from farther east, the area developed in subsequent decades in conjunction with zinc, and later coal, mining.[44] Tensions typical of any newly settled community were amplified by the harsh and mercurial conditions in Illinois; the winter of 1830–1831 devastated settlers, and, as one historian describes, annual anxieties about prairie fires eroded developing community ties:

> Imagine the feelings of the man who, alone in a strange land . . . has his premises surrounded by a sea of standing grass, dry as tinder . . . knowing that a spark or match applied will send a sea of fire wherever the wind may waft it; and conscious of the fact that there are men who would embrace the first opportunity to send the fire from outside their own field, regardless as to whom it might consume, only so it protected their own.[45]

To a large extent, Bonney was a one-man vigilance committee, traveling the area in and around La Salle County, Illinois, in search of accused outlaws. Bonney is aptly described in the 1963 edition of the book as a "bounty-hunter type, seeking reward either in money or in notoriety or both."[46] By his own admission, his overall pursuit of law and order required the occasional accommodation in his own conduct, resulting in what historian Frank Prassel aptly deems his "strange crusade along the edge of the law."[47] While Bonney was principally concerned with shoring up his own reputation, he also produced an account containing all of the requisite features of vigilante narrative. Bonney's "banditti" book also visibly contributed to subsequent accounts, minimally through later uses of his title. And while there is no violence at the hands of Bonney or any other vigilantes in this account, he held and expressed a great many opinions about the merits or detriments of lynching and the practice of vigilantism itself.

One narrative concerns an 1859 consortium of vigilance committees in southwestern Louisiana in an area then called the Attakapas Country.[48] At the time of the vigilante uprising, the Attakapas counties in southwestern Louisiana were inhabited by a complex mixture of ethnic, racial, and class groups. The area was initially settled by French Acadians following their exile from Nova Scotia in 1755.[49] In the decades following the Louisiana Purchase Anglo-American settlers flocked to southern Louisiana to take advantage of the fertile soil and temperate climate. Finding land both scarce and expensive, many of these newcomers traveled further into the western frontier, settling near the Acadians.[50] One of the vigilante leaders' biographers has suggested that the conflict was animated by existing tensions between the French and Anglo communities,[51] but Sarah Russell persuasively argues that area allegiances were considerably more complicated, particularly for those in the wealthy planter class.[52] Russell traces the rising rates of intermarriage and economic interdependency between the two communities, arguing that "cultural differences ultimately could not undermine the cooperation needed to pursue agricultural wealth and safeguard a frontier community where slaves outnumbered free men."[53] Of the 8,934 people counted in the 1860 census of the Attakapas, white people were a 48 percent minority—a demographic condition that surely amplified fears about uncontrolled criminal conditions and slave insurrection.[54] This conjoined hysteria is easily seen in a newspaper article published the day after the famed vigilante confrontation: "From disclosures made by some of the desperadoes, it is evident that if they had triumphed over the committees, they would have excited the negroes to revolt, and God knows what would have been the consequences."[55]

The Attakapas narrative *Historie des Comites de Vigilance aux Attakapas* was written by Alexander Barde, a member of the Cote Gelee vigilance committee, shortly after the movement ended.[56] The Attakapas vigilantes, like the Shelby County Regulators, met opposition in the form of "moderators," a conflict that ended in a dramatic confrontation at the Bayou Queue de Tortue on September 3, 1859. The Attakapas vigilantes were targeting thieves, arsonists, assassins, and those who opposed them.[57] They were generally moderate, most often limiting themselves to whipping and banishing the accused; however, they did shoot two men and hang a man and a woman. An additional "bandit" died during the course of events at Queue de Tortue, because he shot himself in the head to avoid being captured by the vigilantes.[58] As a freestanding text, Barde's account produces a repetition of the elements of vigilante narrative. The overall narrative traces the events leading up to, and justifying, the confrontation at Queue de Tortue. In the course of the account, however, Barde also tells the stories of seven individual vigilance committees, and he makes mention of a number of others.[59] The resulting history offers an eightfold repetition of the same formulaic narrative of vigilante confession and justification.

In 1849, Charles Summerfield's *Illustrated Lives of the Desperadoes of the New World* presented an account of the Cane Hill Company, an 1842 vigilance committee in Fayetteville, Arkansas.[60] Summerfield was, in fact, a pseudonym for Judge Alfred W. Arrington, a district court judge and chronicler of other vigilante movements as well.[61] Arrington was a character in his own right—an on-again, off-again minister turned lawyer who once resorted to extralegal tactics himself when local courts refused to support his filing in an 1839 criminal case.[62]

Fayetteville is located in the northwest corner of the present-day state of Arkansas (still the Arkansas Territory at the time of the vigilante movement in Summerfield's account). In the wake of an 1828 treaty with local Cherokees, settlers from Alabama, Kentucky, Georgia, and Tennessee began to move into the area.[63] At the time of its earliest settlement, the area was densely forested and thickly populated with buffalo herds.[64] With development, the Arkansas Territory was largely divided, economically and culturally, into two agricultural systems; the area along the Mississippi Delta in the east and south were dominated by larger cotton plantation and slave labor, whereas small farmers were more prevalent in the northern and western parts of the territory.[65] More locally, an unfortunate, and ultimately deadly, confrontation between local Cherokees and a pair of bar-owning brothers created tensions and fears in Fayetteville that, by some accounts, still hung over the town the following year when the vigilantes organized.[66] The Cane Hill vigilantes hanged one young woman and five men. They also conducted an elaborate "trial" during which the vigilantes extensively tortured two of their suspects.

William McConnell wrote *Frontier Law: A Story of Vigilante Days* in the 1920s, when he was eighty, with the help of author and scholar Howard Driggs, and it was directed primarily at young readers as a part of the World Book Company's Pioneer Life Series.[67] McConnell included two 1864 vigilance committees in his narrative—one from Payette and one from Idaho City. He was a member of both and, at least according to his claims, a coordinator and strategist. The Payette committee nominally targeted horse thieves, highway robbers, murderers, and those who engaged in trading "bogus" gold dust.[68] The Payette committee eventually hanged two men, explicitly banished one other, and believed their awe-inspiring reputation succeeded in running the remainder of the desperadoes out of town.[69] The Idaho City vigilantes, at least according to McConnell, were able to discourage crime entirely through their tremendous public reputation and without any actual violence.[70]

Located along the central western edge of present-day Idaho, both Payette and Idaho City were mining towns—settled during the "Idaho Gold Rush"

of the 1860s.[71] Drawn by rumors of great profits, miners from Oregon and
Washington and later California made their way into the relatively less navi-
gable, harsher climate of the Idaho Territory to stake their claims.[72] The area
settled quickly; in fact, by 1864, Idaho City was the largest city in the Pacific
Northwest, with over seven thousand inhabitants and over two hundred as-
sorted businesses.[73] Harsh living conditions combined with supply and food
shortages made mining in Idaho a particularly treacherous enterprise—but
the Idaho mines were briefly and immensely profitable.[74] Beyond the usual
claim disputes, the Idaho mining communities were characterized by a number of specific local conflicts. An 1855 treaty between the United States and
the Nez Percé had designated reservation land in central Idaho—minors willfully disregarded the Nez Percé land rights with their push east for gold. The
territory was governed largely by delegated officials from Washington and the
"territory had little or no say over its own affairs or boundaries, which Federal
lawmakers could alter as they saw fit."[75] This so-called "carpetbagging" created disputes about issues of local governance and, in some cases, real debates
about what laws and policies were in effect in the territory.[76] Perhaps most
significantly, like the settlements in Bannack and Alder Gulch, the Idaho gold
rush was concurrent with the Civil War and local allegiances were intense and
divided: "Almost every American in Idaho's mining camps had a friend or
relative fighting on either the Union or Confederate side."[77] While California,
Oregon, and Washington Democrats tended to be pro-Union, a large number
of southern immigrants in Idaho were Confederate sympathizers.[78]

Asa Shinn Mercer's 1894 *The Banditti of the Plains, or the Cattlemen's Invasion of Wyoming in 1892 (The Crowning Infamy of the Ages)* concerns an
1892 vigilance movement in north central Wyoming, in the area around the
Powder River.[79] The first decades of Wyoming's territorial existence were economically limited by the lack of precious metals to mine and the agricultural
challenges inherent to the arid landscape.[80] And while as early as 1868 it was
apparent that the territory's profitable attributes were miles of open grazing
lands, native populations in the northern and central parts of the territory
prohibited settlers from encroaching on these areas.[81] However, following the
discovery of gold in the Black Hills and violent assaults on tribal populations in the territory, the land became more available to cattle speculation.[82]
The ensuing "Wyoming cattle boom" was as brief as it was remarkable: "Its
limited duration is the most important single fact about the Wyoming cattle
boom. Begun in 1878 or 1879, it ran its course by 1883 or 1884, with the hard
winter of 1887 acting as the final curtain for the bonanza hopes of even the
most optimistic ranchers."[83] As aptly summarized by one historian, "Over-
stocking, reckless finance, declining prices, and a shutdown on exports . . .

combined to form a depression in the cattle business; adverse weather conditions precipitated a crisis that led to a panic."[84]

In most cases grazing lands in the territory were federally, rather than privately, owned, so it was essential that *cattle* ownership be clearly determined and easily determinable. Inevitable disputes arose when cattle were transported out of the territory, brought in or "rounded up" from grazing, and with the birth of young unbranded cows or "mavericks" in the herd each spring.[85] The Wyoming Stock Grower's Association (WSGA) made numerous attempts to regulate these disputes, and while the equanimity of the association's practices remains hotly contested among historians, it is indisputable that rancher anxieties over losses in herd size and health following the 1887 winter amplified claims to ownership among large and small ranchers alike.[86] The WSGA paid agents to check brands in train cattle cars; issued "brand books" to aid in the authentication of the various brands and the associated owners; and, most famously, used their political clout to pass "the maverick law," in effect from 1884 to 1887.[87] The association claimed it worked to ensure the economic safety of all of Wyoming's ranchers; small ranchers argued that the WSGA was concerned with protecting only large, corporate cattle interests. This specific dispute was undoubtedly amplified by other long-standing debates in the territory, such as the inevitable tensions between federally appointed and locally elected territorial officials, the movement to statehood, and the reclamation of federally owned lands for the newly formed state.[88]

Mercer's account might best be described as a regulator/moderator narrative within which the warring factions were large-scale proto-corporate cattle ranchers and small independent farmers. The large-scale cattlemen in this account organized themselves as vigilantes to address what they publicly decried as rampant cattle rustling. The moderators in this story were the small rangers and settlers accused of rustling by the corporate cattlemen. Aside from the confirmed lynching of James Averell and Ellen "Cattle Kate" Watson, the number of deaths attributable to any of these vigilantes remains a matter of debate. Mercer accuses them of hanging three men and shooting four others. The aggressions of the corporate cattlemen did indisputably culminate in an attempted assault on the settlers and small ranchers in Johnson County. Their invasion was foiled when the vigilantes arrived in Johnson County to find an unexpected, and massive, armed defense. In an unusual turn of events, the cattlemen remained under siege until they were rescued by U.S. troops ordered in from Fort McKinney by President Harrison.[89]

One narrative concerns the legendary, and enormous, 1856 San Francisco Committee of Vigilance. San Francisco's rapid-fire development in the 1950s was an effect of the California gold rush.[90] Though the mining communities in the Sierra Foothills outside of San Francisco have been described by Susan Johnson as "among the most demographically male events in human history," by the early 1850s, San Francisco's all-male world was beginning to see the arrival of some women and families.[91] What San Francisco *did* share with the more remote mining communities was significant racial and ethnic diversity. In the 1850s, roughly half the city's population was foreign born—nearly five times the national average.[92] San Franciscans were French, Irish, Chinese, Italian, German, black, Mexican ("Sonoran" in the parlance of the day), Chilean, Hawaiian, and British.[93] The population in San Francisco was as mobile as it was diverse: "Among the working classes arriving between 1850 and 1870, only one in ten stayed in the city for three decades; three out of four left within eight years of arriving. Tellingly, when the names of the 120 wealthiest residents of the city were published in 1871 only three of the 509 rich men listed in 1851 reappeared."[94] Fueled by an expanding commercial economy, San Francisco grew rapidly, soon becoming the largest city in the region.[95] Richard Maxwell Brown has aptly, if not poetically, summarized the inevitable tensions that arose as a result of such diversity: "San Francisco was a seething cauldron of social, ethnic, religious, and political tensions in an era of booming growth."[96]

"The Sixty Day Rule in San Francisco of the Vigilance Committee of 1856, by an Eye-Witness, Almarin Paul" is disproportionately brief in comparison to the massive scale of this particular vigilance movement.[97] Paul was a merchant, publisher, and miner in California, coincidentally famous for inventing the "Washoe pan process"—a steam-based technology used to separate gold and silver and used in mines throughout the Rocky Mountain region.[98] As David Johnson accurately asserts, "The 1856 San Francisco Vigilance Committee has commanded the close attention of every scholar of vigilantism. Its more than 8,000 reputed members, its control of the city's most prominent merchants, its paramilitary organization, and its spectacular execution of four men have made it a (perhaps *the*) exemplar of vigilantism."[99] The 1856 committee (re)organized in response to the murder of an outspoken editor and journalist, James King of William. In addition to King's murderers, the committee sought, at least according to Paul, men guilty of "murder, bribery, perjury, ballot-box and jury stuffing."[100] The committee hanged four men and banished a great many others.[101]

There are overlapping social, economic, and civil conditions in the seven locations described by these narratives. As Pfeifer notes in his work on frontier vigilantism, "immigration and westward expansion created new communities where social order and questions of respectability and political power were especially unsettled and contested."[102] Economic opportunities encouraged rapid in-migration to a number of these localities, creating complex social worlds aptly described by Karen Halttunen's notion of the "horizontal society" in which "authority [was] a function not of fixed social status but of fluid self-aggrandizement. In the horizontal society, any man could seize authority over others."[103] Yet while these disordered communities did create anxieties about strangers, social relationships, and civic order, scholars such as Richard Maxwell Brown and Ken Gonzalez-Day have persuasively argued that vigilantes expressed and enforced social relationships and inequalities that mirrored the class stratification and racism of cities and communities in more developed parts of the country.[104] Indeed, as Kent Curtis suggests, the very idea of a "rush" to economic prosperity in a newly developing area was an expression of "the far flung ambitions of an expansionist nation . . . pushing some vision of national economic or political expansion."[105] In the cases of the territorial committees ideas about social and civic order were further complicated by tensions concerning and between nationally appointed and local officials and competing ideas about how to achieve prosperity. Any, or paradoxically all, of these ideas help to explain something about these vigilance movements. But relative levels of civic development and the economic, racial, and ethnic composition of these communities serve as much to differentiate as to analogize the seven localities. Moreover, the individuals who made up the vigilance committees, and the individuals who became the vigilantes' targets, varied widely among these seven, arguably representative, examples.

But in spite of these differences, the narratives about these movements tell an almost interchangeable story. The authors of these twelve histories were driven by an imperative to produce a narrative ordering of potentially ambiguous vigilante violence. In the next section I examine the way that the very act of producing a narrative was, for the authors of these histories, a miniature version of vigilantism—a means of producing order in an otherwise disordered world. Thereafter, I transition to the first three features of the narratives: extraordinary criminal conditions, a failure of the state, and a valorous vigilante response. These features established the necessity of vigilantism. This story is replayed in miniature as the authors begin by drawing connections between the duties of the vigilante historian and the duties of the vigilantes themselves.

## "Men, Do Your Duty": Narrative Obligation

Proper narration was as crucial in the world of vigilantism as crime fighting was, so much so that the culminating act of the 1859 Attakapas committee was to commission Alexander Barde to write its history. The book's epilogue contains a passage that echoes the one from Dimsdale in the epigraph: "At the meeting of November fifth, it was resolved that they would contrive with the other Committees in order to publish the causes and origin of their organizations and the history of their acts."[106] Quite explicitly here, Barde the vigilante historian becomes both an extension of and a spokesman for the Louisiana committees, ensuring that the vigilantes would be given the proper regard in both the immediate and long-term future. As can be seen in the following two passages, the vigilante historian, like the vigilante himself, is bound by an obligation to the public good. The first citation comes from the preface to *The Banditti of the Rocky Mountains*:

> In entering upon the detail of blood, which will startle the most adamantine heart, with a horrifying sense of the depravity to which human nature may descend, it may be well to state in brief, some of the many reasons that have prompted me to this exposure.
>
> First, we will say, that the anxiety of the public to learn the facts and testimony, connected with two of the most heartless desperadoes that have ever infested any locality with their unhallowed presence, or blackened the annals of crime is one of the reasons, and another is, to silence forever any attempt upon the part of their friends, to establish their innocence, or the injustice of their execution.[107]

The passage is nearly identical to one written nearly twenty years earlier by Bonney in *The Banditti of the Prairies*:

> Before entering fully upon our tale of blood, which will thrill every heart with a shuddering sense of the brutality of man, we would premise, by stating briefly, a few of the reasons that have led to this exposure.
>
> The public are desirous of obtaining the fact and testimony concerning two of the most horrible and cold-blooded murders that were ever recorded in the annals of crime; and the possession of such facts as would at once bring the remainder of the perpetrators to a summary and severe punishment. Great have been the depredations of the *organized* band of robbers that once, and still to some extent, infest the western portion of the fair state of Illinois; and the good and honest citizens of Rock Island have had calumny and abuse heaped upon their heads to an unlimited extent by these cowardly ruffians, and that without a single chance of refutation.
>
> To refute, also, the charge of hanging "innocent men," . . . and plainly disprove the many falsehoods that the [criminal gang] have

from time to time caused to appear in the public journals, to sustain the innocent, and fearlessly expose the guilty.[108]

These passages demonstrate the paradoxical tension between the repeating aspiration to establish the necessity of vigilante narrative alongside the framing of this justification in strictly localized terms. I refer, here, to Bonney's reference to "two of the most horrible and cold-blooded murders that were ever recorded in the annals of crime" and the anonymously written reference to "two of the most heartless desperadoes that have ever infested any locality with their unhallowed presence, or blackened the annals of crime." Insofar as the entire point of these official vigilante histories is to establish, absolutely, the "guilty criminal" and the "righteous vigilante," the accounts necessarily make reference to not only criminals but "the worst," "most dangerous" criminals ever known to man. The hyperbole here is more than stylistic; in fact, "extraordinary conditions" presage the necessity not only of the vigilante narrative but of vigilantism itself.

The need to establish, through narrative, the righteousness of vigilante lynchings in both locally believable and universally recognizable ways is the central function of the vigilante histories. And just as vigilantism is asserted as the righteous and necessary response to criminal outrages, so is narrating framed as a valorous but necessary aspect of the vigilante enterprise. The vigilante historians, like the vigilantes themselves, are bound by an honorable albeit unpleasant duty.[109] Per Dimsdale:

> It is not pleasant to write of blasphemous and indecent language, or to record foul and horrible crimes; but, as the anatomist must not shrink from the corpse, which taints the air as he investigates the symptoms and examines the results of disease, so the historian must either tell the truth for the instruction of mankind, or sink to the level of a mercenary pander, who writes, not to inform the people, but to enrich himself.[110]

The same implicit link between vigilantism and vigilante narrative valor can be found in Summerfield's account:

> I have been compelled to relate deadly combats, desperate duels, and bloody assassinations, the mere recollection of which chills the blood in my veins, and excites an involuntary shudder of horror. But I have endeavored also to trace their causes, in the hot, passionate temperament of those chivalrous sons of the fiery South.[111]

Vigilante historians, like Dimsdale and Summerfield, frame their obligation to chronicle the dark corners of American crime and punishment in equivalency to the moral imperative facing the vigilantes; to wit, the proper balance of order and truth had to be maintained no matter how unpleasant the task. The anonymous author, Bonney, Dimsdale, and Summerfield are all responding to a public need for order—in essence, completing the vigilante cycle.

As participants and/or witnesses to the events in question, these narrators (like the vigilantes) perceived themselves as having a unique obligation. In some cases, this was because of their unusually close proximity to the "truth." According to Barde:

> Let not anyone accuse me here of writing fiction, which would be impossible, for I shall be read principally on the scene where this action took place, that is to say in a country which knows the facts almost as well as I do myself, and who would have the right to blame me severely if I wrote untruthfully, when in reality it is so sad and especially so dramatic. I am not writing fiction.[112]

Mercer asserts a similarly unique proximity to the truth, stating in the preface that his book

> is not sent out as a literary production, but an honest statement of the facts as they occurred. Personal acquaintance with the principle actors and accurate general knowledge of the country and its conditions have given me unusual facilities for gathering reliable data.[113]

Middleton's preface contains an even more impassioned version of Barde's and Mercer's assertions:

> I am now in the seventy-fifth year of time from my birth. . . . And I am impelled by a sense of justice and due regard to the memory and the appreciation of my comrades, friends and associates to give to the public in my declining years a true, faithful and impartial account of things that to my own knowledge have so often been misrepresented.[114]

As Middleton states most eloquently, to let the truth go unrecorded would itself constitute criminal neglect.[115]

These authors' assertions of narrative obligation mimic the vigilante story—unordered events and an absence of narrative order are remedied by a valorous vigilante narrator. And these writers conceived of their projects in similarly lofty ways. Summerfield grandly asserts, "I have written not for myself, but for my country."[116] Langford more modestly suggests, "In my view the moral of this history is a good one. The brave and faithful conduct of the Vigilantes furnishes an example of American character, from a point of view entirely new."[117] And Barde, the most florid of all vigilante historians, likens narrative obligation to religious obligation: "Here I am obliged to repeat that which I shall never cease to cry out day and night, as the Mussulmen [sic] cry out the hour of prayer from the Turkish Mosques . . . that justice found itself disarmed before the Attakapas bandits."[118] Be it for God, for country, or the more modestly conceived of "public good," these authors share an abiding obligation to properly narrate vigilante events.

Each narrative established its own necessity by claiming that a record of events was as necessary to the production of order as vigilantism itself. But the story of vigilantism itself began with the assertion that the locality in the narrative, for a variety of posited and variously documented reasons, was plagued by *extraordinary criminal conditions.* This assertion relies on establishing, as each of the narrators attempts to, that a given locality was inhabited by a particularly nefarious gang of "road agents," "banditti," or "desperadoes." This assertion is followed by a corollary premise that, notwithstanding the infestation of "bad elements," the locality suffered *a failure of the state.* A variety of different, often quite complicated, juridical critiques are levied in support of this claim as vigilantes often acted in areas that did, contrary to the myth, have state-sanctioned legal institutions.[119] Once the existence of criminal conditions and ineffective law and order have been "proven," the narrative progresses to its next element—*a valorous vigilante response.* Like the first two claims this assertion is made in localized ways; for example, Dimsdale claims that Bannack was inhabited by the "lawless" man's antithesis— the uniquely moral Bannack miner. But in the assertion of vigilante valor, these narratives also begin to make reference to larger contexts, drawing on national, historical, and religious imagery to shore up the "righteousness" of vigilante violence. And just as the criminals in these accounts are hyperbolically bad, so are the moral vigilantes hyperbolically good; uniquely suited to bring about social order, and uniquely justified in killing to do so. A proper vigilante history can largely be reduced to the progression of these three basic elements—extraordinary criminal conditions, an absence of law and order, and a valorous vigilante response. Of course, these narratives overtly deny the possibility of any such reduction, as the story is told each time as the only one of its kind.

## One: Extraordinary Criminal Conditions

The assertion of extraordinary criminal conditions, by the very nature of its claim to "uniqueness," is made in locally specific, albeit often colorful, ways. Dimsdale, for example, asserts, "It is probable that there never was a mining town of the same size that contained more desperadoes and lawless characters than did Bannack during the winter of 1862–63."[120] These lawless characters, Dimsdale says, "organiz[ed] themselves into a band, with captain, lieutenants, secretary, road agents and outsiders."[121] The band was so organized, according to Dimsdale, that they committed over one hundred murders and operated according to a secret and elaborate system of signals and codes.[122] The deception of the Montana road agents was so complete that, according to *Banditti of the Rocky Mountains* and Langford, their password was "I am innocent" or simply "innocent."[123] A declaration that, paradoxically, when made as a "gallows speech" not only failed to deter the vigilantes but offered a final proof that they were executing a guilty man.

Dimsdale attributes the remarkable upsurge in crime to the discovery of gold: "The stampede to the Alder Gulch, which occurred early in June, 1863, and the discovery of the rich placer diggings there, attracted many more of the dangerous classes, who, scenting the prey from afar, flew like vultures to the battlefield."[124] Alexander Barde presents a similar formulation, albeit specific to criminal conditions in southwestern Louisiana: "On February 1, 1859, society found itself divided into two camps, of which one was fortunately more numerous than the other, but which seemed to be outflanked on all sides by the audacity of the second: the first camp was that of honest men, the other was that of bandits."[125] Barde's bandits, like Dimsdale's road agents, were supremely well organized, having "regimented themselves and formed an order and unity which would have been worthy of admiration, if the forces of that army had been employed in the defense of society."[126] And, of course, Barde asserts that the well-organized "army" of bandits was unique, even among criminals:

> The soldiers were the scum, the most foul, the most abject; those who were loathsome of soul as well as of body; those who did not know even by tradition that there is a God, and that morality exists . . . and those who would kill in cold-blood because they did not know the meaning and significance of the word conscience.[127]

But while property crimes are central in both Dimsdale's and Barde's accounts, the Attakapas narrative necessarily makes reference to different local economic conditions: "Pirates from all parts of the country were drawn to the Attakapas country, and soon it was infested with a band of outlaws who knew how to trap the unprotected herds, the hope of the poor worker or the wealth of the well-to-do class."[128] Demonstrating the adoptability and adaptability of the formulaic features of vigilante narrative, Barde's "pirates of the prairies" are simultaneously interchangeable with Dimsdale's road agents and entirely different insofar as they are unique to the Attakapas landscape. Dimsdale's road agents are locally produced and defined by a mining economy, robbing coaches and worthy miners of currency and gold. Barde's bandits, on the other hand, steal livestock.

Every vigilante history makes reference to a similarly locally defined, and singularly nefarious, group of outlaws. Mercer's account is populated by an alleged infestation of cattle rustlers and the desperado vigilantes who wrongly accuse them. About the latter he asserts, "The invasion of the state of Wyoming by a band of cutthroats and hired assassins in April, 1892, was the crowning infamy of the ages. Nothing so cold-blooded, so brutal, so bold and yet so cowardly was ever before recorded in the annals of the world's history."[129] Bonney would disagree, asserting about three murders in his locality, "A more cowardly, cold-blooded murder was never committed. The annals of crime have no record which more fully awakens the deepest execrations of the human heart."[130] But it shouldn't be surprising that Bonney thinks these local murders were uniquely appalling, given his assertion that "the Valley of the Mississippi River from its earliest settlement has been more infested with reckless and blood-stained men, than any other part of the country, being more congenial to their habits and offering the greatest inducements to follow their nefarious and dangerous trade."[131] Langford, like Dimsdale, believes that the Alder Gulch bandits reigned supreme in criminal history:

> Nowhere else, nor at any former period since men became civilized, have murder and robbery and social vice presented an organized front, and offered an open context for supremacy to a large civilized community. . . . I cannot now remember the instance, within the past three hundred years, when the history of any country records the fact that the criminal element of an entire community, numbering thousands, was believed to be greater than the peaceful element.[132]

However, according to the vigilante historians, such criminal overthrows were actually quite common, having already taken place in Texas, Louisiana, Arkansas, California, and Illinois.

In all of these cases, the narratives describe localities beset by unimaginably bad and dangerous criminals, singularly dangerous because they were born of local conditions that were especially conducive to particular kinds of crime.[133] In this way, vigilante narrative was uniquely suited to express localized social anxieties, be those anxieties related to the mercurial economy of gold rush California, the vicissitudes of open-range grazing in Montana, or the social unrest of a post-emancipation South. Of course the formulae and its adaptability were never acknowledged in the narratives themselves. In the repetition of the element of extraordinary criminal conditions, the thrust of vigilante narrative is already clear—extraordinary events call for extraordinary actions. While vigilantism was a widespread phenomenon, these histories make it clear that the interpretation of extralegal punishments or executions needed to be managed. In other words, to ensure that a given killing be perceived as an "execution," and not a "murder," these narratives had to establish that criminal conditions were so singular and horrifying that all the usual measures of response were rendered useless, creating what Peter Silver calls, in his work on narrative constructions of Indian wars in early America, "a remarkable collective delusion fueled by fear."[134]

## Two: The Failure of the State

The accounts progress to their second common element—a failure of the state—in order to counteract the presumption that regulating crime was the right and responsibility of the government. Western folklore imagines a vast and unordered frontier landscape in which vigilantes were forced to control crime during initial phases of settlement. The vigilante narratives reveal a much more complicated and interesting relationship between vigilantes and the law. Levi Ashcraft's account seems, at first, to describe a criminal geography in the Republic of Texas defined by its existence beyond the reaches of the state:

> At the time our history properly commences in 1838, although the Regulators were not organized until sometime afterwords [sic], Texas was almost in a state of anarchy. . . . It was almost impossible for the government, yet in its infancy, and without adequate resources for its own support, to extend that supervisory care over the inhabitants which it is now happily able to do. Beset as it were [sic] on the one hand by the Mexicans, and on the other by the repeated incursions of hordes of wild and merciless savages . . . the government found but little time for the regulation of the internal affairs of the county, and was indeed powerless to preserve the ascendancy of law and order. Add to this the fact that Texas then furnished an asylum for all the murderers, thieves, swindlers and reckless desperadoes in the United States, and the reader

will not be surprised that lynch code with all its horrors and severities was adopted, and, when it suited the caprice of the majority, rigidly enforced.[135]

This passage from Ashcraft's account marks the transition from the extraordinary criminal conditions claim to the assertion of an absence of law and order. Vigilantism was justified on the grounds that local citizens faced with lawless conditions and the failure of the state had no choice but to take the law into their own hands. But the failure of the state in this account, and in the other histories as well, is not simply because of the remoteness of Shelby County.[136] As Ashcraft continues his narrative, it becomes clear that law and order was not so much absent as corrupt and ineffectual. Ashcraft continues:

> The members of [the criminal] gang were . . . in the ascendancy in Shelby county, and as a consequence controlled the local elections. . . . By these means when one of the clan chanced to be detected in the commission of an offense against the laws they were enabled quietly to effect his escape, and thus prevent an investigation calculated to endanger their safety.[137]

According to Ashcraft, the sheriff and his deputies were corrupt, witnesses gave false testimony or "disappeared" under mysterious circumstances, and court proceedings were run by a hapless puppet of the desperadoes, Jonas Phelps. Ashcraft describes Phelps as a man "too lazy and indolent to be an active member of the clan, but his principles, or otherwise his entire want of any such useless commodity, pointed him out as a fit instrument to be used by them as occasion should require; and he was therefore elected to the honorable but not very lucrative office of Justice of the Peace."[138] Following his initial assertion that the Republic of Texas virtually lacked any civil structures, Ashcraft spends a considerable portion of his narrative describing how ineffectual these (non)existent structures were.

Lest Phelps's elected office seem like an anomaly, Daggett's description of the judge in nearby Harrison County offers even more colorful evidence of the dissolution of law and order: "Judge Hansford was another bird. . . . He . . . came to Texas and took up the profession of law, and liked a rascal better than an honest man. He got mixed in with . . . certificate frauds, and moved up in Harrison County. He became judge of the District Court, got drunk and puked on the docket, and General Rusk adjourned court for him."[139] In essence, to cite Daggett's (abbreviated) summary of law and order, "courts were a farce."[140] Characters like the hapless Phelps and the vomiting Judge Hansford consistently occupy "official" positions in these narratives. Either at the mercy of outlaws, or outlaws themselves, these officials repeatedly fail to acknowledge, let alone eliminate, the marauding outlaws. But the important thing about these descriptions is that they undercut interpretations of vigilantism as the righteous practice of citizens in frontier areas so remote as to be outside the reach of the state.[141] Ashcraft, like many of the vigilante narrators, advances two contradictory premises. The first is that Shelby County, and the Republic of Texas at large, were too far beyond the control of the state to have any legal structure whatsoever. But he then colorfully describes the legal structures that were in Shelby County, all the while detailing their corruption and ineffectiveness. The complexity and intermittent illogic of such claims about the absence of law and order can be succinctly summed up by Langford's bizarre assertion in his account of the Alder Gulch vigilantes: "Practically, they had no law, but, if law had existed, it could not have afforded adequate redress."[142] This seemingly paradoxical statement serves the essential function of simultaneously delegitimizing extant legal institutions while providing a contingent justification for the vigilantes' usurpation of community control.

McConnell's account also engages in an "if not absent then corrupt" formulation: "The Indian and other troubles stimulated the forwarding of numerous requests to Washington for the establishment of a military post in Boisé Valley. The Settlers wanted protection not only from the Indians, but from a truly more dangerous class of savages, the lawless whites."[143] But the account doesn't stop with this claim that Boisé City was remote and needed additional governmental support and structure. He subsequently devotes two chapters to documenting juridical malfeasance in the new territorial capital of Boisé City, painting a picture of near-absolute bureaucratic corruption. He points to jury fraud, asserting, "When occasion required the speedy summoning of jurors, hangers-on around the court rooms, often there for the purpose of being summoned, were called by the sheriff or his deputies to act as jurymen."[144] He also notes suspicious electoral procedures, claiming:

> It was noticeable that the sporting class [*sic*] were taking great interest in the delegates who were to attend the nominating conventions that year in Boisé County. It was equally noticeable that the rank and file of our citizens, the business men and those who toiled in the mines, paid no attention to the matter; but few of them even knew when the primaries and nominating conventions were to be held. It was an easy matter, therefore, for the lawless characters to control the nominating conventions of both political parties.[145]

Finally, McConnell suggests that the second session of the Territorial Legislature in November 1864 created still further juridical mayhem:

> The work of this session was devoted largely to amending and repealing the acts of the first [legislative] session. One of the acts repealed was "An Act Concerning Jurors," which did not place sufficient power in the sheriff's office to protect "their friends" from the penalties of the law by selecting jurors friendly to certain interests. A new statute was then enacted under the provisions of which the sheriff and his deputies could secure a jury which would either convict or acquit, as desired.[146]

Boisé City's criminals were as organized as Dimsdale's and Barde's lawless gangs, and McConnell suggests that they managed to take over not only the community but the legal system itself. He claims they succeeded because "those who managed to seize control of the government—the gamblers, highwaymen, horsethieves, and 'bogus-dust' operators, with the keepers of their resorts . . . stood together."[147] And here McConnell, and the other narrators who emphasize the supreme organization of the desperadoes, foreshadow the corresponding organization of the vigilantes. To be organized, in these narratives, is to have power.

These narratives suggest that law and order were not so much absent but, like in Ashcraft's and McConnell's accounts, corrupted by local criminal interests; as a result, vigilante historians, in order to justify vigilante lynching, engage in complex juridical critiques.[148] These critiques focus on jurisdictional disputes (or failures, like McConnell's) and/or flaws within the legal system itself. Barde's critique of the legal system focuses on juries and false testimony: "Justice found itself disarmed before the Attakapas bandits, because the law found itself powerless through two absurdities of our criminal legislation: the almost unlimited right of recusation and the power of witnesses."[149] Summerfield's critique of the juridical system targets lawyers:

> Backwoodsmen view the disciples of Blackstone as their worst foes, who rescue every culprit from the clutches of justice. It is the lawyers who pick holes in every indictment. It is they who wheedle and mystify the judge. The arrival of a lawyer, therefore, in a new settlement, is regarded as the most serious calamity—an evil omen of coming misfortunes.[150]

Summerfield's critique subtly mirrors Langford's two different ideas about lawlessness, as he associates increased settlement and "civilization," rather than remoteness and a lack of civility, with increasingly lawless conditions. Here, as in Langford, lawlessness is not so much an absence of law as it is a diffuse social state wherein the vigilantes perceived that the state was failing to control criminal conditions. But in all of these cases, "lawlessness" is asserted as the precondition of vigilantism and as a preliminary point of jurisdictional dispute with an allegedly failing state. The vigilantes asserted a self-sanctioned authority over their communities by minimizing the presence or legitimacy of sanctioned law and order.

The jury tainting, false testimony, corrupt legislation, and legal wrangling described by these vigilante historians suggest that the criminally besieged and systematically unprotected communities were left with no choice.[151] *If* criminal conditions were bad enough and *if* these criminal conditions were allowed to continue because of an absence of law and order, then a vigilante response would seem not only necessary but inevitable. And this is precisely the function of the first and second features of vigilante histories. Once a vigilance committee was formed, and certainly once it began to engage in public violence, events demanded a narrative justification. The narrative constitution of these violent events as legitimate or justified required that these narratives produce a compelling and convincing case for the organization of a vigilance committee.

While the first two features of the vigilante narrative worked together to establish legitimacy for the vigilantes, the assertion about a failed state offered a slightly different constitutive benefit than the allegation of extraordinary criminal conditions did. While allegations about extraordinary criminal conditions were most effectively made in locally specific ways, the notion of a failed state borrowed its paradoxical central logic from a myth about national identity. Hubert Howe Bancroft, in his nineteenth-century history of popular tribunals, deemed vigilantism an expression of the "people's right to revolutionize" and the vigilantes' allegations of state failure can be largely understood in these terms.[152] Vigilante legitimacy relied on the idea that the nation's citizens retained some power outside of the state. In one of vigilantism's most poetic ironies, vigilance committees often drew up constitutions upon forming, and these constitutions drew liberally and unabashedly on the U.S. Constitution for language and form. These vigilante constitutions were established in direct opposition to the state while simultaneously paying homage to its manifestoes and its foundational ideals about the prerogatives of a people to advance and protect their own interests. In this way, vigilantes managed to be both extra- and antigovernmental and virulently patriotic at the same time.

# Three: The Valorous Vigilante

In progressing to their third common feature, the narratives assert that these publicly violent men were not merely justified but genuinely righteous; accordingly, just as each locality was characterized by singularly lawless conditions and a singular absence of legal protection, so was each community populated by the desperadoes' antithesis—the valorous vigilante. The valorous vigilante, like the nefarious road agent, is a product of the locality, made "good" by precisely the same conditions that have made others "bad." Summerfield's version of the valorous vigilante is literally cultivated in the new territory as the "'Cane Hill Company' . . . was composed mostly of laboring men, old settlers and honest [sic] who had *worked* themselves out of comfortable homes in that once gloomy wilderness."[153] Dimsdale's valorous vigilante is more figuratively produced by the particulars of a mining community:

> The remarks which truth compels us to make, concerning the classes
> of individuals which furnish the law-defying element of mining camps,
> are in no wise applicable to the majority of the people, who, while ex-
> hibiting the characteristic energy of the American race in the pursuit of
> wealth, yet maintain, under every disadvantage, an essential morality,
> which is the more creditable since it must be sincere, in order to with-
> stand the temptations to which it is constantly exposed.[154]

Dimsdale defines the valorous vigilantes' morality in contrast to the criminal conditions that surround them; yet like the road agents they are a product of a mining community. And in both of these cases, the valorous vigilante is both a locally produced and a mythically national figure—the American settler courageously overcoming hardship in a hostile, uncivilized wilderness.[155] But as we can see in Dimsdale's and Barde's accounts, this formulaic assertion was, like the assertion of extraordinary criminal conditions, entirely adaptable to local social conditions and ideological requirements.

The vigilante, in order to be valorous, needn't just be a product of American national myths. Barde's entire account, for example, is populated by classical Greek and European historical references to such an extent that the vigilantes themselves are described as a kind of "who's who" of history:

> The people, with as much imagination as Alexander Dumas, had
> placed a halo around those who were going to fight for the purification
> of the country. For some, they wore belts of red or green silk, like those

worn by members of the Comic Opera; also the undervest of the inhabitants of the Apennines or Abruzzi and a cocked hat crowned with
flowers. To those poetic soldiers they had given a poetic chief; he could
and would be Fra Diavolo, honest man dressed in velvet from head to
foot having rows of ribbons on his vest. To others the vigilantes would
be Puritans of the time of Cromwell, wearing leather jackets and iron
helmets, who would go to war warmed with heavy muskets while sing-
ing the glorious psalms of the reformed church of England; for others
they would cover their faces with black masks like the Italians of the
Middle Ages or the villains of the opera; and they would wage war at
night, like Indians or like the bands of Rob Roy.[156]

Barde's description captures the way that vigilante valor can be cast in both
localized and universal ways. The description is local insofar as it captures the
ethnic admixture of the Attakapas (Acadian) community, but these multiple
references also make the vigilantes universally heroic, interchangeable with valorous characters from other periods and regions. And valor need not even be
consistently constructed within the same vigilante history. Barde goes on to
liken the vigilantes to the soldiers of the American and French Revolutions
and, most dramatically, to Christ on Judgment Day.[157] Offering the ultimate
certification of the vigilantes' righteousness, even an "outlaw" targeted by the
vigilance committee in Grande-Pointe exudes, "If the Committees strike with
justice which I do not doubt that they do, they act as good citizens, for they are
but doing that which Christ will do at the last Judgement; they are separating
the good from the bad."[158]

    In other accounts, such as Ashcraft's, vigilantism was unquestionably a
matter of patriotic duty. But in cases when two vigilante groups vied for authority, their patriotic valor could be muddied by "the public's" confusion
over which vigilante group more successfully embodied national ideals. Regarding support for the Shelby County Regulators' leader, Ashcraft asserts:
"[Eph Daggett], as well as many other good men, was blinded by prejudice
in-so-much that they did not regard the lawless acts of Moorman in their true
light, but looked upon him as a public benefactor whose motives were pure
and patriotic."[159] But, according to Ashcraft, true vigilante patriotism was revealed when the Regulators finally went too far: "The hanging of Jamison on
the public square, and in a few feet of the court house, appeared an intentional
insult to the laws of the land, which the Regulators had set out to uphold. The
patriotism of many who had been quiet spectators of the many scenes of lawless violence, was now aroused."[160] Summerfield's vigilantes are also aroused
by patriotism: "A company of lynchers were [sic] raised, amounting to four

hundred men, and a regular committee of *thirty* was organized, under a constitution as eloquent in its declaration of rights, and as precise in its definition
of specific lynching powers, as the Constitution of the American Union in
its enumeration of the separate elements of federal jurisdiction."[161] Vigilante
groups, perhaps not surprisingly, reenacted the moment Summerfield describes again and again. The drafting of a committee constitution enabled the
vigilantes to take up their extralegal practices in the name of national ideals
and patriotism. As with the paradoxical patriotism associated with allegations
of a failed state, vigilantes were able to lay claim to the nation and its symbols
while openly and unapologetically defying the authority of the government.

The most sweeping and inclusive understanding of vigilante valor can
be found in Paul's account of the San Francisco committee. His narrative
includes the following lengthy excerpt from one of the committee's public
proclamations:

> Great public emergencies demand prompt and vigorous remedies. The
> people suffering under an organized despotism which has invaded their
> liberties, squandered their properties, usurped their offices of trust and
> emoluments, endangered their lives, prevented the expression of their
> will through the ballot box, corrupted the channels of justice, have now
> risen in virtue of their inherent right and power. All political, religious
> and sectional differences and issues have given away to the paramount
> necessity of a thorough and fundimental [sic] reform and purification
> of the social body.
>
> We have spared and shall spare no effort to avoid bloodshed, but,
> undeterred by threats of opposing organizations, shall continue peaca-
> bly [sic] if we can, forcibly if we must, this work of reform to which we
> have pledged our lives, our fortunes, and our sacred honors.[162]

Paul follows the excerpt by observing, "When one gives thought to the excitement of the community at the time when no man was neutral, the address
must be considered as having a true American ring to it."[163] The "American
ring," of course, can be partially attributed to the document's similarity to the
U.S. Declaration of Independence. But the committee's proclamation goes far
beyond merely equating vigilantism and patriotism; it associates vigilantism
with an expression of natural rights, the means to social purification, a sacred
duty, and the amelioration of all manner of social differences. This particularly sweeping assessment of vigilante valor offers a partial explanation for the
appeal of vigilante practice itself. Repeatedly framed as a necessary response
to real conditions, vigilantism was always susceptible to local adaptation and

deployment. In other words, one could be a vigilante, and therefore valorous, in a range of different and locally defined ways. Inevitably, the converse became equally as true—to be valorous, one could be a vigilante.

Langford was aware of this multidirectional pull between valor and vigilantism, suggesting that it was only by virtue of vigilante practice that men could differentiate themselves from the lawless commotion. Following the discovery of a brutally murdered corpse, the vigilante spirit was ignited:

> These appalling witnesses to the cruelty and fiendishness of the perpetrator of this bloody deed roused the indignation of the people to a fearful pitch. They went to work to avenge the crime with an alacrity sharpened by the consciousness of that long and criminal neglect on their part, but for which it might have been averted. They felt themselves to be, in some degree, participants in the diabolical tragedy. In the presence of that dead body the reaction commenced, which knew no abatement, until the country was entirely freed of its bloodthirsty persecutors. That same evening, twenty-five citizens of Nevada subscribed an obligation of mutual support and protection, mounted their horses, and, under the leadership of a competent man, at ten o'clock started in pursuit of the murderer.[164]

And, according to Langford, once the valorous spirit had been aroused, it could only be maintained with still further vigilante violence. Having hanged one man, the committee was more or less obligated to hang others, for "if what they had done was right, it would be wrong to permit others equally guilty to escape."[165] And here Langford, alone among the narrators, manages to capture the ambiguity of the figure of the valorous vigilante. His if/then statement implies, but does not directly address, the reverse possibility. If what the vigilantes had done was *wrong*, then they had not executed a criminal; they had committed a murder. And so, he asserts, they had to continue to assert their position within, and in relationship to, the law—they had to keep executing people. And Langford, himself a vigilante, continues the process with the production of his narrative, taking great pains to certify that the thirty deaths in Bannack and Virginia City were not crimes, but inevitable and just acts.

Each of the vigilante histories attempts to produce a narrative of inevitability. Rich in local details about both crime and juridical failure, the narratives seem to move naturally toward succeeding chapters in which executions, brutal punishments, and/or particularly notorious criminals are profiled. On their own terms, these narratives were stories about local communities—about the particular anxieties associated with rapid-fire economic growth, the anonymity of newly developing settlements, and unresolved questions about how these new groups of people might live together. These local stories worked, however, because they relied on a simultaneously familiar and eminently unique-seeming formula—a formula that allowed vigilantes to be local heroes and paradoxical patriots.

## Narrative as Truth: The Vigilante Record

In 1869, Henry Plummer's family, upon learning of his death, decided to travel from New York City to Bannack to ensure that his murderers were prosecuted. Langford, himself in New York City at the time, was summoned by Plummer's siblings to discuss their brother's untimely demise. Langford recorded the visit that he and a colleague paid them:

> I . . . found them to be well-educated, cultivated people. They were very eager in their desire to find and punish the murderers of their brother, and repeatedly avowed their intention to leave, almost immediately, in pursuit of them. . . . Finding them resolved, we concluded that, rather than allow them to suffer from the deception they labored under, we would put in their hands Dimsdale's "Vigilantes," with the assurance that all it contained relative to their brother was true. . . . The following day we called upon the brother, who, with a voice broken by sobs and sighs, informed us that his sister was so prostrated with grief at the revelation of her brother's career that she could not see us. He thanked us for making known to them the terrible history.[166]

Dimsdale, a man who wanted to "prove not only the necessity for [the vigilantes'] actions, but the equity of their proceedings," succeeded in framing Plummer's death for his family as an execution rather than a murder. According to Foucault, "the narrative of murder settles into [a] dangerous area." "Dangerous" because, as Foucault observes, it "posits the relation between power and the people."[167] These narratives served precisely this function for the vigilantes, positing—as in the case of Plummer's family—their position within, against, and above the law.

According to Barde, "History watches only those whom it admires."[168] Foucault's "Tale of Murder" introduces a more complicated understanding of history, suggesting instead that history's narrative *decides* whom it, and we, will admire. The *events* in the vigilante narratives are not, categorically, heroic events. In fact, they might be perceived as distinctly *un*heroic, often involving confrontations between hundreds, or thousands, of vigilantes and one or a few "desperadoes." And while some of these narrators, like Dimsdale, make a point of arguing that vigilantes were never cruel, or excessive, the fact is that they were sometimes remarkably sadistic.[169] The vigilantes' historians produced these accounts to justify the violent practices of the vigilantes. In doing so, they made recourse to a set of formulaic elements that sought to establish the necessity and inevitability of their actions. Their repetitive assertion of extraordinary criminal conditions, an absence of law and order, and the valor of their own practices created the basic justification for a range of extreme and often questionable practices. And notwithstanding the vehemence of these justifications, the narratives' subsequent assertions about *orderliness* and *public popularity* offer further evidence of how indeterminate the practices of the vigilantes really were.

# 2

# Heroic Stories

*Vigilante Ideals and Lynching Truths*

A n ideal vigilance committee convened and acted in an organized and evenhanded manner in response to uncontrolled criminal conditions and was roundly supported and applauded by its community for doing so. This story of vigilante practice is told again and again by vigilantes, their official historians, and their later admiring chroniclers. But this construction, like the "Bible Belt pornography" of the southern lynching narrative, has only an approximate relationship to real lynching events.[1] In this chapter, I examine two secondary features of this frontier vigilante narrative—orderliness and public popularity—in order to demonstrate that the narrative of ideal vigilantism was important to the vigilantes themselves, not just their historians. My analysis in this chapter continues to draw on the most important critical premise developed within scholarship about southern lynching. Ida B. Wells and her successors effectively proved that the stories lynchers tell about their practices are not necessarily true. This crucial observation applies not only to southern lynching but to lynching in the frontier as well. The organizational and procedural practices of vigilantes did *not* guarantee equitable proceedings for those tried by the committees. In fact, between the lines of the vigilantes' own justificatory histories lay the traces of their own farcical engagements with the law. Vigilantes were *not* universally respected and adored by their communities; in fact, they were frequently criticized, challenged, and openly accused of breaking the law. But even in the presence of these less than ideal truths, vigilantes were aware of and sought to both attain and present themselves according to an idealized version of vigilantism. The bulk of this chapter focuses on two particularly vivid, though not unique, vigilante events in order to examine the way in which the narrative ideals of "orderliness" and "public popularity" were produced. By magnifying each of these events, it is possible to see the subtle accrual of narrative during, around, and after these violent moments. The chapter concludes with examples from the larger collection of official vigilante histories.

The first event comes from Charles Summerfield's *Illustrated Lives of the Desperadoes of the New World*, a narrative about a vigilance committee in northwest Arkansas.[2] Summerfield, recall, was a pseudonym for Alfred W. Arrington, a minister turned lawyer. I focus here on Summerfield's account of the 1842 Cane Hill Company's "trial" and execution of five men. This trial reveals the peculiar way in which vigilantes adopted, and adapted, the forms of state-sanctioned court proceedings to advance their own aims and to instantiate the narratives subsequently told about them. Organization and orderliness function in a particular way in this trial for both the vigilantes and their public, serving what might best be described as a legitimizing, though not necessarily legitimate, function. The second event comes from the Alder Gulch, Montana, vigilance committee of 1864 and concerns the ideal, but forcibly constructed, public popularity of this movement. As discussed at length in the Introduction, Captain J. A. Slade was executed by this committee for defying their self-asserted authority and jurisdiction—he literally tore their arrest warrant to shreds. But Slade's spectacular and troubling execution was not the only occasion in which the Alder Gulch committee acted swiftly and forcefully to eliminate challengers and detractors. Public popularity, as the story of this committee reveals, was willfully, violently, and successfully constructed by these vigilantes. I conclude the chapter by opening a discussion as to how, in the presence of these less than ideal vigilantes' pasts, vigilantism became idealized within the context of a broader western history.

The cases and documents I use make it possible to identify differences between the events surrounding a given vigilance committee or lynching and the way that these events were narrated by vigilantes and their historians. The inaccuracies in the narrative accounts are interesting in their own right—creating an opportunity for revised historical interpretations of some particularly well-known frontier vigilance committees.[3] But my central concern here is with how the narrative of ideal vigilantism functioned alongside the practices of the vigilantes to not only legitimate but inform their actions. This unusual relationship between narrative and practice is analogous to Foucault's work in the "Tales of Murder" essay, wherein he analyzes the relationship between Rivière's murderous actions and his confessional narrative.[4] Foucault asserts:

In Rivière's behavior memoir and murder were not arranged simply in chronological sequence—crime and then narrative. The text does not relate directly to the deed; a whole web of relations is woven between the one and the other; they support one another and carry one another in ever-changing relations.[5]

In Rivière's case, Foucault suggests that the murder itself was an enactment of a preexisting narrative—of "a memoir stored beforehand in the memory."[6] Foucault's notion of a "web of relations" between violence and narrative provides a provocative way of thinking about the function of lynching narratives and their intermittent inaccuracies. As the examples in this chapter will demonstrate, there is a constitutive and reciprocal relationship between the idealized narrative of vigilante practice and what actual vigilantes did to conform to these narratively constructed ideals. Indeed, one aspect of this constitutive and reciprocal relationship was revealed in the last chapter through the ways that historians designated by the vigilantes produced idealized accounts of committees' activities. That impulse is present in this chapter as well, but the examples I look at here also reveal that vigilantes conformed their own practices and activities to the narrative of ideal vigilantism—what Foucault calls, in the case of Rivière, "a memoir stored before hand in the memory." The vigilantes' attempts to perform narrative ideals served to shore up, and make ever more indelible, the formulaic vigilante narrative that circulated among regions and vigilance committees—creating, in effect, yet another layer of constitutive reciprocity between event and narratives. The "web of relations" here operated not only at the level of individual vigilance committees (or, as in Foucault's Rivière example, with respect to single deeds and narratives) but also among multiple vigilance committees' deeds and narratives and across periods and regions.[7]

One example of the complex relationship between lynching event and narrative can be seen by returning to the Mark Twain lynching account. As a reminder: In August 1901 a young woman was attacked, though *not* sexually assaulted, on her way home from church in Pierce City, Missouri.[8] Three men were lynched for the crime. Twain's treatment of the story, however, makes recourse to the predictable figures associated with a southern lynching tale—a black male *sexual* predator, a white female victim, and a heroic white male who attempted to but could not protect her. In Twain's account, the narrative formula of southern lynching comes to stand in for actual events, making the subsequent lynching violence meaningful and comprehensible in a particular, if not terribly accurate, way. Twain's intention may have been good—the retelling is included in his vitriolic antilynching screed "The United States of Lyncherdom" (1901)—but the effects of his narrative constitution of this violence were considerably more complex.[9] Twain relied centrally on the formulaic narrative associated with lynching in the turn-of-the-century South—a reliance that, in this case, misrepresented the actual events in Pierce City. The specific result here was to contribute to the wider misperception that the young white woman had been raped by a black man (or men). Twain's point, a good one certainly, was that no crime justified mob brutality. Nonetheless, Twain's commentary worked to shore up deadly falsehoods about black men sexually assaulting white women. The false deployment of this formulaic narrative was replayed over and over again in the Jim Crow South, producing what Ida B. Wells first argued was a rape myth and what Jacquelyn Dowd Hall called, over a century later, "Bible Belt pornography." In Foucault's words, a complex "web of relations" existed between violent events and narratives about this violence.[10]

A web of relations can also be traced within the production of stories about particular lynchings and/or vigilantes in the frontier, and between these particular narratives and narratives about frontier vigilantism more broadly. The vigilante narrative was composed of certain predictable features such as uncontrolled criminals and valorous vigilantes. As Foucault suggests, the temporal relationship between event and narrative can be complicated—a preexisting narrative might invite and enable certain actions. In the case of the vigilantes' historians, a preexisting and formulaic narrative may have been the most effective means of constituting and legitimating a set of events. But it might also mean—as in Rivière's case and as in the case of the vigilance committees in this chapter—that events themselves were an enactment of a preexisting story. Ultimately, the web surrounding vigilante events and narratives comprised all of these possible relations.

This chapter demonstrates the way that the complex web of relations between vigilante event and vigilante narrative worked. In all of these examples, the practices of actual vigilantes departed from the constructed narrative of ideal vigilantism. But even in the presence of these less than ideal practices, the vigilantes made gestures toward *performing* the ideal characteristics contained in the vigilante narrative. So, for example, while the Cane Hill vigilantes were not being legitimately orderly, they made a tremendous show of orderly practice. While the Alder Gulch vigilantes were not universally popular, they went to great lengths to make it appear as if they were. A narrative of ideal vigilantism carried and supported the practices of the vigilantes in a series of complex relations, all of which were characterized by a reciprocal exchange between idealized narrative descriptions and the peculiar ways in which actual vigilantes attempted to enact these ideals.

This chapter also reveals a different but important use for the archived documents of vigilantes. In the case of the Cane Hill vigilantes, a close reading of the official history written by Charles Summerfield about the committee reveals some internal contradictions. The narration of events is largely critical of the vigilantes, yet the portions of the narrative that discuss vigilantism abstractly, or in general terms, are insistent about the benefits of vigilante organizing. Summerfield's account reveals a clear tension between the obligations of the vigilante historian to create an idealized account of the vigilantes and this narrator's awareness that these vigilantes' actions weren't entirely ideal. Summerfield's ambivalence was as personal as it was ideological. In 1839, he convened a vigilance committee of his own when Fayetteville courts refused to support his prosecution of a murderer.[11] But Summerfield's *own* willingness to resort to extralegal means didn't mean he couldn't see the grievous flaws in the practices of the Cane Hill vigilantes—a relatively common occurrence among vigilante practitioners who understood their own practices as necessary and legitimate while refusing to endorse any and all vigilantism. This familiar tension produced, in this case, a paradoxical but intriguing record. It becomes particularly clear here that these narratives serve less to offer an accurate view of past events than to help us see how the vigilantes and their historians were using narrative to constitute and/or legitimate certain practices. In this light, the formalized and idealized claims made by Summerfield as well as the parts of his narrative that contradict or complicate these idealized claims are equally useful. In the case of the Alder Gulch vigilantes, the presence of multiple official histories along with private documents of some of the leading members of the vigilance committee reveal how the idealized narratives were functioning for the vigilantes. In all of the cases in this chapter, it becomes clear that the narrative of ideal vigilantism was not only the formal conceit of the vigilantes' historians but a crucial and constitutive construction for the vigilantes as well.

## "Hang Him First and Try Him Afterward": The Myth of Orderly Justice

Late one evening in 1840, three men entered a home on Cane Hill in northwestern Arkansas and fatally stabbed a man named Wright.[12] The men then shot and used a dagger to dismember two of Wright's daughters. Wright's wife and his four remaining children escaped with their lives, although their twelve-year-old son remained permanently impaired from a severe head injury sustained during the attack. The three men lit the house on fire before fleeing from the scene, thereby alerting neighbors to the bloody crime. Within hours, a crowd of horrified onlookers had gathered around the remains of the three slain Wrights and their home. By noon the following day, the crowd numbered in the thousands and included the local vigilantes—the Cane Hill Company— as well as their thirty-member executive committee. Such an admittedly brutal crime provoked the vigilantes, and they vowed to act immediately. The vigilantes' leader, Captain John West, swore that they "would never give over the search until the murderers were discovered and the foul deed avenged!"[13] The desire for vengeance quickly overwhelmed the would-be lynchers, and rather than engaging in any sort of investigation, they proceeded to hold a trial immediately. Given that the committee had no one in particular to put on trial, the proceedings were necessarily a bit unusual.

The trial began with a diffuse, community-wide interrogation:

> The first act of the committee marked the heights of desperation to which the excitement had risen. They passed a resolution that every man in the community should prove, by other testimony than his own, his precise "whereabout" [sic] on the fatal night of the murder. That was placing every man's life at the mercy of chance, to establish a precarious *alibi*! And to show that they were resolved to carry out the rule of evidence to its extreme consequences, with the utmost rigor, every member of the committee and company, at the outset, was required, and actually succeeded in substantiating the *marvellous* [sic] *alibi*.[14]

Five men were singled out during this initial phase of the Cane Hill Company's trial. The vigilantes' procedural ingenuity was quickly revealed during the interrogation of their five suspects. The first man, William Collins, struggled with the vigilantes and, as a result, was beaten with fists and clubs and "tickled [in the] ribs with bowie knives."[15] The committee's efforts to subdue their suspect backfired, in a sense, when Collins's submission to their brutality made him begin to appear incompetent:

> [Collins's] response was a tissue of contradictions. Every sentence was a falsehood, which always seemed to be uttered for the purpose of augmenting the suspicions against himself. So that the committee of thirty at last concluded that he was an idiot; and as he established the *sine qua non*, alibi, he was restored to liberty for the time being.[16]

Though Summerfield does not state this explicitly, it appears as though the committee, irregular though its interrogation may have been, had a working idea about legal competence.

The second suspect, John Patterson, was examined and his case "terminated pretty much in the same manner."[17] The third man, Thomas Jones, vociferously challenged the committee's authority during his interrogation, "and some of the committee began to talk about *burning*."[18] Only after a respected community member verified Jones's whereabouts on the night of the murder was he also released. The committee's fourth suspect, James Barnes, reacted differently to the committee's assaults, such that "the clearness of his statement and the promptitude of his replies to all interrogations, manifestly disconcerted the committee. . . . It was only when a proposition was made to bring up his wife for examination, that he lost, for one instant only, his sublime self-control."[19] On the basis of the corroborating testimony of his wife, and that of two other witnesses, however, Barnes was released as well. The committee's final suspect, Ellerey Turner, was then brought before the vigilantes.

Summerfield included a transcript of Turner's interrogation, "in the *exact* words of the questions and answers, as nearly as [he could] recollect them," which contains the following excerpts:[20]

> Uncle Buck.[21] Mr. Turner, will you please inform the committee where you were on the night of the murder of Wright and family?
>
> Turner. I wish first to be informed what right you have either to question or suspect me?
>
> Uncle Buck. It is needless to talk about that. We have all gone through the same examination, and you must do so too.
>
> Turner. But you were not examined in chains?
>
> Uncle Buck (Disconcerted.) There was no ground to suppose we were murderers.
>
> Turner. And what grounds have you for supposing that I am a murderer? . . .
>
> Uncle Buck. (With increasing ferocity,) It is suspicion enough, that you seem unwilling to tell *where* you were when Wright's family was butchered.[22]

When Turner refused to answer any of the committee's questions, they prepared a brush fire; whether it was created to torture or execute him is unclear.[23] Faced with this immanent possibility, Turner's fiancée, Rose, intervened and confessed to the committee that the couple was together on the night of the murder and that Turner had refused to admit as much to protect her honor. But the committee refused to hear Rose's testimony because she was engaged to Turner.

Uncle Buck. Then, in that case we cannot admit your bare, unsupported evidence, my pretty maiden. We are sorry for you; but we
must be governed by the legal rules of evidence.

Rose. But have you any proof against Ellerey?

Uncle Buck. That is not to the purpose. We have laid down the rule, that
every person must prove his innocence or bear the consequences.
There is no other method of avenging the atrocious murder.[24]

The eventual testimony of a witness to Rose and Ellerey's unchaperoned tryst
convinced the committee to free Turner. The committee, having released their
five primary suspects, "then held a secret meeting, from whose sitting all strangers, all spectators were excluded; and soon adjourned indefinitely."[25]

The interrogation phase of the Cane Hill trial contained many irregularities and innumerable legal infractions, but, according to Summerfield, matters
only deteriorated after the five men were released. The committee rearrested
the men to conduct a second trial. This time, they attempted to provoke a
confession from Patterson by whipping him "till his bare back was cut into
ribbons of gory skin, and the blood ran down and stood in red puddles at his
feet."[26] The committee denied his pleas for water and to see his wife and child
before dying. In desperation, Patterson finally confessed to the murders and,
after further coercion, to the involvement of the four other men. All five men
were sentenced to die, and two days later, they were hanged. Two years later, a
group of Cherokee men delivered two men, the Price brothers, to Fayetteville,
twenty miles east of Cane Hill. Because five men had already been hanged
for the Wright murders, the Price brothers believed they were safe and confessed to the crime.[27] Partially as a result of interference from the Cane Hill
Company, no witnesses appeared at the Prices' state-run trial, and they were
discharged from custody.[28] And so, as Summerfield ends the story, "the guilty
went free, and the sinless were lying in their cold graves."[29]

Vigilantes often engaged in such "legal proceedings," or trials.[30] Given
their intrinsic location outside of state-sanctioned juridical structures, these
proceedings took on an ambivalent cast, neither wholly replicating nor com-
pletely distorting the formulas and practices of sanctioned legal proceedings.
Legal historian Lawrence M. Friedman aptly summarizes this ambiguity by
stating, "The 'trials' run by the Vigilance Committees were highly irregular;
but they never quite descended to barbarism, and they would not have been
totally unrecognizable to a lawyer."[31] His characterization correctly captures
the strange paradox of vigilante trials—conducted, on the one hand, in defiance or circumvention of state-sanctioned legal proceedings, and yet making
use of many of the same forms and practices, albeit in remade or distorted

ways. These paradoxical proceedings, I argue, were one of the ways in which vigilantes produced their own conduct in accordance with one significant feature of the vigilante ideal—orderliness.

Summerfield's account of the Cane Hill Company reveals his own ambivalence about the committee's activities. It is clear that he became *more* distressed with the committee as events progressed; he praised the committee's organization, neutrally described the first interrogation, criticized the second trial and Patterson's torture, and vehemently decried the executions. The escalation of events, in fact, formed the basis of Summerfield's sense of narrative obligation—he wrote the account based on a pre-execution request from Ellerey Turner. Summerfield's change in tone throughout the narrative indicates that the vigilantes' actions during the weeks following the murders and arson grew increasingly illegitimate. In other words, even if the committee's initial mechanism of narrowing suspicion was remotely equitable, the resulting interrogation did not, to use Friedman's terms, produce "arguments and doubts"; rather, the proceeding worked against the five men, actually making them *become* guilty. Paradoxically, the vigilantes became more "orderly" and less equitable in even measure.

This dangerous direction of events is already evident during the first interrogation when Ellerey Turner demanded that Uncle Buck explain why he was under suspicion ("What ground have you for supposing that I am a murderer?") and Uncle Buck reframed Turner's challenge as evidence of his guilt ("It is suspicion enough, that you seem unwilling to tell *where* you were when Wright's family were [sic] butchered."). Turner increased, rather than diminished, his vulnerability to the committee by challenging their authority— "I wish first to be informed what right you have either to question or suspect me." Whether Turner was "right" in any legal or moral sense, Uncle Buck's reply—"It is needless to talk about that"—accurately and fatally summarizes Turner's position within the proceeding. Challenging the vigilantes' authority and identifying the explicit illegality of the proceeding made Turner seem more, rather than less, guilty in the committee's eyes. Yet in spite of the "guilty-seeming" conduct of the five suspects during the interrogation—as evidenced by fighting back, seeming dishonesty, an inability to answer questions, and challenges—the vigilantes pursued an orderly performance rather than an expedient resolution and released the men pending further and more compelling "evidence" of their guilt.

By this point, however, it would seem the men were doomed.[32] Their conduct during the initial interrogation had made them seem guilty to the committee. And as a result of their harsh treatment at the hands of the vigilantes, the five suspected men began to voice public criticism of the committee.

According to Summerfield, "From the irritation produced by the memory of those shameful wrongs, the *five* who had suffered most keenly, had, as a matter of course, said many hard things concerning the Cane-Hill lynchers, in which censure their friends had joined, and a strong tide of popular feeling was beginning to flow in their favor."[33] The five men's public criticism of the committee directly challenged the vigilantes' claim to authority in, and on behalf of, their community. The committee rose to this challenge, and after some strategic wrangling and maneuvering, rearrested the five men. But the men were still not lynched; instead, the committee reconvened to conduct its second proceeding, a three-day trial. While the initial proceeding had been public, the new trial was not, but, according to Summerfield, "thousands of anxious spectators collected at Boonsborough, from all parts of the country, even from southern Missouri, and from the Indian Territory."[34]

Summerfield's painstakingly detailed description of the geography of the Cane Hill area explains how this technically *private* proceeding was actually a public spectacle. He describes the committee's "hall of justice" as "a beautiful little cone of a peak near the centre of the Cane-Hill group."[35] On the western slope of this hill, "beneath a mighty oak . . . the committee of thirty organized their court."[36] At the base of the hill, and on the other side of a stream, lay the town of Boonsborough. In this town, and "in full view of the peak," thousands of spectators gathered, "anxious to penetrate the mystery in which [the committee's] . . . proceedings were shrouded."[37] But the crowds' anxious participation in the trial was limited to a long view from the bottom of the hill, as the stream was guarded by "a chosen band of twelve—men of known and desperate daring."[38] The vigilantes' trial was "private" only in the sense that the crowds of interested community members were not allowed to hear the testimony of the witnesses or the deliberations of the committee. But the occurrence of the trial itself was a matter of central public interest, as the proceeding unfolded dramatically on the hillside above the town.

Summerfield's account of this second proceeding is worth citing at length, both because it captures the local color of the trial and because Summerfield, a judge, had a keen eye trained on the legitimacy of the vigilantes' ideas about legal practices.

> Through the intervention of a friend I was permitted to be present at the deliberation of the committee, and to see and hear everything that happened. Several other members of the bar obtained the same permission. This time the committee sat several days in succession. Many witnesses were brought before them and examined; but their testimony

was exceedingly slight. It mostly related to looks; tones of the voice; mysterious gestures; words let fall in fits of intoxication; expressions of hatred towards the men, or the actions of the Cane-Hill Company, uttered in a state of passion, by those now doomed to be the victims, or by their relatives and friends. All the rules of legal evidence were outraged; all the ordinary methods of proof were set at nought. Hearsay, vague rumor, were solemnly installed in authority. A shake of the head, a shrug of the shoulders, were regarded as unquestionable proofs of guilt. A change of countenance from red to pale, observed even by moonlight, was gravely related as an infallible symptom of a conscience ill at ease; and every word disapproving the proceedings of the lynchers was set down as a positive proof of murder.[39]

At the end of the third day, "Romping Ann" Stockton traveled up the hill to appear before the committee. "Red-haired, red-eyed, brazen-browed, and half-drunk," she testified that her lover, John Patterson, had confessed to the murder and had implicated the four other men.[40] As a result of her testimony, Patterson (as noted above) was brought back before the committee; tortured; and, along with the others, sentenced to die. Summerfield concluded that Stockton had been paid for her testimony "by some *infernal* in the service of the company, to trump up the story, *so as to give a pretext of justice to the vengeance which many regarded as already too long delayed*."[41] This final phrase in the passage from Summerfield makes it clear that while an interest in swift justice remained salient a month following the murder, the justice had to have at least the *appearance* of legitimacy.

The cultivation of this legitimacy is evident in all stages of the vigilantes' actions—requiring committee members to produce alibis, initially releasing the five suspects, conducting a second three-day trial (notably witnessed by attorneys), drawing on witness testimony, and going to great lengths to secure a "confession" from Patterson to justify the executions. But this of course raises the question—how "legitimate" could any of these strange procedures have seemed to an onlooker like Summerfield? The absence of an alibi offered no real proof of guilt, the released men were already doomed, the second trial was long but farcical, the vigilantes' star witness was a drunken woman of "ill-repute," and they brutally tortured Patterson physically and emotionally to make him confess. But in spite of all these strange and unfair practices, heartily and critically narrated by Summerfield himself, the paradoxical answer to the question is that the vigilantes' efforts to legitimize their actions produced the desired effect.

According to Summerfield, organization is at the center of vigilantism and is what distinguishes the practice from mobocracy. Regarding those who criticize lynching, he asserts:

> [They] are not only perfectly unacquainted with the real causes of lynching, but also profoundly ignorant of the formal proceedings in the courts of the lynchers. They suppose these assemblages to be mere mobs. . . .
>
> Such a view is utterly incorrect. A company of lynchers have almost nothing in common with a common mob. They have, so to speak, always, a written constitution and *organic law*; a committee of examination, who hear the evidence against the culprit, under oath; deliberate, and pass sentence. They have regularly elected officers, whose duty is not only to *catch*, but to *hang*.[42]

Yet Summerfield, as noted in the previous chapter, was also keenly aware of the ways that vigilantes were unhampered by the strictures of sanctioned (if not organic) law. He wrote:

> Backwoodsmen view the disciples of Blackstone as their worst foes, who rescue every culprit from the clutches of justice. It is the lawyers who pick holes in every indictment. It is they who wheedle and mystify the judge. The arrival of a lawyer, therefore, in a new settlement, is regarded as the most serious calamity—an evil omen of coming misfortunes.[43]

These two seemingly paradoxical ideas accurately describe the Cane Hill Company. The vigilantes "organized," Summerfield claims, "under a constitution as eloquent in its declaration of rights, and as precise in its definition of specific lynching powers, as the Constitution of the American Union in its enumeration of the separate elements of federal jurisdiction."[44] And there was, in the course of the trial, "a committee of examination" who heard evidence against the accused and passed sentence. Yet the Cane Hill Company was able to make contingent and flexible use of all these procedures and practices such that their process was both expedient *and* legitimized.

In other words, the fact that the Cane Hill Company was organized and orderly established them, within Summerfield's definition, as legitimate vigilantes as opposed to a murderous mob. And the fact they were still able to achieve their desired ends made them superior to the bureaucratically hampered state. Summerfield documented but could not reconcile the conflict between the real and imperfect Cane Hill vigilantes and his abstract ideal of vigilantism. The potentially ephemeral distinction between "good" insurgency and "bad" mobocracy had been an issue since the nation's beginnings. As Carroll Smith-Rosenberg notes, political thinkers in the early national period were preoccupied by the question: "How popular could popular sovereignty become before anarchy ensued?"[45] The very political impulse that legitimated vigilante organizing—and democratic insurgency more generally—always threatened to exceed the bounds of contextual acceptability. Vigilante defenders drew on ideas of "organization" and "moderation" to establish the line of demarcation and the vigilantes' location on the proper side of these distinctions.

Summerfield was not the only vigilante enthusiast to draw on "organization" as a requisite feature of vigilantism. The same idea can be seen in a passage from Hubert Howe Bancroft's *Popular Tribunals*, in which he offers a distinction between the dignity of vigilance committees and the horrors of "mobocracy":

> Wherever we find a body of armed members of the community acting contrary to law or in opposition to officers of the law, be it composed of the best citizens or the worst, be its existence a necessity, its acts productive of social well-being, or otherwise, if it is an organized band, acting under fixed rules, acting with coolness and deliberation, with good intentions, determined to promote rather than to defeat the ends of justice, such a body is what upon the Pacific Coast has become [*sic*] to be known as a Committee of Vigilance. Though it may have the same object view, and though it may accomplish the same results, if the body or association be not organized or officered, if it be without constitution, by-laws, rule, or regulation, acting under momentary excitement or in the heat of passion, careless of the administration of justice, swayed only by resentment, intent on making a display, infuriate, unreasonable, vengeful, it is a mob, though composed of doctors of divinity.[46]

For Bancroft "lynch mobs" can be rightly criticized for vengeful, disorganized violence, but "proper" vigilantism is characterized by order, deliberation, and procedure. The Cane Hill Company meets Bancroft's objective criteria for vigilantism versus mobocracy; they were organized *and* officered, had a constitution, and deferred the initial heat of passion following the Wrights' murders long enough to hold three separate proceedings. In other words, consistent with Summerfield's and Bancroft's ideal forms of vigilantism, the Cane Hill Company was justified and valorous in what they did. The paradox here is that they were also fatally wrong.

Bancroft additionally suggests that qualitative distinctions can, and should, be made between vigilance committees and lynch mobs. These distinctions require that we ask: Was the Cane Hill Company acting "with coolness and deliberation" and "good intentions"? Were they "determined to promote rather than to defeat the ends of justice"? While Summerfield is critical of this particular vigilance committee's procedures and practices, they still meet the threshold of "intention" outlined by Bancroft. However perverse and unjust the committee's practices may have been, they were not random or exclusively ill-intentioned. But no amount of good intentions or ephemera of procedures mitigates the fact that the vigilantes murdered five men. Except that, paradoxically, it is precisely the ephemera of procedures that might mitigate this fact for Bancroft and Summerfield. The formalistic and procedural aspects of the Cane Hill Company's lynchings served to legitimize the violence for the lynchers themselves and for their later chroniclers. In other words, the committee's deliberate though farcical trial practices served to constitute the committee's practices in relationship to the vigilante ideal of orderliness. There is little wonder then that the vigilantes were intent on appearing to be orderly, for in doing so they also appeared to be legitimate.

The aspiration to "orderliness," however, couldn't usurp vigilantism's central and defining aspiration to expedience. Friedman makes it clear that one of the significant appeals of vigilantism was its community-sating immediacy:

> The men of the mob had the satisfaction, grim though it was, of a justice that lay literally in their hardened hands; they pulled on the ropes themselves, not through surrogates. Regular courts would never have been so swift. To many people, punishment is twice as satisfying when it works with white-hot immediacy, when the arguments and doubts of a trial do not disturb its naked emotions.[47]

"White-hot immediacy" aptly characterizes the moment in which the outraged community in Cane Hill gathered around the smoldering remains of the Wright home and the vigilantes' leader vowed to "avenge the foul deed." But it was a month and two proceedings later before the company had established the (admittedly) dubious basis for executing five men. It is impossible to determine with certainty, based on Summerfield's account, the degree of "inevitability" associated with these lynchings. But close attention to the way in which events unfolded suggests that while the proceedings served a partially legitimate function, the *symbolic* significance of the trials was equally, if not more, important to the vigilantes.

Drawing partially on the idea of swift justice, vigilantism is also explained as an intervention into ineffectual, absent, or corrupt state criminal prosecution. Brown offers an extensive, and elegant, analysis of this possibility in his chapter "Lawless Lawfulness: Legal and Behavioral Perspectives on American Vigilantism."[48] His review of legal writings from the late nineteenth and early twentieth centuries identifies three ways in which period legal experts supported and defended lynch law—economy (insofar as lynching reduced the public's cost for supporting trials), popular sovereignty (as lynching was a direct expression of public opinion), and efficiency (as the vigilantes circumvented the excesses and absurdities of state-sanctioned court proceedings).[49] Brown identifies this third aspect of vigilantism—efficacy and efficiency—as the most frequently occurring, and compelling, justification for vigilantism in these writings. He asserts:

> Whether behaving legally as lawyers or judges or extralegally as participants in lynch law these leaders of late nineteenth-century America were motivated by their desire to repress crime. To them the law, rigorously applied, seemed to hamper justice, whereas lynch law enhanced it. It is this that explains why some founders of state bar associations could also be unashamed participants in lynch law. They saw no contradiction. . . . The illuminati rationalized the practice of vigilantism and sought reform not through aggressive law enforcement to suppress lynch law but though modification of the regular system of law and order in ways that would have accentuated the simplicity, certainty and severity of vigilantism.[50]

According to Brown, period legal experts described and justified vigilantism by making reference to the vigilantes' seemingly superior procedural practices. But just as Friedman's idea about speedy justice doesn't explain the extended procedural delays of the Cane Hill vigilantes, the vigilantes' legal defenders would be unable to explain why the vigilantes engaged in extended procedures that deferred "simplicity" and "certainty" in favor of intricate procedural performances. Not only did these proceedings significantly delay any ultimate punishment; they also involved deliberate, albeit distorted, adaptations of state trial procedures. If the central draw of vigilantism was its ability to circumvent compulsory procedural elements, the Cane Hill Company would have, and certainly could have, more successfully done so. Instead, the committee made deliberate use of the forms of state law in order to further establish their organizational legitimacy.

This strategic deployment of state law is clearly documented in the details of the first two proceedings. During the initial interrogation, the committee rose to James Barnes's challenge—"The clearness of his statement and the promptitude of his replies to all interrogations, manifestly disconcerted the committee"—by drawing his wife into the proceedings—"It was only when a proposition was made to bring up his wife for examination, that he lost, for an instant only, his sublime self-control." Only moments later, however, Uncle Buck correctly "remembered" that spousal testimony was, as a matter of law, inadmissible.[51] He rejected Rose's defense of Ellerey ("We cannot admit your bare, unsupported evidence") by grandly reasserting statutory law ("We must be governed by the legal rules of evidence."). In fact, the committee was not governed strictly by *any* laws, regarding evidence or anything else, but references to the rule of law, like this one, reinforced the vigilantes' claims to legitimacy. The committee's use of state law was characterized by adaptation, as well as irregular adoption. The initial proceeding began with an assertion that all men were guilty until proven innocent, a notion "not totally unrecognizable to a lawyer" as an inversion of a constitutionally guaranteed trial. At the second, longer trial Summerfield notes that "all the legal rules of evidence were outraged" and that the committee heard from a "steady stream of sworn witnesses."[52] This is a colorful assessment of the proceeding to be sure, but it helps to capture the committee's irregular recognition of the forms governing a state-run trial.

A drive toward increased prosecutorial efficiency and efficacy does not explain why the vigilantes would bother to engage with, and rework, the familiar procedural elements of a trial. Bancroft disparages those who harshly criticize the extralegality of vigilantism, asking, "Were it not better they should turn their attention to the root of the matter and rectify the necessity that engenders them? Strip from law its trammels, its hypocrisy, humbug, and technical chicanery, and mete the evil-doer quick and certain punishment."[53] Bancroft's assertion reveals the degree to which a narrative of ideal vigilantism was used to justify and defend a range of different, even contradictory, practices. Procedural elements enacted by the state were regarded as "technical chicanery," but these same elements enacted by the vigilantes indicated careful deliberation and right-mindedness and distinguished them from unchecked mobs even when, as in the Cane Hill case, these orderly practices resulted in illegitimate and deadly violence.[54]

Summerfield's account of the Cane Hill trial is unusually colorful and detailed, but there is nothing unique about the proceeding itself. Vigilantes engaged in all manner of "legal" proceedings to shore up their legitimacy and establish themselves positively with respect to the vigilante ideal. The

1851 San Francisco Committees of Vigilance held lengthy proceedings during which witnesses submitted "character testimony" about those suspected of criminal activity.[55] The Payette, Idaho, vigilance committee's first order of business was to "prosecute" those participating in the bogus gold dust trade.[56] The 1868 vigilance committee in Laramie, Wyoming, held a "formal and impartial trial" and condemned six men to death and banished forty others.[57] In all of these cases, the "trials" took place without the presence of the accused men.

In a chapter devoted to vigilantism in Idaho, Bancroft praises the vigilantes for their ability to work creatively, and effectively, outside of the law. He asserts: "What follows forcibly illustrates the difference between the ability and energy of court officials and the average man of business in ferreting criminals and bringing them to punishment. Every thought and action of the one is hampered by form, while the other is free to employ his wits and to follow them."[58] While Bancroft is overlooking the extent to which "proper" vigilantism was quite formalized, he is quite correct that vigilance committees demonstrated remarkable creativity in devising new kinds of trial proceedings. The "employment of wits" found a vigilance committee in Lafayette Parish questioning a group of murder suspects at the gravesite of the murder victims.[59] A suspected murderer in Bannack was transported to the location where the victim's body was found for interrogation.[60] Creative reconfigurations of trial settings, such as these, or trial procedures, such as those in Arkansas, California, Idaho, and Wyoming reveal the range and complexity of vigilante legal proceedings.[61] These proceedings slowed the passions of swift justice and deliberately engaged with state law in aspiration to legitimacy and in order to enact the vigilante ideal of *orderliness*. This cultivation of procedural legitimacy lent itself, in turn, to the constitution of another important component of ideal vigilantism—*public popularity*.

## "It Don't Change the Real State of Facts": The Myth of Popular Justice

In mid-December 1863, a young man from Nevada City named Nicholas Tbalt was hired to collect a pair of mules from the outlying valleys.[62] When days passed and Tbalt did not return, the mules' owners began to suspect that he'd stolen their livestock. Their misperception came to light a few days later when a local hunter came across the young man's dead body concealed in a sagebrush thicket. Tbalt's corpse was conveyed to Nevada City, where "hundreds of people from Nevada, Virginia City and the other towns in the gulch" saw for themselves that "the body . . . bore the marks of a small lariat about the throat, which had been used to drag him, while still living, to the place of concealment."[63] Twenty-five outraged men convened a posse and left Nevada City in search of the murderers.[64] They apprehended three men—John "Long John" Frank, George Ives, and George "Old Tex" Hillerman—and brought them back to Nevada City. The posse, and their supporters, decided to hold their own trial in Nevada City instead of transporting the suspected murderers to Virginia City and into the hands of the local authorities. It wasn't that there was no state-sanctioned law and order in the area; it was that the posse didn't *like* the local authorities. Specifically, they suspected that the sheriff, Henry Plummer, was the leader of an elaborately organized criminal gang whose members included their suspects—Frank, Ives, and Hillerman. On the basis of this belief, they were doubtful that the men would be convicted in a sanctioned criminal trial. Better, they felt, that they should try the men themselves.

Like many of the life-and-death determinations of the vigilantes, the decision to try the case in the miners' court in Nevada City was made on the basis of a "popular vote."[65] But the solicitation of the public's opinion had to be carefully managed to ensure that the outcome of the vote matched the vigilantes' plans. Vigilante prosecutor Henry Fisk Sanders recorded the procedural decision as follows:

> James Gi[bb]on and one or two other friends of Ives had joined in the discussion and assumed to vote, but their votes being challenged, it was decided that they did not possess the requisite qualifications for electors, and their votes were rejected, and proposition to turn them over to the miners' sheriff, at Nevada City was carried; whereupon Gibbons left rapidly on horseback for Virginia City, to advise friends of Ives that he was in peril and to secure the attendance of lawyers.[66]

Here and throughout the trial an association with any of the accused men— in this case, Gibbon's friendship with Ives—disqualified men from being a legitimate part of the "popular."[67] The vigilantes' qualitative assessments about "popular opinion" mirrored their assessments of local criminal courts— anything not to their liking didn't exist.

Ives's trial began the next day in front of a gathering of 1,500 to 2,000 miners; the crowd included numerous friends of the defendant, who had rushed seventy-five miles from Bannack to turn the crowd in his favor.[68] Ives's trial, like the proceeding in Cane Hill, was an imaginative admixture of sanctioned and concocted practices. Ives was prosecuted by Sanders and Charles Bagg and defended by four attorneys—H.P.A. Smith, J. M. Thurmond, Colonel Wood, and John Ritchie. The assembled miners reserved the right to hear and intervene in the investigation, and the twenty-four-member advisory commission/jury was made up of twelve representatives from each of the two mining districts. The defense attorneys sought recourse throughout the trial to statutory law but were soundly overruled. "Long John" testified against Ives (or, to use Dimsdale's description, turned "state's evidence") and was released. Hillerman was tried and found guilty of general association with Ives but, being an older and unthreatening man, was only banished. The trial concluded after three days, when twenty-three of the twenty-four-member miners' jury returned a guilty verdict and Sanders's motion to hang Ives received majority support from the crowd.[69] According to Sanders, Ives's last words on the scaffold were, "I'm not guilty of *this* murder."[70]

One week later, Nevada City's vigilance committee officially organized, but not everyone in the community welcomed the arrival of the vigilante organization. According to Sanders:

> Immediately after the organization of the committee it was confronted with a challenge as to its right to act or exist. Divers [*sic*] and sundry persons, not all of whom belonged to the criminal classes, sought to organize a counter society to resist its action, and lawyers prepared for it a declaration of its purposes and a pledge of fidelity to them and unity of action.[71]

In another document concerning this incident he notes:

> The lawyers identified with this movement were quite in earnest and enthusiastic in propagating its tenets, and were insisting on occasions, in season and out of season upon the sacred right of trial by the constitution and laws of the country qualified to discharge official duties. The vigilance commitee [*sic*] decided that the most effectual way to suppress this movement was to signify to these lawyers that their presence in this community was undesirable and that they should retire. One of them was sent to the Three Forks of the Missouri and the other to Utah, where upon reconsideration the vigilance committee directed the other one to follow.[72]

Even more explicit than their earlier strategy of disenfranchising dissenting voices, the would-be vigilantes elected to remove detractors from the community altogether.

This was actually the second occasion on which a "moderating" party had attempted to organize in Alder Gulch. Sanders also notes that Sheriff

Plummer "conjured up a vast host in the shape of a vigilance committee, and spent . . . ten days endeavoring to incite the alarm of his neighbors lest a blood-thirsty gang of miners organized as a vigilance committee should come to Bannack and hang a large number of its most respected citizens."[73] Plummer's efforts to organize a "moderating" party had begun during Ives's trial and had done little to discourage the rapidly organizing vigilantes. Of course, the vigilantes had already decreed that Plummer and his associates were criminals, not defenders of the law, and their attempts to challenge the vigilantes were easily dismissed. The second attempt at a moderating party was spearheaded by the attorneys who had defended Ives at his trial. These men, with their relentless invocation of sanctioned, statutory law seemed to present a much more substantial threat to the newly formed committee.

Sanders had actually anticipated the possibility of anti-vigilance sentiment and recorded his concerns about the possible effects of these sentiments on public perceptions of the committee. He and committee cofounder Paris Pfouts had agreed that community opinion about the vigilantes would need to be properly fostered early on, for "the large class which exist [*sic*] in every community who, not seeing the exigency, are indifferent to the public's movement, would be swayed hither or thither according as the enterprise was a success or failure in the first instance."[74] As the details of Ives's trial and the detractors' banishments reveal, the vigilantes made concerted efforts to ensure that their initial activities were perceived as successful. Friedman makes a particularly wry and astute observation about the Montana vigilantes, asserting, "It was 'popular justice,' to be sure, but antipopular as well."[75] He is referring specifically to the ways in which committee members "criminalized" behaviors that they disdained but that were highly popular in other sectors of the community—swearing, drinking, and prostitution. Friedman's observation points to another, more insidious, aspect of this committee's relationship to the "popular" as well. The Alder Gulch vigilantes worked deliberately and forcefully to produce and enforce the public's positive perception of them. For public popularity, like orderliness, was a key feature of ideal vigilantism.

A passage written by western cultural scholar Richard Slotkin perfectly captures the link between "public popularity" and the figure of the ideal vigilante.

> Vigilantism represents itself as the expression of the will of civilized society as a whole. . . . But for the vigilante the pretense is thin: in every case, he acts as the agent of only one class or element in his society, asserts his privilege to act and administer violence as if it were mandated by the whole, and even circumvents the will of the majority

to achieve his ends. The vigilante identifies his enemy as a tribelike entity within society, devoted to conspiratorial codes of secret purpose and procedure. Yet the vigilante's own procedures are mirror images of those followed by the tribe or dangerous class he attacks. Since that class probably represents the interests and views of some part of the community—however small—there will always be those who will plausibly assert that it is the vigilante movement that is the conspiracy against the whole, and the supporters of vigilantism, who are the tribe within the settlements, the dangerous class.[76]

Slotkin's assessment underscores the degree to which the court of public opinion was both a central and potentially dangerous defining realm for the vigilantes. Ives's last words on the scaffold, "I am not guilty of *this* murder," exemplify the central vulnerability of vigilante practice—the nebulous relationship between violence as a means of punishing criminals and violence as a criminal practice. Ives's final challenge to the vigilantes invited the Alder Gulch community to read his "execution" as a murder. Public support (or at least the illusion thereof) was not only desirable but essential if the vigilantes were to be regarded as extending or supplementing social order, for public opinion could mean the difference between legitimate vigilantism and vigilantism perceived as antisocial, criminal behavior. The Alder Gulch committee's awareness of this distinction is marked by Sanders and Pfouts's early organizational scheming.

The decision to hold Ives's trial in Nevada City was the inaugural public moment for the would-be vigilantes. The posse had already acted on its own self-conceived authority in arresting the three men and bringing them back to the outraged citizens of Nevada City. Releasing the three men into Plummer's custody at that point would have forestalled the growing vigilante fervor. The "vote" about where to hold the trial was skillfully manipulated to produce a "popular decision" to keep Ives in Nevada City and under the vigilantes' control. The disenfranchisement of dissenting voices likely would have occurred regardless of the dissenters' racial identity. Sanders's assertion that Gibbons was "a friend of Ives" makes this particularly clear—identifying dissenters as either outlaws or outlaw sympathizers was the easiest way for the vigilantes to ensure that all "legitimate" public opinion fell in their favor.[77] This same strategy reappeared when Sanders attempted to mediate a dissenting juror's opinion in the minds of the assembled miners. In suggesting the execution, he exhorted: "The dissenting juror is one of the road agents, beyond all reasonable doubt. I advise hanging the prisoner immediately. There are many lawless people assembling to free him."[78] Many of Ives's friends *were* assembled in the crowd; they had gathered to support and attempt to defend him. But their "popular perspective" on the trial and execution had been subdued by the hundred or so guards surrounding the outdoor courtroom, armed with shotguns and rifles.[79] As Slotkin observes, "The vigilante identifies his enemy as a tribelike entity within society, devoted to conspiratorial codes of secret purpose and procedure."[80] The Alder Gulch committee made consistent reference to the intricately organized outlaws in their midst, using both the alleged existence of and affiliation with this conspiratorial body as the force against which they positioned themselves and as the principle means of constituting their place within the larger social order.

Sheriff Plummer's attempt to organize a moderating party was dismissed by the vigilantes with further recourse to the same strategy—his call for civil order was attributed to his personal fear of the vigilantes as opposed to his elected position as sheriff. But the attorneys who organized a moderating party presented a more profound challenge to the committee. Some of these men had defended Ives during his trial and were keenly aware of the innumerable legal infractions involved in his conviction and execution. The vigilantes were unable to accuse these men of being outlaws themselves—they were "divers [sic] and sundry persons, not all of whom belonged to the criminal classes." And the moderating party was *technically* in the legal right—"insisting on occasions, in season and out of season upon the sacred right of trial by the constitution and laws of the country qualified to discharge official duties." These men worked to swing public opinion against the vigilantes. To resolve this threat, the vigilantes removed them from the community altogether. The success of the Alder Gulch committee's enforcement of their own "popularity" can be seen in an account of this incident, written thirty years later by Bancroft. He states, "Two lawyers, Smith and Thurmond, were driven from the territory by the exasperated people for attempting to clear the banditti when arrested."[81] The vigilantes' own prosecutor, Sanders, was both more honest and ambivalent in his record of the incident. The "people" did not banish Ives's attorneys—the vigilantes did. But the slippage of this attribution in Bancroft's record of the committee is crucial. It marks the degree to which the vigilantes had successfully established their particular ideas about criminality as an expression of *popular* justice.

Richard Brown has eloquently argued that "popular sovereignty" was the cornerstone of the nineteenth century "doctrine of vigilance."[82] In fact, for Brown, variant levels of public support provide a qualitative mechanism for analyzing nineteenth-century vigilantism.

Two "models" of vigilante movements developed. One was the "good" or socially constructive model, in which the vigilante movement dealt

with a problem of disorder straightforwardly and then disbanded. . . .
The other model was the "bad" or socially destructive one, in which a
vigilante movement encountered such strong opposition that the result
was an archaic and socially destructive vigilante war.[83]

He goes on to assert that "some movements were run according to the ideal
theory of vigilantism whereas others were not."[84] But this is a complicated distinction to make within the practices of committees like the one in Alder Gulch.
Inarguably, when vigilantes encountered powerful moderating movements these
conflicts resulted in heightened levels of social disorder. Engagements such as
the brutal Shelby County Regulator/Moderator War were "socially destructive"
virtually by definition. But movements that met with less powerful opposition,
such as the Alder Gulch committee, may not have been actually *run* according
to "the ideal theory of vigilantism." Rather, as revealed by the would-be moderators' banishments, these movements may have been produced by their members
to *appear* as if they were run according to this ideal.

Vigilantism did not, really could not, successfully address its critics—
particularly if its critics, like the moderating party in Nevada City, were drawing attention to the illegality of the committee's practices. Public popularity
was a key feature of ideal vigilantism, necessary to shore up and strengthen the
tenuously self-conceived authority of the vigilantes. Extralegal violence, particularly executions, required at least the appearance of widespread community support. Vociferous objections, accusations of criminal conduct, and calls
for a return to civil authority threatened the fundamental logic of vigilantism.
In truth, even a failure to enthusiastically support the vigilantes could prove
fatal. Sanders was keenly aware of vigilantism's vulnerability to challenges, as
is revealed in his explanation of Slade's lynching:

> He was executed for high treason. With great deliberation he locked
> horns with the Vigilance Committee, defied its authority, poured upon
> it all manner of vituperation, flouted its action, and spake of it with
> unmeasured contempt. The Committee was compelled to abdicate its
> functions or then and there vindicate its right to be and to do.[85]

Sanders's rather lofty assessment aside, it should be recalled here that Slade, in
fact, thought he *was* a member of the vigilance committee. Surprised at becoming a target himself, Slade failed to take the committee members seriously when
they arrested him for being drunk and disorderly and capriciously tore up their
warrant. This lack of respect constituted a profound threat to the vigilantes, and
they responded by violently, and publicly, making their authority clear.

Accusing critics and detractors of being outlaws, or doing away with them altogether, was common practice for nineteenth-century vigilantes. When the challenges developed into full-scale regulator/moderator conflicts, such as those in Shelby County, Texas, the Attakapas region in Louisiana, and the Powder River region in Wyoming, small local wars erupted. But even individual challenges to the absolute authority of the vigilantes, like Slade's, could prove fatal for the vigilantes' opponents. A man banished by the Laramie committee refused to leave town and was hanged as a result.[86] When a ferry crew in Payette, Idaho, challenged the local vigilance committee the men barely escaped with their lives.[87] And, as Summerfield repeatedly suggests in his account of the execution in Cane Hill, five innocent men were executed by vigilantes they refused to join and dared to criticize. None of which is to suggest that these vigilantes did not enjoy some level of local support in their communities. But when this support wavered, or when it was complicated by local objectors, the vigilante ideal required that the committees enforce support for their practices by whatever means necessary. When traces of the vigilantes' violent enforcement of their ideal popularity disappeared, they and their practices came to stand in for the rest of the community as "popular justice." The complex exchange between narrative ideals and real events can be seen in the accounts of the Cane Hill and Alder Gulch vigilance committees as well as these other cases. In all cases, the Foucauldian "web of relations" involves both marked departures from narrative ideals of "orderliness" and "public popularity" and the attempts of the vigilantes to reframe their own actions in accordance with these ideals.

*An ideal vigilance committee convened and acted in an organized and even-handed manner in response to uncontrolled criminal conditions and was roundly supported and applauded by its community for doing so.* The Alder Gulch committee described themselves as conforming to this ideal regardless of the fact that when people *didn't* fall in line with their plans for the community, they banished them from Montana or hanged them—like Slade. And the Cane Hill Company perceived themselves as ideal, even though their "orderly" practices led them to murder five innocent men. Narrative has played an essential role in constructing a record of ideal vigilantism out of the less than ideal practices of these vigilantes. For each of the committee's official historians found a way to tell the story of their local vigilantes in accordance with the narrative of ideal vigilantism. But within these narrative accounts of ideal vigilantism are traces of the less than ideal ways in which the vigilantes acted and traces of the ways the vigilantes attempted to alter their practices in accordance with an ideal form of vigilantism. Throughout the bulk of the nineteenth century, a narrative of ideal vigilantism carried and supported the practices of vigilantes in a series of ever-changing relations, all of which were characterized by a reciprocal exchange between idealized narrative descriptions and the peculiar ways in which actual vigilantes attempted to enact these ideals.

## Ideals and Facts: The Vigilante Record

Given the apparent gap between the vigilante ideal and the lynching practices of vigilantes in the frontier, how did the ideal narrative construction of vigilantism come to permeate the historical record about the frontier vigilantes? The answer can be found partially in the history of history itself. Henry Fisk Sanders (1856–1930) was both the prosecutor for the Alder Gulch committee of 1864 and the founding president and historian of the Montana State Historical Society. His extensive manuscripts include encyclopedic writings on early Montana history and, of course, a number of detailed and positive accounts of the vigilantes. Charles Coutant (1840–1913), while not documentably a vigilante himself, was an avid proponent of the committees in Cheyenne and Laramie. He was the Wyoming State Librarian from 1901 to 1905, which means he was also the custodian of the State Historical Society. He wrote extensively on early Wyoming history, and his manuscripts also include detailed and positive accounts of the feats of the local vigilance committees. Hubert Howe Bancroft (1832–1918), pioneer historian of California and the West, devoted two enormous volumes of his series on Pacific states' history to vigilance movements: *Popular Tribunals*, volumes 1 and 2. He also succeeded in obtaining all of the records of the 1851 San Francisco Committee of Vigilance and a large portion of those of the 1856 committee. The records are held in the archive that bears his name at the University of California, Berkeley. Samuel Asbury (1872–1960) was a devoted Texas historian and collector and can be credited with collections across the state of Texas, some of which include the one-of-a-kind manuscripts of official vigilante histories such as those written by Ashcraft and Daggett. These men played, both figuratively and materially, central roles in producing the vigilante archive and in establishing the relationships between the local vigilantes and the remainder of territorial and early state history. These men, to return to Hayden White's theory of historical narrative, all shared a central responsibility for making "events" into "facts."

Amid a detailed account of Cheyenne's civic development, Wyoming historian Charles Coutant paused to reflect on the historian's burden:

> He who attempts to write a history is placed at a serious disadvantage
> as compared with the writer of fictions works—whether what is termed

the "Popular Literature of the day" or the dime novel for as between them there is a difference in degree but not a difference in principle— for the latter who can invent his own facts and dress them up in the necessary amount of what Webster once termed "sentimental flap doo- dle" to make them readable wheras [*sic*] the writer of history must take facts as they exist and if he succeeds in so arranging and placing them before the public as far as possible in chroniological [*sic*] order so as to make of them logical and systematic portions of the whole subject he will be fortunate.[88]

Coutant's humility notwithstanding, his production of historical narrative in- volved a good deal more than simply "arranging" events in chronological order. In fact, his work offers the occasion for a revealing set of comparisons—a way to understand the relationships among vigilante events, fact making, and the archive.

I cite extensively from Coutant's manuscripts on the Cheyenne commit- tee here to demonstrate the narrative maneuvers used to make imperfect local lynching practices into the records of ideal vigilantes. Regarding lynching in general, Coutant states:

> Where the law is supreme and unobstructed and can be promptly and efficiently enforced, lynch law is never justifiable and should never be resorted to, where however the authorities are powerless to act—of [*sic*] if they do so act with public enemies openly or covertly—then it some- times happens that lynch law is the only apparently practicable way by which life and property can be protected, then the case is far differ[en]t— but even then should never be resorted to until all other means have been tried and found unavailing.[89]

Coutant is advancing a familiar principle of ideal vigilantism here—the req- uisite precondition of absent or corrupt law and order. But *corruption*, he unequivocally states, was not the problem. He asserts:

> He who should either by voice or pen assert or insinuate that there ever was a time in the history of Cheyenne when its authorities operated openly or covertly—or were in the slightest degree in sympathy—with the lawless element which was such a wretched and unholy burden to the city during the early days would be little else than a libeller and a gross falsifier.[90]

Within Coutant's fairly rigid definition of justified vigilantism, and given his absolute statement that there was no legal corruption in Cheyenne, we would have to assume that there was a complete absence of law and order.

But when a vigilance committee left three men tied together in the street and wearing a warning from the vigilantes, the following editorial appeared in the *Cheyenne Leader*:

> We seriously think that there is but little need of their presence or attention here. So far the officers of the law have with an exception or two done their duty, in the matter of arresting offenders promptly, and bringing them to the bar of justice.
>
> In this city, we regret to say, that this self-constituted body has commenced proceedings in a rash manner. Their threats and intimidations toward officers of the U.S. Government who have been honestly performing their duties, as required by law, is out of place entirely, and should be disregarded. . . . The Vigilance Committee, even though it may number 200 members, cannot minister force or authority enough, to commit all manner of questionable acts with impunity. The intimation "Beware of Vigilantes" has no terror for honest men; and our advice to Vigilantes is to beware of each other![91]

According to this account, law and order was neither corrupt nor absent in Cheyenne. It may or may not have seemed unsatisfactory to the local vigilantes, but dissatisfaction with the law was not, in Coutant's estimate, a satisfactory basis for vigilantism. But despite this logical flaw, Coutant was an avid supporter of this committee and grandly asserted, "The noble men who composed the advance guard and who struggled so long and faithfully to preserve law and good government in Cheyenne . . . never did prove untrue in the slightest degree to the best interests of their fellow citizens."[92] Within Coutant's own assessment of ideal vigilantism, there was no justification for these vigilantes' usurpation of authority; paradoxically, he claims these vigilantes were "noble men" acting in "the best of interests of their fellow citizens."

Coutant clearly asserted that vigilantism "should never be resorted to until all other means have been tried and found unavailing." But again, this ideal did not quite play out at the level of local lynching practices. On March 20, 1868, the Cheyenne vigilantes lynched Charles Martin, an accused but acquitted murderer, and Charles Morgan, an accused *but untried* mule thief. There was a widespread belief that Martin's acquittal had been a mistake, but the *Cheyenne Leader* still decried his extralegal execution:

Does this justify the subversion of all law, and the assumption of supreme right to take dark vengeance upon offenders by an unauthorized
and illegal band of midnight assassins? Mob spirit is the insanity of over
zealous citizens, and is countenanced by no principles of manliness,
honor, nor bravery, and we sadly miss our calculations if the majority
of respectable citizens of Cheyenne approve of the transactions of last
evening. . . .

We call upon all in authority, in the name of an outraged people,
and violated laws, to aid in bringing to justice these mob spirits that
are running loose among us. That the guilt of murder is equally theirs,
with the most guilty criminal of the land, we do solemnly maintain,
and believe all honorable citizens will concur in the sentiment we aver.[93]

Coutant's narrative record of Martin's lynching was infinitely more neutral-
ized and focused principally on the public debauchery of Martin on the afternoon of his acquittal.[94] More importantly, however, Coutant omitted Morgan's
lynching from the historical record altogether. Morgan, having only been accused of but not yet tried for stealing a mule, was also lynched by the Cheyenne
committee—an execution that wholly contradicted Coutant's ideal version of
vigilantism wherein "all other means have been tried and found unavailing."
In fact, *no* other means had been tried or found unavailing in this case. This
particular event of vigilante violence was entirely inconsistent with the "noble"
picture of the Cheyenne vigilantes that Coutant wanted to create, and as a
result, this violent event simply disappeared from his narrative version of historical fact. Far from merely arranging "events" in chronological order, Charles
Coutant—like Sanders, Bancroft, Asbury, and the official vigilantes historians
before them—was a maker of fact. And these men produced the narratives
about the vigilantes that constituted their violent practices as expressions of
the vigilante ideal.

# 3

# John/the Victim/the Heathen

*Hubert Howe Bancroft and the Making of Western History*

Vigilantes and vigilante historians were initially responsible for the narrative construction of vigilante practice as heroic—for making, to borrow Foucault's formula, "the stuff of history from street brawls."[1] But the vigilantes and their early chroniclers were not exclusively endowed with the power to narrate their location within larger regional historical narratives. This privilege resided with the group of men who were, in fact, positioned to create inaugural regional pasts—both archival *and* narrative—and to locate the actions of the vigilantes within these newly minted histories. As Richard Slotkin notes, "Writers in each section (of the country) attempted to create a rationale of American history in which the history and the cultural attitudes of their own section would emerge as the moral quintessence of the American national experience."[2] Men such as Charles Coutant in Wyoming, Wilber Fisk Sanders in Montana, and Samuel Asbury in Texas were able to amplify, obscure, and remix events from the past in ways that altered the qualitative location of vigilantism within larger histories.[3] To an even greater extent than any of these men, Hubert Howe Bancroft ennobled his local vigilance committees—the San Francisco Committee of Vigilance of 1851 and the San Francisco Committee of Vigilance of 1856—making these men the central actors in local historical dramas; larger regional stories; and, ultimately, important symbolic figures within a national narrative about citizenship.

To do this, Bancroft, like the men who had written accounts of specific vigilance committees before him, had to stretch the truth a bit. But Bancroft's interest in recasting vigilante practices in a positive light was different from that of the vigilantes. First, Bancroft was not a vigilante himself; while he was deeply (and conspicuously) invested in shoring up the legitimacy and heroism of the two vigilance committees in San Francisco, this investment had nothing to do with mitigating interpretations of his own violent actions. Bancroft's own reputation did not hinge on the proper interpretation of the violent practices of the vigilance committees in San Francisco. Except—and this leads to a second important characteristic of Bancroft's work on vigilantism—Bancroft's sense of his own significance, as a collector and narrator of a specifically western past, did hinge on his narrative about the significance of vigilantism as a regionally distinct practice. The vigilantes, for Bancroft, marked the zenith of what was distinct and distinctly possible about what he deemed "the Pacific States Region." The significance of the vigilantes to Bancroft's overall understanding of regional history was made abundantly clear when he devoted two enormous volumes of his thirty-nine-volume Pacific states' history series to "popular tribunals" (see Appendix B). Bancroft was acutely self-conscious about himself as a historian and about the process whereby he produced both his archival collection and his written work. Because of this, he left not only the multiple thousand-page volumes of the Pacific states' history but hundreds of pages of research notes, chapter drafts, and interview transcripts. By looking closely at Bancroft's unpublished and edited manuscripts, we can see not only the traces of Bancroft's attempts to write favorably about vigilantism but his ruminations on what was at stake in these historical practices. Simply put, Bancroft *knew* he was stretching and obscuring the truth in his writings on vigilantism. An illuminating example of Bancroft's historiographical sleight of hand can be found in the draft of a chapter written for but deleted from the published version of *Popular Tribunals*, volume 1: "Vigilance in Northern California."[4] The story at issue concerns the theft of gold dust in a mining community in Diamondville in 1857. In fact, the story demonstrates a number of things about vigilantism that Bancroft wanted to de-emphasize or erase from the historical record altogether—unpleasant details and realities that had long compromised ideal characterizations of vigilante practice such as racial violence and torture.

The story Bancroft tells begins in a familiar way. "Gold in tempting quantities being discovered," miners rushed to form a settlement near Butte Creek in 1857. After naming this new settlement Diamondville, Bancroft reports, "the next thing to do was to hang somebody. . . . Fortunately for the purposes of that little crude community providence sent a lamb for the sacrifice. In form and color it was like a Chinaman; and it was seen robbing the sluice." Bancroft's critical distance from these vigilantes, here made manifest by his cynical characterization of the necessity of a hanging to the formation of a crude settlement, is both amplified and complicated by what comes next. The account of "the Chinaman's" capture reads, in Bancroft's draft, "~~John was seen~~ The ~~victim was~~ heathen was detected by a watchman and shot" (see Figure 3.1). The two eliminated descriptors offer an all-too-vivid demonstration of the way in which vigilantes were legitimated, and their victims dehumanized, in Bancroft's history more broadly. This narrative dehumanization makes sense in light of what comes next—an account of John's multiple gunshot wounds, his semi-strangulation, the removal of his queue, and his ultimate pleas to be taken to a countryman to get money to pay his accusers back. Bancroft tells us that John was unable to get the money from his friend and "some were now for hanging what remained of John upon a tree. But others said no; what advantage should accrue from extinguishing the little light remaining in that uncircumcised lump." The phrasing here, like Bancroft's use of the objectifying "it" earlier in the passage, marks an inhuman and dehumanizing act of narrative violence, as does Bancroft's removal of the story in its entirety from his history of vigilantism. Bancroft sensed, quite correctly, that this story represented a number of vigilantism's quite real and quite devastating flaws: Vigilantes' claims to fight crime all too easily became an excuse for targeting those with lesser or no social power, vigilance committees frequently resorted to extreme and sadistic forms of violence, and vigilantes often dehumanized the objects of their control. None of these truths helped to support Bancroft's desired characterization of vigilantes as ideal citizen subjects.

Bancroft's work in the *Popular Tribunals* volumes is marked by a series of these types of erasures and narrative interpolations. In this way, Bancroft's work was as defined by the mutually constitutive relationship between event and narrative as was the work of the official vigilante historians before him. Importantly, however, this mutual constitution occurred not only at the level of historical narrative but at the more complicated intersection of event, narrative, and archive. In this way, Bancroft helped to produce the singularity, heroism, and historical status of the San Francisco Committee of Vigilance of 1856 as well as the singularity, heroism, and status of vigilantism itself. Some of these effects can be seen by examining what I might here call "the shadows" of Bancroft's accounts—the deleted passages, the logical inconsistencies in the accounts, and the chapters that were relocated elsewhere in the series. The remaining sections in this chapter address Bancroft's biography and the Pacific states' history project, the *Popular Tribunals* volumes and Bancroft's interest in vigilantism, the sources and methods Bancroft used to write the *Popular Tribunals* volumes, the story that Bancroft ultimately told about the San

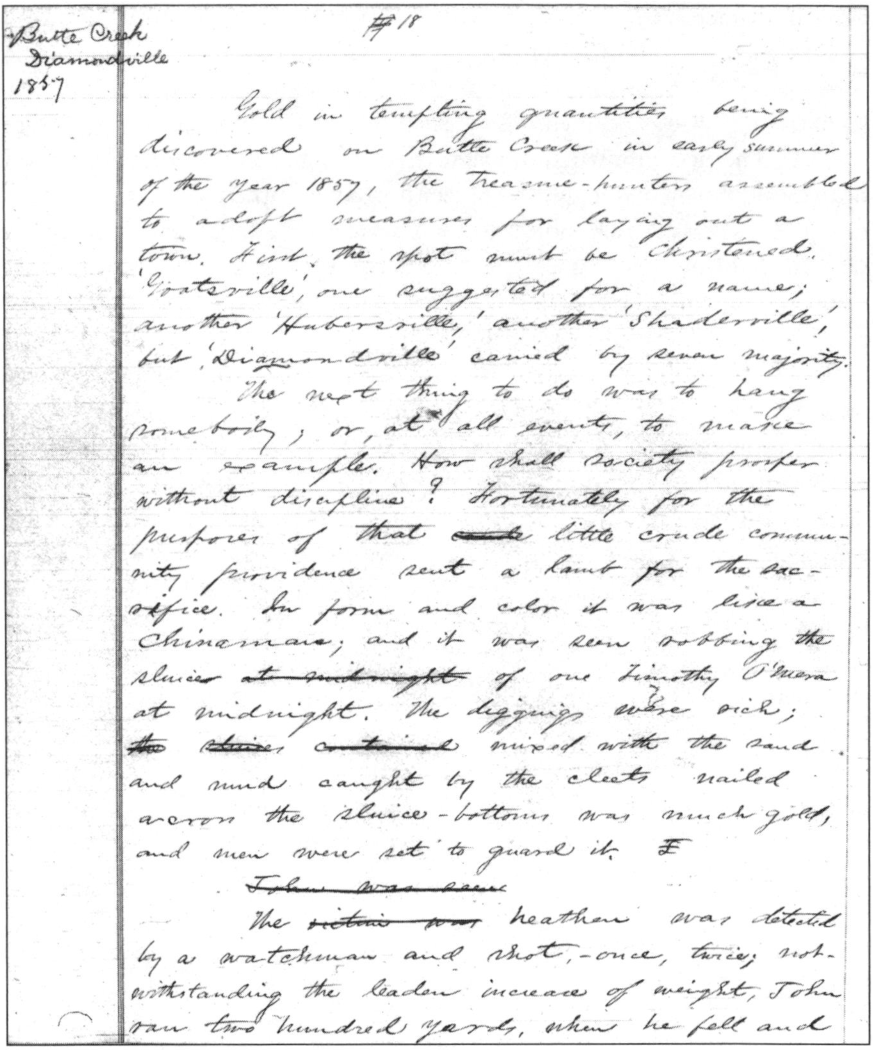

Butte Creek
Diamondville
1857                          #18

Gold in tempting quantities being discovered on Butte Creek in early summer of the year 1857, the treasure-hunters assembled to adopt measures for laying out a town. First, the spot must be Christened. 'Goatsville', one suggested for a name; another 'Hubersville,' another 'Shadersville,' but 'Diamondville' carried by seven majority.

The next thing to do was to hang somebody; or, at all events, to make an example. How shall society prosper without discipline? Fortunately for the purposes of that ~~one~~ little crude community providence sent a lamb for the sacrifice. In form and color it was like a Chinaman; and it was seen robbing the sluice ~~at midnight~~ of one Timothy O'Mera at midnight. The diggings were rich; ~~the sluice contained~~ mixed with the sand and mud caught by the cleets nailed across the sluice-bottoms was much gold, and men were set to guard it.

~~John was seen~~

The ~~victim was~~ heathen was detected by a watchman and shot,—once, twice; notwithstanding the leaden increase of weight, John ran two hundred yards, when he fell and

**Figure 3.1:** From Hubert Howe Bancroft, "Vigilance in Northern California," Records of the Library and Publishing Companies, BANC MSS B-C 7, Bancroft Library, University of California, Berkeley.

Francisco vigilantes, and the story of race and violence that Bancroft helped to erase from the history books. The chapter concludes with a closer look at Bancroft's idealized work on the San Francisco committees within the context of the broader history of vigilantism and the history of the western United States.

## The Works of Hubert Howe Bancroft: Methodological, Historical, and National Origins

Born in Ohio in 1832, Hubert Howe Bancroft arrived in San Francisco in 1856 to open a bookstore. He was successful as a bookseller and stationer and began to collect materials concerning the West.[5] His early collection, by all accounts, was specific only as to region and included newspapers, secondary materials, and original manuscripts. Enjoying the financial comfort of his successful book and publishing business and lured by the promise of his own collection of rare books and manuscripts about the West, Bancroft believed he could produce a bigger, better, and more accurate history of his beloved Pacific states region. Bancroft was also deeply invested in becoming a historian; indeed, he considered history writing "among the highest of human occupations."[6] Between 1883 and 1890, the Bancroft Publishing Company produced a thirty-nine-volume series titled *The Works of Hubert Howe Bancroft*. By way of introducing the first volume, Bancroft wrote, "The characteristics of this vast domain, material and social, are comparatively unknown and are essentially peculiar."[7] And indeed, Bancroft's Pacific states domain *was* vast, comprising the area stretching between Central America in the south; Alaska in the north; Hawaii in the west; and Wyoming, Utah, and Idaho in the east. Though Bancroft originally imagined that he would write the entire series himself, the project proved too large, and he ultimately employed a team of researchers and writers who gathered sources and prepared material for the studies. The majority of the series is arranged geographically (see Appendix B). The exceptions to the geography-based volumes come at the beginning and end of the series. The series begins with *Native Races*, volumes 1–5, designed to "rescue" the original inhabitants of the region from obscurity. Bancroft considered the *Native Races* volumes "preliminary" to the "soul and centre" of his project and deemed volumes 34–39 "supplemental."[8] Volume 34, *California Pastoral*, and volume 35, *California Inter Pocula*, are concerned with the respective effects of Mexican culture and the gold rush on the evolution of political, social, and cultural life in California but are, according to Bancroft, less "condensed" or "solid" history than creative compendia containing the wealth of intriguing stories he was unable to include elsewhere in the series.[9] Volumes 36 and 37 of Bancroft's series, *Popular Tribunals*, portend to tell the stories of vigilance committees in the West.[10] The series concludes with volume 38, *Essays and Miscellany*, and volume 39, *Literary Industries* (Bancroft's scholarly autobiography).

Bancroft's biographers, William Caughey and Harry Clark, have written extensively about the controversies surrounding the collaborative work done on the series. Caughey's carefully researched table, "Apportionment of

Authorship Credits for Bancroft's 'Works,'" reveals that twenty-one of the individual volumes were written entirely by Bancroft's staff.[11] Bancroft himself
wrote varying percentages of fourteen of the volumes, ultimately writing only
four of the books entirely on his own. Inevitably, tensions arose regarding the
substantive contributions of Bancroft's writers, specifically concerning his unwillingness to share authorial attribution. Each of the central figures on Bancroft's staff—Henry Oak, William Nemos, and Frances Fuller Victor—made
attempts to lay claim to their contributions to the series through, respectively,
an alternative scholarly (auto)biography (Oak's *"Literary Industries" in a New
Light*); a notarized statement released after Bancroft's death; and a display at
the San Francisco Midwinter Fair of rebound volumes bearing Victor's name
as the author.[12] Notwithstanding these controversies, Caughey and Clark both
acknowledge that Bancroft's methods were innovative; his use of a research
staff, his collection of primary materials about the region, and the biographical manuscripts he and his staff amassed enabled him both to produce what
remains a principal archive for the region and to coordinate the production
of *The Works*, a series that seems to hover ambiguously between archival (or
primary) and historical (or secondary) document.[13]

The series was produced over the course of seventeen years.[14] A central
component of Bancroft's production and sales strategy involved the procure-
ment of subscriptions for the entire series, an approach that enabled Bancroft
to "borrow" against the future of *The Works* in order to create the time and
money he needed to achieve such a massive undertaking. Bancroft's sales staff
campaigned heavily for the subscriptions, encouraging potential buyers to believe in the monumental significance of a history of the region. In some cases,
this "monument making" extended as far as the explicit exchange of mention in the history for subscriptions—making him, as aptly summarized by
Richard White, "the late nineteenth century['s] . . . most successful historical
entrepreneur."[15] It would be too simplistic to suggest that the exchange of
money for historical fame affected the ultimate narrative in the series; in fact,
Bancroft's argument, as expressed by his well-trained sales staff, was fundamentally sound. *The Works* did represent an early attempt to centralize a history, region, and population largely overlooked in other early histories of the
nation. The significance of this was twofold. First, however suspect *The Works*
might have been as a historical project (and, indeed, this very suspicion is my
principal concern here), the collection and scope of information represented in
the volumes have a continuing historiographical impact. As Bancroft gathered
information and sources to produce the Pacific states volumes, local events
and local sources assumed a particularly regional significance. In this sense,
Bancroft's project had an epistemological impact, producing new possibilities

of regional knowing and new categories of specifically "regional" knowledge. I contend, also, that the series exceeds its own purported ambitions by not only laying claim to a local history but positing a larger ideology about the nation—an ideology that Bancroft was specifically interested in theorizing through his work on vigilance committees. For in the *Popular Tribunals* volumes, Bancroft was able to use the figure of the vigilante as a limit case for theorizing the unique character of the West and the significance of the West within the larger context of the United States.

## The Works and Popular Tribunals: Metonymies of Citizenship

The *Popular Tribunals* volumes are noticeably distinct within the context of the larger series. The volumes fall within the portion of the series that Bancroft deemed "supplemental," but volumes 34 through 39 do not all supplement the series in the same way. *California Pastoral* (volume 34) and *California Inter Pocula* (volume 35) are, in effect, social commentary. Bancroft took a free hand in interpreting phenomena in these books, by his own admission "weaving [in] fancies of [his] own" and indulging a "free use of words" to preserve what he considered the "originality and beauty" of his extra material.[16] The final two volumes in the series are supplements in the more literal sense of the word, allowing Bancroft to include commentary on a range of other authors and historians (*Essays and Miscellany*, volume 38) and analyses of his own methods and practices (*Literary Industries*, volume 39). The *Popular Tribunals* volumes (36 and 37) are concerned with a particular subject; interregional by design, the two texts reveal a topical obsession that is demonstrated nowhere else in the series.

These volumes are also two of the mere four that Bancroft actually wrote by himself.[17] Remarkably, neither Caughey nor Clark, both of whom devote considerable attention to the controversies surrounding Bancroft's writing staff, focus on the volumes that Bancroft *did* write. Arguably, these texts tell us more about Bancroft's historical scholarship than the collaborative work done elsewhere in the series does. Though Bancroft initially reviewed major portions of the series before publication, over time the principal members of his staff became almost entirely responsible for the published texts. It is, in other words, virtually impossible to think critically about Bancroft as a historian in the context of the vast majority of the series, since his relationship to the project was largely as a series editor and rarely as either primary researcher or author. The *Popular Tribunals* volumes are materially exceptional in this respect because we are able to see the mechanics of Bancroft "doing history"— working with sources and producing narrative.

At the outset, Bancroft envisioned his historical account of vigilantism as "an episode of Californian history which would occupy three or four chapters," but the project grew as he worked on it, "the subject constantly assuming larger proportions and with its increased proportions larger importance."[18] In response to this increased significance, he revised the estimated length of the work upward until he "found that not less than three volumes would be necessary in which properly to present the subject to the public."[19] In some sense—and this is borne out by Bancroft's unpublished reflections on the vigilante project—this extended work was a misstep with respect to the larger series. He wrote, "I very much regretted this, as did also my friends. It was thought by all of us to be too large, out of proportion to the other work I was doing."[20] Indeed, why did he produce over 1,400 pages of writing on a topic that was by definition exceptional, even in the Pacific states region with which he was obsessed? Bancroft offers a partial answer early in the first volume of *Popular Tribunals*, asserting that the practice of popular justice achieved its "broadest proportions" in the U.S. West.[21] Having traced a history of popular tribunals that stretches from "Clodius" and the gladiators in Cicero's Rome through Robespierre's "Committee of Public Safety" in 1793 up to modern etymological disputes regarding the origin of the term "lynch law," Bancroft understood the popular tribunal as a practice of global and transhistorical magnitude. If then, as he asserts, the practice reached its conceptual zenith in his own region of interest, it makes a certain amount of sense that he centralized this achievement in his work on the Pacific states.

In fact, Bancroft made this very argument to explain the significance of his work on vigilantism. According to Bancroft, not only did popular tribunals crop up with unusual frequency during the development of the western portions of the United States; the popular tribunal as a concept reached its ideal incarnation, the vigilance committee, in this period and region. Even more specifically, in Bancroft's historical schema, the vigilance committee reached *its* ideal incarnation in the San Francisco Committee of Vigilance of 1856. In terms of Bancroft's understanding of the issues of historical significance here, even if the volumes *were* regrettably long or disproportionate in the context of *The Works*, the story was so unique, and uniquely *local*, as to be indispensable within the context of the larger history.

But here I think it is necessary to invert Bancroft's assertions about historical significance. Preliminarily, and as a mode of interpreting both his published and unpublished work on the topic, I would argue that Bancroft's ideas about the singular importance of popular tribunals (or vigilantism—given that Bancroft's asserted distinction between the two is hardly axiomatic) invert and obscure the real reasons he devoted such extended periods of time and such a vast number of pages to the topic. In fact, Bancroft's musings on the topic expose two things. First, vigilantism and his own evolving relationship to it and opinions about it reveal that Bancroft wanted the series not only to give a *history* of the Pacific states region but, in drawing on the geography, period, and population of the region, to offer a theory about national citizenship itself. The *Popular Tribunals* volumes offered Bancroft an occasion for reflecting on issues such as citizenship, social difference, and the relationship between American identity and emerging structures of the nation. Moreover, I argue that it is worth being suspicious of the idea that the popular tribunal evolved into an ever-more perfect manifestation in the western United States (let alone an ideal version in 1856 San Francisco); instead, I suspect, the 1856 San Francisco vigilance committee was constituted as the pinnacle of popular justice precisely because Bancroft "researched" and narrated this status into being. This historiographical achievement both marks a crucial moment within the larger history of vigilantism and lynching within the United States and demonstrates the way that narrative and event defined these practices at the level of historical writing and the archive.

## Making a Past: Bancroft and the *Popular Tribunals* Volumes

A brief look at the structure of the *Popular Tribunals* volumes is enlightening with respect to the idea that Bancroft was largely responsible for fabricating the historical significance of the San Francisco vigilance committees. Volume 1 of *Popular Tribunals* (volume 36 in the larger work) is 749 pages long. Bancroft opens the book with two introductory chapters reflecting on the philosophical issues concerning social and civic systems of order, justice, and the state and tracing some "ancient roots" of popular tribunals. Bancroft's third chapter, "Engendering Conditions," telescopes toward San Francisco through a history of Spanish colonial politics in Mexico and the later discovery of gold in California. Thus, Bancroft arrives at the first of his real interests: the San Francisco Committee of Vigilance of 1851. For the next 367 pages, Bancroft provides a detailed account of this committee's organization and actions, wrapping up, in chapter 26, "Before the World," with a series of newspaper clippings documenting wide-ranging reactions to the vigilantes. In the second half of volume 1, Bancroft presents a series of geographically framed chapters such as "The Popular Tribunals of Utah and Nevada" and "The Popular Tribunals of Arizona, New Mexico, and Mexico." In volume 2 (volume 37 in the larger work), Bancroft arrives at his principal topic of interest and devotes all 748 pages to the San Francisco Committee of Vigilance of 1856. The distribution of content in these volumes reveals Bancroft's unabashed obsession with the San Francisco committees, as does his dedication of the second volume to William Coleman, "Chief of the Greatest Popular Tribunal the World has ever Witnessed."[22] This devotion marks a shift from Bancroft's preface to the first volume wherein he expresses a certain ambivalence about popular tribunals:

> During my researches in Pacific States History, and particularly while tracing the development of the Anglo-American communities on the western side of the United States, I fancied I saw unfolding into healthier proportions, under the influence of a purer atmosphere, that sometime dissolute principle of political ethics, the right of the governed at all times to instant and arbitrary control of the government.[23]

How can we understand Bancroft's ultimate and conspicuous fascination with the San Francisco vigilantes given his initial awareness of the geographic breadth of the vigilante impulse as well as his apparent skepticism regarding the practice?

On some level, Bancroft's fascination with the San Francisco committees is unsurprising—vigilante practice itself was taken up and justified in intensely localized terms.[24] Vigilantes understood their own practices as principally related to the local conditions in which they operated, rather than as subsidiary to the larger, transregional practice of vigilantism. In other words, any story a given vigilance committee told about itself was defined and constituted as a story about a particular time and place—San Francisco in 1856 or Alder Gulch in 1864—rather than as a story about the merits of vigilantism, per se. In fact, vigilance committees were often vehemently critical of other vigilance committees—narratives of justification were most effective when they convincingly appealed to extraordinary local conditions. Supporting the vigilance practices of others undercut the claim that local conditions were particularly exceptional. The San Francisco Committees of Vigilance of 1851 and 1856 were, by the logic of their participants, both related to and justified by the conditions and history of San Francisco. Bancroft's initial interest in writing a transregional history of vigilantism was a radical proposition that gave way, in the final incarnation, to vigilantism's own logic of localism. Given that Bancroft's library and research team were located in San Francisco, and that the project evolved in close association with members of the two committees, this turn to localism is hardly surprising. Though this is not surprising, it is interesting to look at the ways this happened. In part, because the process whereby Bancroft's reflections on popular tribunals generally turned into an homage to the San Francisco committees specifically reveals something about how narratives of heroic vigilantism became established as historical truth.

It should also be noted that Bancroft's initial aspiration to write a history of popular tribunals in the vast domain of the "Pacific states" was incredibly ambitious if not impossible. As Richard Maxwell Brown has asserted, it is impossible to determine just how many individual vigilance committees convened following the inception of the practice in the United States during the Revolutionary War.[25] This is no less true for the century leading up to Bancroft's publication of the *Popular Tribunals* volumes in 1887. Minimally, we learn from Brown, the period saw 108 vigilance committees in Bancroft's region of interest, including "large" (or what Brown deems particularly important) committees in California, Colorado, Idaho, Nevada, New Mexico, Wyoming, Washington, and Montana.[26] Though Bancroft was unusually successful in procuring primary documents and biographical statements from throughout the region on a range of topics, he never had access to equivalent documents for vigilance committees outside of San Francisco. Given that he spent months maneuvering former members of the two San Francisco committees into relinquishing what were thought to be compromising and controversial papers for his study, it is easy enough to understand that he simply didn't have analogous documents for other large committees.[27] Bancroft's accounts of other committees relied heavily on secondary sources such as published histories (specifically what I refer to as "official vigilante histories," such as Thomas Dimsdale's concerning the Alder Gulch committee of 1864) and newspaper accounts. Interestingly, though Bancroft was clearly suspicious of these types of sources as representative of the truth about the San Francisco committees, he relied on such documents in writing histories about committees in a range of other Pacific states' localities.

While researching vigilantism in San Francisco, Bancroft was cautious and thorough, employing a variety of techniques and sources to arrive at his "definitive" account. First, Bancroft tells us, he contemplated newspaper sources and other histories of the period regarding the question of vigilantism.

> Spreading before me six or eight of the chief journals of the day, I had in them so many eye-witnesses of the facts, written by keen fact-hunters while the incidents were yet warm, and thrown out among a people who knew as much of what was going on as the newspaper reports themselves.[28]

But this approach proved unsatisfactory for Bancroft, since these sources revealed to him only "the outside of the subject," so he set about obtaining firsthand accounts of vigilantism in San Francisco and, most importantly, conducting a series of interviews with members of the 1856 committee.[29] These interviews became a part of Bancroft's expansive biographical manuscripts collection and include twenty-five transcripts documenting Bancroft's interviews with individual members of the vigilance committee of 1856 (see Appendix B). The majority of the interview transcripts are approximately 20 pages in length, one notable exception being the 175-page manuscript documenting Bancroft's interview of William Tell Coleman, the "great chief" to whom he dedicates the second volume.

We can observe this much of his process through his own disclosures in *Literary Industries*. We can know a bit more by looking at the two research notebooks concerning vigilantism that are contained in the Bancroft archive; here, we can see something of *how* Bancroft used the interview manuscripts (e.g., the sections he identified as significant or the manuscripts that were used more and less frequently). The two roughly two-hundred-page notebooks are scrapbooks composed of small pasted notes highlighting portions of the interview manuscripts Bancroft found unusually interesting, references to other sources (e.g., newspaper articles or published histories) and clippings or long transcripts from other documents. All of the pasted scraps and notes are marked "Cal, 1856, vigilantes" and many bear additional topical subheadings. The research notebooks allow us to trace, partially, Bancroft's use of the interview manuscripts—for example, we can note his frequent citation of the interviews with Isaac Bluxome, John Manrow, and William Coleman as well as the complete absence of some of his other subjects. We can see that Bancroft drew extensively on John Hittell's *A History of the City of San Francisco and Incidentally of the State of California; and, A Guidebook to San Francisco*, a work produced by Bancroft's own publishing company in 1878.[30]

Though these sources are intriguing, the provenance of the vigilante research notebooks is unclear, and it is difficult to make definitive claims about the trajectory of Bancroft's research for the *Popular Tribunals* volumes. The notes for the larger collection, Bancroft Reference Notes (ca. 1870–1885), indicate that the 265 research notebooks in the archive "were compiled by the staff of The Bancroft Library in the 1870's and 1880's to facilitate the writing of Hubert Howe Bancroft's histories."[31] Given that Bancroft wrote, and therefore possibly did the research for, the *Popular Tribunals* volumes on his own, it is possible that notebooks 264 and 265 were compiled by some part of Bancroft's team *after* he wrote the *Popular Tribunals* volumes. It is also clear that the notebooks represent only a portion of the research used in writing the *Popular Tribunals* volumes. The notebooks refer only to the 1856 San Francisco committee, and there is no indication of how Bancroft went about his work on the 1851 committee and even less information concerning how he worked on the committees outside of San Francisco. Not all of Bancroft's "scraps" have been processed by the Bancroft archivists, and it is entirely possible there are equally extensive notes concerning the committees in the remainder of the "West." Though, in truth, this seems unlikely. Using chapter 35, "Popular Tribunals of Montana," as an example, it seems as though Bancroft relied on newspaper clippings and published work—in this case, Thomas Dimsdale's *The Vigilantes of Montana*.[32] Last, the chapter drafts for the two *Popular Tribunals* volumes—both those that were published and those that were either deleted or moved to another part of the series—reveal Bancroft's concerted attempts to shore up the legitimacy of vigilantism.[33]

Before moving to a close reading of Bancroft's sources alongside his published account, it is useful to remember that the San Francisco Committee of Vigilance of 1856 organized after a popular newspaper editor, James King of William, was murdered. In addition to capturing and punishing King's assassin(s), the vigilantes were concerned with alleged corruption in San Francisco's political and legal systems. It is not within the scope of this chapter to arbitrate the issue of political corruption in San Francisco or to assess whether skullduggery was as rampant as the vigilantes contended. I do not argue that the members of the vigilance committee in San Francisco were the city's "best men" or that they were merely the most powerful. There are a significant number of secondary sources that attempt to do this kind of historical work (with varying degrees of success).[34] I am much more concerned with the process whereby we come to believe we know the answers to questions such as these. Specifically, as these interpretive concerns relate to vigilantism and lynching, I am interested in using Bancroft's work as a means of tracing how the vigilantes' narratives evolved into conventions about region and how vigilante constructions of "heroism" became further linked with constructions of national identity. Finally, Bancroft's work reveals how constructions of racial and ethnic difference, violence, and exclusion were linked, and erased, from the ideal narrative of vigilantism.

## "The Serpent's Variegated Glitter": Heroic Narratives among Clay Footed Men

In an exquisite passage deleted from the published historiographical reflections in *Literary Industries*, Bancroft acknowledges the trouble he had reconciling the men around him in San Francisco with his heroic account of vigilantism.

> Among many other lessons learned while writing this work one in particular presented itself more pertinent than ever before. It was never to come too near the object about which you wish to write well. There

is nothing which so saps enthusiasm as intimacy. Near men and near events are tame in outline, bald, crude, soulless in appearance; or, if brilliant and fascinating, there is too much of the serpent's variegated glitter even in the best of them.[35]

But, of course, Bancroft was often in quite close proximity to the subjects of his *Popular Tribunals* volumes—a proximity that affected him negatively, as is reflected in the remainder of the passage.

> Now there are no men on earth whom I respect and admire more than the leaders of the Vigilance movements of 1851 and 1856. No one ever received me with greater cordiality when I visited them or appeared more willing to do all in their power to serve me and yet after studying the character and thinking and writing of one of them for a week or two, to meet him then was like a wet blanket to me and my work. I always had the blues after such an encounter and I soon learned that if I wished to write well concerning a person, truthfully even, I must keep away from him.[36]

"Writing well" about vigilantism (and the vigilantes themselves) was not, despite Bancroft's elision, perhaps at all the same as writing "truthfully" about them. In fact, Bancroft's intriguing admission here reflects a marked gap between his narrative aspirations and his cognizance of events—or, as is the case here, individuals. Perhaps the most intriguing aspect of this confession is Bancroft's decision to resolve this dilemma by removing himself from the company of the real vigilantes rather than by reconciling his account to the men he actually encountered.

Indeed, the idea that the vigilantes were—however hyperbolic Bancroft's prose might be in this instance—worthy of more respect and admiration than any other men on earth while simultaneously provoking a level of despair for Bancroft reveals that he was aware of the ways in which his account of the San Francisco vigilantes was conceptually disconnected from the real world around him. Alternately less interesting ("bald" or "crude") and less genuine (exhibiting "the serpent's variegated glitter"), the San Francisco committee members were of less interest to Bancroft as real men than as figurations within a theory of ideal citizenship and the nation. In effect, Bancroft interpolated these real historical individuals into a narrative tableau wherein *he* constituted their heroism. Bancroft wasn't always an advocate of vigilantism, and he wasn't initially a booster for the 1856 committee. Among his notes for the project one finds a few early notations reflecting his ambivalence about "mobs" or what he called in the passage cited previously "the sometime dissolute principle of political ethics, the right of the governed at all times to instant and arbitrary control of the government."[37] The evolution and significance of Bancroft's opinions can be traced through his work on the Law and Order Party, his theorization of the vigilante as the ideal citizen, his treatment of the period *after* the committee disbanded, and his erasure of the connection between vigilantism and racial violence.

At times, Bancroft asserts that his accrued respect for vigilantism was, paradoxically, an effect of his growing disagreement with the *anti*-vigilance position—specifically, in this case, the Law and Order Party. This idea appears in *Literary Industries* wherein he narrates the evolution of his beliefs about vigilantism:

> I had not proceeded far in my investigations before I became convinced that *the people* were not only right, but that their action was the only thing they could have done under the circumstances. I arrived at this conclusion in summing up the arguments of the opposite side. The more I examined the grounds taken by the law and order party, the more I became convinced that they were untenable, and so I became a convert to the principles of vigilance through the medium of its enemies, and before I had heard a word in their own vindication.[38]

The Law and Order party's unwavering support of the government was problematic for Bancroft on a number of levels. The state, as far as Bancroft was concerned, was intermittently subject to corruption, susceptible to the interests of the wealthy, and often just plain incompetent. In principle, Bancroft was committed to the right of "the people" to supersede the periodically corrupt and/or inefficient machinations of its government; or, as he puts it most plainly in a passage deleted from the published work, "I claim that the majority of any people possess the right to revolutionize."[39] But while the right to "revolutionize" was important to Bancroft, he made a point of defending the actual 1856 committee against charges of revolutionary activity: "The vigilance committee movement was no revolution, neither did any member wish in the least degree to subvert or overthrow the laws."[40] At the simplest level, this assertion is simply illogical—by definition, vigilantism always subverts, and frequently overthrows, the law.

Of course, Bancroft knew that the San Francisco committees had effectively "subverted" the law, making his claim to the contrary worth considering. Schematically, the contradiction here is actually quite similar to the one reflected in the passage about Bancroft's disappointment with the real vigilantes. The tension here, again, is between constructed narrative ideals and the real events (and individuals) Bancroft was nominally writing about. Bancroft's growing disdain for the Law and Order Party reflected his unwillingness, at least theoretically, to privilege the prerogatives of the state over those of the people. Given that he was writing the *Popular Tribunals* volumes contemporary to the emergence of ever-increasing numbers of state (legal, bureaucratic, and economic) structures in San Francisco, his defense of the right of vigilantes can be understood as standing in for the reservation of a larger set of rights in the face of, and in opposition to, a growing state.[41] But—and this is the crucial contradiction where the nominally nonrevolutionary San Francisco committees are concerned—Bancroft was better able to defend the importance of the vigilante *ideal* here than any actual vigilantism. Bancroft disdained actual "revolutionary" activity—along with mobs, social unrest, and "turbulent disorderly rabble."[42] In fact, Bancroft's distinction between most negative forms of popular tribunals and the ideal San Francisco vigilance committees relied centrally on his narration of these particular vigilantes as bureaucratically well ordered. This narrative construction, whether accurate or not, was fundamentally at odds with the revolutionary principle whereby Bancroft justified their organization and practices.

In opposition to what Bancroft characterized as the "religious" devotion of some to state structures, stood "the people"—an idealized, fully equal mass of heroic citizens.[43] It is no coincidence that Bancroft elected to use "the people" in the passage about the Law and Order Party as a stand-in descriptor for the vigilance committee. In fact, the notion that the 1856 committee represented an ideal manifestation of democratic citizenship—and, here, "democratic" is best understood as drawing on an integrated notion of national and economic participation—is at the core of Bancroft's ideal narrative version of civic vigilantism. His ideological commitment to the vigilantes seems fully comprehensible given his characterization of their conduct in the face of unthinking defenders of the state.

> When I saw this element banded in support of law, or rather to smother law, and opposed to them the great mass of a free and intelligent people, representing the wealth and industry of the state, merchants, mechanics, laboring men, bankers, miners, and farmers . . . when I saw these men drop their farms and merchandise and rise as one man to vindicate their dearest rights, the purity of the polls, safety to life and property,—when I saw them rise in their single heartedness and integrity of purpose . . . when I saw them vilified, snarled at, and threatened with extermination by pompous demagogues who had

placed themselves in power,—I was moved to strong expression, and found myself obliged repeatedly to revise my writing and weed out phrases of feeling which might otherwise mar the record of that singular social outburst which I aimed to give in all honesty and evenly balanced truthfulness.[44]

Indeed, Bancroft was obliged. Though not, as he claims for a second time in this passage, to historical truth so much as to an ideal narrative characterization of the vigilantes and of vigilantism more broadly (i.e., one that "weeded out" unpleasant truth). For this idealized citizenry represented not only the best of San Francisco but a particular version of idealized national citizenship. This ideal citizenship was crucial to Bancroft and his larger historical project because it conceptually and materially privileged the western United States and its territories as the origin of the nation's future. This narrative gesture transplanted the long heroic figure of early national patriotic insurgency (the antitax regulator, the colonial revolutionary) into the West and enabled Bancroft to make an argument that Frederick Jackson Turner would make with infinitely greater impact six years later—American political subjectivity and identity were, at their core, western. For Bancroft, this idea was represented by the figure of the vigilante; for Turner, it would be more vividly represented by a metaphoric frontier.[45]

The evidence suggests that Bancroft was well aware of the actual lack of truth and balance at play in his account. And while Bancroft *was* careful to revise his writing to publish only the most idealized account of the vigilance committees, both his own drafts and the documents in the archive allow us to see other aspects of the story. In a deleted passage about the 1856 committee, Bancroft writes, "At that time, the summer of 1856, state and municipal offices as a rule were filled by Southerners and Democrats, clannish and partisan in the extreme. Naturally, those who sympathized with them in politics, on the subject of slavery, or who were tinged with their false ideas of chivalry . . . joined the ranks of the law and order party."[46] It is interesting, certainly, to note Bancroft's association of southern chivalry with the anti-vigilance movement, given that false ideas about southern chivalry would be used to justify southern vigilantism, qua lynching, in a few short years. But it is also important to note that the two opposing sides in the vigilance debate in San Francisco were not representing, as Bancroft suggests in the published and idealized narration, abstract ideas about the merits of a free people and the prerogatives of the state. In fact, as Bancroft's own deleted writings make clear, the vigilance question in San Francisco was deeply informed by a pre–Civil War political historical context.

This can be seen even more clearly in the biographical manuscript concerning Clancy John Dempster, one of the elected vice presidents of the committee. According to Dempster:

> The secret of the greater part of the opposition to the Vig[ilance] Com[mittee] was the bitter feeling on the part of the pro-slavery party which had long controlled the State and which, unable to manipulate the Vig[ilance] Com[mittee], looked with dread to it's [sic] peaceable disbandment as in that case its leaders would remain the future leaders of the people. The chiefs of the party were even then preparing to cut the Pacific States loose from the Federal Union and to lend more support, if not physical assistance, to the establishment of a slave empire.[47]

Specifically, here, Dempster is attempting to explain the protracted and armed conflict that transpired between the vigilance committee and the Law and Order Party after the committee had completed its nominal anticrime and corruption work. More generally, the passage makes it clear that the vigilantes themselves were cognizant of the issues surrounding both their own movement and the opposition that it faced. Infinitely less abstract than Bancroft's metahistorical characterization of a conflict between a potentially domineering state and a free and rational people, Dempster's account acknowledges that the debates in San Francisco concerning the vigilance committee were actually about real political and economic issues that were already and materially on people's minds.

Dempster's commentary offers more than a complex view of the political historical context for the 1856 vigilance movement; the committee officer was also cognizant of the differentiation of roles *within* the committee. He asserts, "I should wish to enlarge in [sic] the cheerful sacrifice of their time by laboring men [and] the risks they took which did not, to such an extent at least, affect the more prominent members of the Vig[ilance] Com[mittee]."[48] Dempster's reference here to "laboring men" (or, as he deems them earlier in the passage, "the rank and file") is posited in contradistinction to prominent members—presumably, officers such as himself.[49] Dempster's manuscript was of particular interest to Bancroft, who calls it "a most able and eloquent narration, prepared for me with great care, a narration in which the heart-beats of the movement seem to pulsate under his pen."[50] Dempster was not only a ranking committee officer; he was the custodian of the committee's records and the one who reviewed all the other interview transcripts to clarify and supplement the existing accounts.[51] But in spite of Bancroft's awareness of the quality of this particular interview manuscript, Dempster's arguably more realistic account of power differences *within* the vigilance committee—along with the differential risks and benefits associated with these inequities—did not find its way into Bancroft's idealized account of equal citizen subjects "rising as one man." John Manrow, another of Bancroft's interview subjects, gives us another perspective. He reports there was, "[A] great fear on the part of bankers, merchants and newspaper men of mobs," which the vigilance committee ameliorated by "post[ing] guards to keep *the people* quiet."[52] It is difficult, in light of Bancroft's adamant characterization of the committee's membership as "the people," to discern who "the people" feared by these business leaders and held back by the vigilantes might have been.

While vigilance committees inevitably justified their practices in local terms, the effects of their practices were hardly ever so discreet or contained—a reality that both Manrow and Dempster also address. Not surprisingly, the San Francisco committee of 1856 garnered considerable attention throughout Northern California. So much so, in fact, that following their disbandment a number of other area committees sought both support and official "franchise" status from the San Francisco committee. Manrow reported on the committee's reaction to this phenomenon:

> There was another thing that bothered us a good deal. The Committee received from all sections of the state, from towns and precincts, documents expressing a desire on the part of the people to organize Vigilance Committees to act in their respective localities, as branches of ours. We replied to them that we could not undertake to extend our organization in that way, that our Committee was simply a local matter, that we could not amalgamate with them but must confine our operations within their present limits.[53]

According to Dempster, the committee was equally besieged by local requests for assistance:

> The Ex[ecutive] Com[mittee] by every mail received innumerable letters asking for redress of grievances. Women desired protection from brutal husbands or from those who, under promise of marriage, had robbed them of their virtue. Many of these letters were from native Californians—people who could neither speak nor understand English.[54]

These effects are hardly surprising—the 1856 committee had staged four dramatic public executions and engaged in a series of warlike maneuvers with the Law and Order Party. The vigilantes' authority, whether legitimate or not, was undoubtedly conspicuous and awe inspiring. But these inevitabilities were not easily reconciled with Bancroft's characterization of the San Francisco committee's successes. His treatment of the period *after* the committee disbanded is limited to an aggrandizing account of the remarkable improvement in electoral and judicial proceedings.[55] In other words, Bancroft's narrative only acknowledges the specifically localized and contained effects of the San Francisco committee. This again demonstrates the ambiguous conceptual space from which Bancroft attempted to legitimate both vigilantism as an abstract prerogative of citizenship and the San Francisco Vigilantes *without* simultaneously legitimizing any form of vigilantism (or "popular tribunal") that compromised the reputation of either. Of course, this paradox of exceptional justification was characteristic of not only Bancroft's account but of vigilante justification itself. This helps to explain why, as both Manrow and Dempster report, the San Francisco vigilantes were reluctant to help other vigilance committees; as had always been the case with vigilante justification, legitimacy was constitutionally and definitionally local and particular. In recognizing the legitimacy of other committee's aspirations to vigilantism, the San Francisco committee necessarily weakened their own assertions about what made their actions uniquely necessary.

The San Francisco Committee of Vigilance of 1856, like *all* vigilance committees, legitimized their practices through a series of narrative claims (criminal conditions, a failing state, etc.). The "official history" written by Almarin Paul, analyzed in the previous two chapters, demonstrates this. Paul's justificatory narrative, like others of its kind, laid claim to local conditions and specificities in order to secure legitimacy for explicitly illegal practices—as always, extraordinary conditions required an extraordinary response. And as was also always the case, the narrative justification and the terms in which it was articulated obscured, distorted, and/or erased events and individuals that compromised or contradicted the idealized narrative characterization. As the prior chapter demonstrates, this is the process whereby the ambiguous practices of vigilance committees were constituted through narrative as legitimate and heroic.

Looking at Bancroft's work, we can begin to see how the narrative of ideal vigilance created to justify the practices of individual groups of vigilantes was ever-more indelibly inscribed into regional and national history. Bancroft's narrative constitution of the San Francisco committees reproduced their most idealized narrative self-conceptualization at the level of a secondary historical account. In so doing, Bancroft reinscribed the San Francisco committees' idealized claims about themselves. This process of reinscription also occurred in Bancroft's treatment of vigilance committees outside of San Francisco as he relied heavily on the official vigilante histories produced to legitimate and justify the practices of these vigilantes. Bancroft was not only complicit with the narrative distortions in the original accounts—by relying on these accounts as transparent and truth-telling primary documents—he was also actively engaged in obscuring, distorting, and erasing discontinuous events and individuals to shore up his own, nominally multiregional, account of popular tribunals.

To strike the proper narrative balance, Bancroft's story had to achieve a particular and specific scale—simultaneously local and metahistorical. In one sense, the story of vigilantism in San Francisco was opportunistically constituted by Bancroft as heroic in strictly localized terms. The relationship between events in San Francisco and larger national debates about slavery alternately compromised and contradicted this account. As Bancroft privileged one-dimensional local justification over larger contextual complexities, he adhered to the vigilante narrative logic of localism. At the same time, Bancroft was locating his locally framed story of the San Francisco vigilance committee(s) within the context of an abstract narrative about idealized and active citizenship. He was thus able to argue that the vigilantes' opponents, the Law and Order Party, were actually enemies of an independent-minded and agential citizenry rather than a group of people who held opposing, but valid, opinions on the vital debate of the day over slavery. Inequities among the vigilance committee members went unmentioned in Bancroft's epic account, as did the more gruesome aftereffects of the committee's "successes."

## Vigilantism, Race, and Violence

Though the two volumes of *Popular Tribunals* end chronologically with the final days of the 1856 committee, Bancroft actually wrote quite a bit of work on post-1856 vigilance activity in Northern California. A number of these stories document racial violence, extreme violence, or both. So conspicuous was the evidence of the relationship between vigilantism and racial violence that Bancroft's original version of *Popular Tribunals* contained a chapter titled "The Crusade against Foreigners."[56] This chapter, as its title suggests, documents a series of particularly gruesome incidents wherein vigilantes targeted individuals—for example, Chinese mine workers or Mexican laborers—in diffuse and violent ways. The accounts, drawn from eyewitnesses and newspapers, are unsurprising to anyone familiar with southern lynching narratives and confirm the relatively recent scholarly suspicion that we must attend to the issues of racial and ethnic difference in studies of lynching in the West.[57] In effect, alleged criminal accusations and "prosecutions" initially targeting individuals were swiftly redrawn as the racialized criminalization of entire groups of "similar" people. As a result, whole segments of the population fell prey to figurative and real aggression enacted by some group of vigilantes. The story about John that opens this chapter offers an example of this kind of racial violence as do stories about the brutal torture and executions of Mexicans, natives, and Chinese.[58]

This type of information was inconsistent with Bancroft's larger narrative frame in *Popular Tribunals* and he moved the sections of the "Crusade against Foreigners" that he found particularly interesting to volume 38 of the Pacific states' history, *California Inter Pocula*. The volume, a loosely arrayed series of reflections on the social and political order in California, includes chapters such as "Gambling," "Drinking," and "Dueling" along with Bancroft's work on racial violence, which can be found in chapters such as "Some Chinese Episodes." From the outset of the chapter we learn that these episodes will not be happy ones:

> In the annals of our coast there is no fouler blot than the outrages perpetrated at various times and places upon Indians, Mexicans, and Chinese. Viewed from any standpoint the aspect is revolting. As a free and forward nation we fling over the walls of a close despotism sentiments which would have disgraced feudalism. As a progressive people we reveal a race prejudice intolerable to civilization; as Christians we are made to blush beside the heathen Asiatic; as just and humane men we slaughter the innocent and vie with red-handed savages in deeds of atrocity.[59]

Bancroft had found ample evidence of such revolting racist behavior in his research on vigilantism in Northern California but clearly felt this story was better told as an aspect of gold rush history generally, rather than as a grim but quite real aspect of the history of *Popular Tribunals*. Deleted passages from the "Crusade against Foreigners" chapter offer ample and vivid evidence of this darker side of vigilantism. Bancroft notes in the draft, "White skins were very fashionable among the miners; Indians, Africans, Asiatics, Islanders, and the Mixed breeds of Mexico and South America they detested."[60] It is hardly surprising, then, that when the miners convened and acted as vigilance committees, their treatment of those they regarded as the "others" in their midst was hardly even handed; indeed, Bancroft makes this very clear.

> As I have said, the Chinese were summarily treated by the mob ~~vigilance committee~~, so were Mexicans and Chileans, particular [*sic*] if the offence had been committed against an American but the poor naked

native was scarcely high enough in the scale of humanity to command the deliberations of the august local tribunals. Let one of these outraged wanderers once turn and strike a blow in the defense of his insulted wife or children, and straightaway the cry is raised; men with rifles mount their horses, ride over to the rancheria, and shoot down men, women, and children innocent and guilty promiscuously.[61]

The passage includes yet another of Bancroft's revealing strikethroughs (see Figure 3.2). To note that the difference between a "revolting racist mob" and a civilized and evenhanded vigilance committee is narrative is almost banal in light of Bancroft's evident struggle with terms here. It bears noting again that Bancroft suffered from the paradox of detesting mobs while wanting to venerate his local vigilantes. This paradoxical logic is particularly interesting here because editing decisions such as the one in this passage reveal that Bancroft was cognizant of his power to produce a particular historical impression. In real historical terms, and Bancroft knew this, the difference between a vigilance committee and a mob was merely and simply linguistic. So thorough was Bancroft's erasure of the association of vigilantism and racial violence that his published work on the 1856 San Francisco committee includes his claim that "no class of person was more greatly benefited by the Vigilance Committee than the Chinese."[62] The vulnerability of vigilantism to racist impulses, well documented by Bancroft in his unpublished manuscripts, is replaced by the explicit association of vigilantism and benevolent treatment of the Chinese population in San Francisco.

Bancroft's unpublished drafts also offer evidence of vigilantism's violence and chaos after 1856. The enormous San Francisco committees of 1851 and 1856 may well have inspired those who lived in the mining committees north of San Francisco to take the law into their own hands, but the committees did not seem to inspire these newly formed vigilance committees to be particularly evenhanded or moderate in their use of violence. And while the vigilance committee trials of the San Francisco committees, like others, may have been farcical, many of the committees that followed in their wake ceased having trials altogether. This enabled Bancroft to make use of a strategy long employed by the vigilantes' own historians—the association of "good" local vigilantism with orderly practice and the condemnation of the bad practices of vigilantes elsewhere as *dis*orderly and mob-like. Bancroft's prejudices are evident in the following passage on "mobocracy" among miners in Northern California.

We have seen that the mob-law of the miner, appealing as it does to brutalizing passions, and executed under the influence of momentary days, unless they should first obtain a permit from a committee of three appointed by the meeting. Every mining-camp should appoint selectmen to whom all foreigners in the district should deliver up their arms. So said the miners of Tuolumne, two thousand and more being present this Sunday at Sonora,

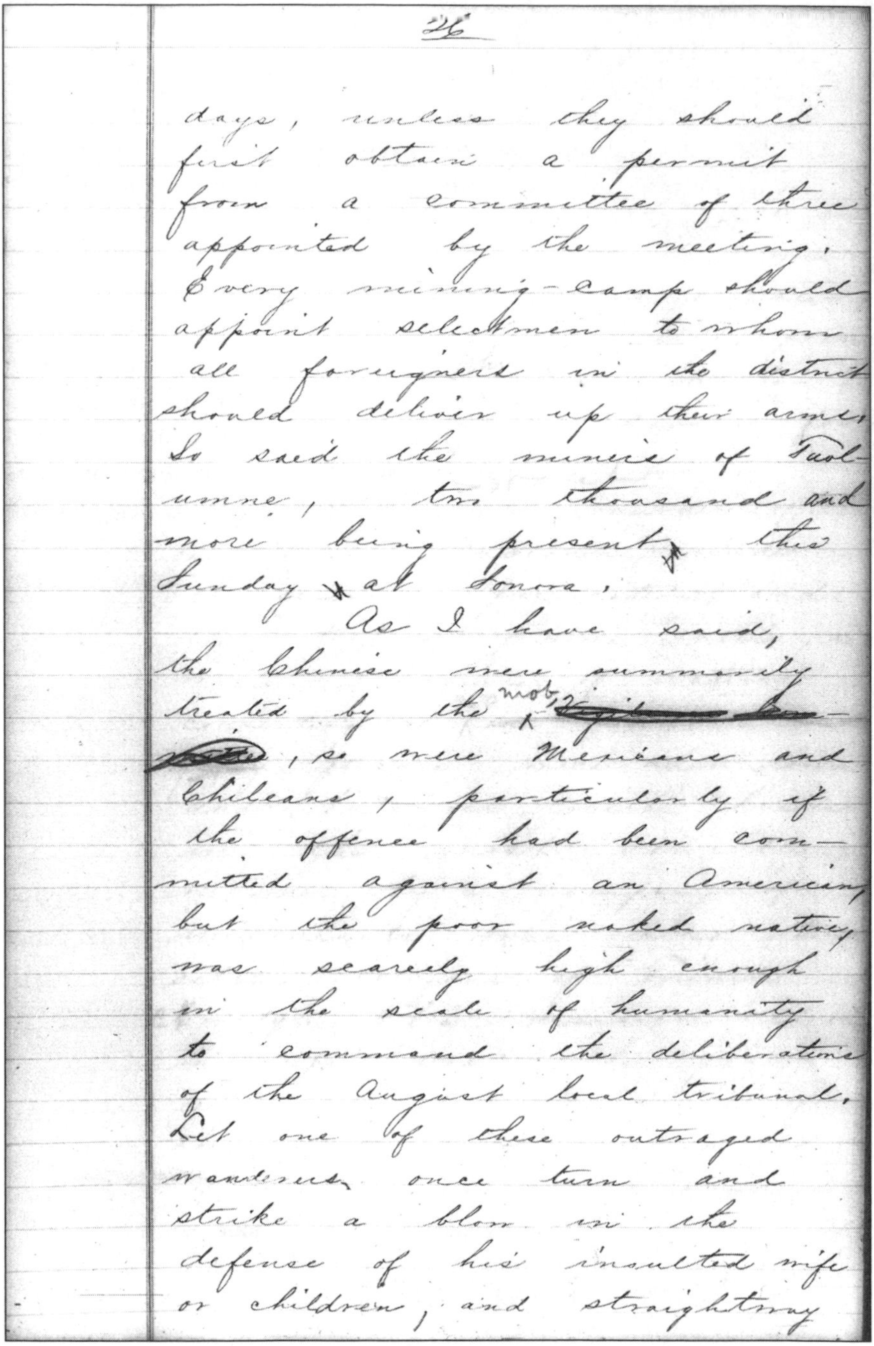

As I have said, the Chinese were summarily treated by the mob, so were Mexicans and Chileans, particularly if the offence had been committed against an American, but the poor naked natives was scarcely high enough in the scale of humanity to command the deliberation of the August local tribunal. Let one of these outraged wanderers once turn and strike a blow in the defense of his insulted wife or children, and straightway

**Figure 3.2:** From Hubert Howe Bancroft, "The Crusade against Foreigners," Records of the Library and Publishing Companies, OS Box 16, folder 19, BANC MSS B-C 7, Bancroft Library, University of California, Berkeley.

excitement and strong drink, is a very different affair from organized vigilance, dispassionately, conscientiously, prayerfully if you will, and unselfishly watching the welfare of the commonwealth, using force only when all other means fail, using its power with moderation, tempering justice with mercy, and gladly relinquishing its distasteful duties the moment it can do so with safety.[63]

This venerated vigilantism was the opposite, Bancroft continually insisted, of what he called "mobocracy . . . where hiccoughing gold-diggers adjudged their fellow-creatures to death, and swung them into eternity amidst the drunken orgies of modern bacchanalia."[64] But this qualitative distinction, like so many others attendant to stories about vigilantism and lynching, was only and wholly narrative.

Bancroft's erasure of the violence and mayhem enacted by vigilantes was hardly unique. Those who had produced the idealized vigilante histories before him had also tried to minimize gruesome and bloody details in the interest of making vigilantes seem orderly, moderate, and even tempered. In spite of this, ample evidence exists to suggest that vigilantism often produced extreme sadism. This matters, of course, because the relative moderation of frontier vigilantism has long been used to distinguish it from southern lynching. In this conventional differentiation, frontier *vigilantes* are moderate and evenhanded, whereas southern *lynch mobs* are frenzied and sadistic.[65] While there are important historical shifts associated with pre-1880 vigilantism in the West and post-1880 vigilantism in the South, it is also extremely useful to recognize the force and effect of gestures such as Bancroft's strikethrough. Indeed, to a great extent, this small narrative sleight of hand acts as the metonym for the way that our historical understanding of vigilantism and lynching has evolved overall. Sadistic and immoderate violence was not only an aspect of vigilantism in California; indeed, similar stories can be found in every other region of the United States as well.

## Vigilantism, Violence, and the Body

In 1841, the Shelby County Regulators traveled to Louisiana to capture a man suspected of thievery. The regulators, unable to shoot the man in cold blood, advised the man to run and then shot him as he made his escape. According to an article in the *Redlander*, the vigilantes then "cut him in pieces, and hanged the fragments in trees."[66] The regulators were, it would seem, keenly aware of the power of public violence and its symbols. In 1838, they captured a man named Brown suspected of stealing a horse from a traveler from Tennessee.

According to Levi Ashcraft, the incident "was a splendid opportunity to make capital both with the Tenneseeans [*sic*] and with the citizens of the county."[67] Ashcraft includes a lurid account of Brown's treatment at the hands of the vigilantes:

> Poor Brown was dragged from his place of confinement protesting most solemnly his innocence, and carried to a dreary swamp a short distance south of the town, where he was entirely denuded of his clothes, tied to a tree and whipped till his back wore the appearance of a raw beefsteak. He still continued to assert his innocence, but to no purpose—he was undergoing the sentence of a court from whose stern decrees there is no appeal. The green grass under his feet had changed its color to scarlet; the leaves were clotted with his blood; yet the blows ceased not; stripe after stripe fell upon his bare and bleeding back, thick, fast and furious; the lynchers taking the whip by turns as one would become exhausted or revolt at the horrid cruelty of the scene.[68]

But the regulators were not satisfied with the brutal flogging. Ashcraft's account of the incident concludes:

> On the beech tree to which he was tied some ingenious artisan has carved his effigy. The design represents a gallows, the figure of a man below with a rope around his neck; under the whole is inscribed in rough capitals "A. F. Brown for horse stealing," a sort of hieroglyphic clause in the lynch code to warn all similar offenders of the fate which awaited them.[69]

Midway through his history of the Montana vigilantes, Dimsdale argues that the criminal set was actually lucky to fall into the hands of the Alder Gulch committee, insofar as the vigilantes did not engage in cruel, excessively sadistic violent practices. "The truth is," he asserts, "that the Vigilance Committee simply punished with death men unfit to live in any community, and that death was, usually, almost instantaneous, and only momentarily painful."[70] The supposed moderateness of vigilante violence was a peripheral component of the vigilante ideal. According to this ideal, "mobs" were cast as sadistic, extreme, and gratuitously violent, whereas vigilance committees were characterized as moderate, evenhanded, and controlled. This particular component of idealized vigilantism served a peculiar function attempting to mitigate the central fact that lynching was always, at its core, an act of violence. Dimsdale's idealized assertion that violence was an unfortunate side effect of vigilantism overlooks entirely the complex, and intermittently extreme, ways in which vigilantes made deliberate use of the symbolic power of their violent authority.[71]

The Shelby County Regulators' dismemberment of a dead body clearly indicates that a quick and painless execution was not these vigilantes' exclusive aim. Simple executions proved unsatisfactory to a number of other vigilante groups as well. An 1868 lynch mob in Wyoming made a point of hanging the corpse of a "criminal," already dead from multiple gunshot wounds.[72] The Alder Gulch vigilantes hanged a man already dead from gunshot wounds and the crowd fired over one hundred bullets into the corpse before taking the body down and burning it along with the dead man's house.[73] In 1870, suspected cattle thieves Ami Ketchum and Luther Mitchell were "hand-cuffed together, stripped, and partly skinned, then burned alive, then hanged up and left by cattle men to hang there several days."[74] The practice of taking "trophies" from lynched bodies can also be found in this period. According to Brown:

> The habit appeared early in the history of American vigilantism with the display in Kentucky in 1799 of the head of Micajah Harpe, one of the brother duo of fearsome outlaws who had plagued the Tennessee-Kentucky settlers until checked by regulators. Trophies were still being taken as late as 1891 when in the frontier community of Rawlins, Wyoming, a leading citizen, Dr. John E. Osborne—a future governor of Wyoming—participated in the vigilante hanging of the ferocious bandit, George (Big Nose) Parrott. The next day Dr. Osborne "skinned 'Big Nose' George and cut away the top of the skull, in order to remove the brain. The skin was tanned and made into a medical instrument bag, razor strops, a pair of lady's shoes, and a tobacco pouch. The shoes were displayed in the Rawlins National Bank for years."[75]

These incidents were admittedly rarer in frontier lynching than they were later in the South. The important thing, though, is that according to the vigilante ideal, they should never have happened at all. Vigilantes were not supposed to delight in the violent aspects of vigilantism; ideally, they were supposed to merely tolerate the violence of lynching as an undesirable means to a desirable end.

Such an idealized version of vigilantism obscures the ways in which vigilantes understood and made use of the real *and symbolic* violent logic of lynching. An understanding of the force of symbolic violence explains why the Shelby County Regulators carved the hanged effigy of a man they did not actually execute into the tree where he was flogged. Cutler recounts a similar incident in Boston, where, "on the night of September 10, 1835, a gallows was erected in Brighton Street, Boston, in front of Mr. Garrison's house, with two ropes suspended therefrom. On the crossbar was the inscription 'Judge Lynch's law.'"[76] In 1868, vigilantes in Cheyenne, Wyoming, produced an even more creative version of a symbolic lynching. When three men arrested for theft were released on bond, they were found the following morning, unharmed, but tied together and bearing a canvas placard that read:

$900 stole | Thieves. | 500 Recovered.
*F. St. Clair,    E. De Bronville,*
*W. Grier.*
City authorities please not interfere
*until* 10 *o'clock*, A.M.
Next *case* goes up a *tree*
*Beware of Vigilance Committee*[77]

In June of 1863, the women of Virginia City successfully forestalled the public hanging of three men convicted of murdering a deputy sheriff. The morning following their release, on the gallows erected to hang the men, were two hanged bear cubs with a sign stating:

Two Graves for Rent
Apply to
X. Beidler[78]

This incident occurred less than six months prior to the vigilantes' hanging spree and accurately foretold their coming power in the community.

These incidents acted as what Levi Ashcraft calls "hieroglyphic clauses in the lynch code,"[79] clearly projecting the violent and deadly authority of the vigilantes. Moreover, these incidents reveal the degree to which vigilantes themselves recognized the important relationship between their authority and their ability to enforce this authority through violent practices. Violence was never simply a side effect of vigilantism—lynching was the centerpiece of vigilantism, and lynching was always an act of violence. From this perspective, it is not surprising that lynching in the South became increasingly sadistic, extreme, and perverse at the turn of the century. These lynchers learned the practice from those who had acted before them, in both southern and western frontier regions. Sadistic lynching practices did not *develop* during the period of southern racial lynching; rather, these practices became more common, more frequent, and—most tragically—more acceptable to those who either enacted or witnessed these scenes. But this increase in frequency does not mean that the lynchers who came before them really *were* ideally moderately violent; it merely means that the vigilantes, their historians, and their advocates successfully mitigated these macabre departures from the ideal in the historical record.

## "The Greatest Popular Tribunal the World Has Ever Witnessed": Historical and Historiographical Implications

Historians, in general, love the San Francisco Committee of Vigilance of 1856. To quote David Johnson, "The 1856 San Francisco Vigilance Committee has commanded the close attention of every scholar of vigilantism. Its more than 8,000 reputed members, its control of the city's most prominent merchants, its paramilitary organization, and its spectacular execution of four men have made it a (perhaps *the*) exemplar of vigilantism."[80] In his masterful study of vigilantism, *Strain of Violence: Historical Studies of American Violence and Vigilantism*, Richard Maxwell Brown chooses the committee for the book's only chapter-length study, and the San Francisco vigilantes are central in Christopher Waldrep's transregional work on vigilantism as well.[81] As a scholar of vigilantism, I have always been intrigued and baffled by the well-entrenched fascination that seems to characterize historical treatments of this committee. Johnson's assertions are certainly true—the committee *was* extraordinarily large and was a well-organized body that controlled important municipal bodies and executed four men. But these characteristics are not singular to the 1856 San Francisco committee. The earlier 1851 San Francisco committee was just as well organized and bureaucratically embedded, and many other vigilance committees, for example, the 1864 Alder Gulch committee, were considerably more deadly.[82] If size really *does* matter, the 1859 consortium of vigilance committees in the Attakapas region of Louisiana, with four thousand members, could also be considered a vigilante benchmark. But these committees are limited to either regional significance (as is the case of the committee in the Idaho Territory) or virtual obscurity (as is the case with the Acadian vigilantes).

Bancroft's archival and historical obsession with the two San Francisco vigilance committees cannot be disentangled from the nominally "real" significance of the groups. Simply put, Bancroft manufactured the historical significance of these particular vigilantes and simultaneously produced three associated and lasting historiographical effects. First, the narrative accounts used by vigilantes to justify ambiguous violence were preserved at the level of regional history. If, as Foucault suggests, "narrative makes the stuff of history from street brawls"[83] and local vigilance committees were intent on narrating their particular street brawls into history, then Bancroft acted as their willing accomplice. Local histories—such as Dimsdale's about the Alder Gulch committees or the more glorified versions of events offered by San Francisco committee members in their biographical interviews—were enshrined as "primary sources." Street brawls narrated as history became "History."

Second, the sanitized and glorified accounts of vigilantism associated with this newly produced history became, by virtue of their placement within Bancroft's project, uniquely and distinctly western. In other words, the "popular tribunals" of the "frontier West" began to seem *and thus became* distinct from the lynch mobs of the South. This regional difference can be most notably discerned through the disappearance of racial difference and violence from Bancroft's history. The year 1892 was the deadly highpoint of southern lynching; the two *Popular Tribunals* volumes were published the following year. Bancroft's conceptual and imaginary difference between "good" frontier lynching and "bad" southern lynching took hold as a historiographical convention. But Bancroft's unpublished materials reveal that this difference was as much a factor of narrative—what was and was not included in his story of vigilantism in the West—as it was a reflection of stark differences between actual lynching events in the 1890s.

In spite of these two major historiographical effects on the continuing history of lynching and vigilantism, it is unclear that Bancroft was specifically committed to vigilantism, per se. As his notes and deleted passages suggest, Bancroft disliked rabble, disruption, and disorder. And vigilantes themselves—the actual living, breathing men who were members of the San Francisco vigilance committee—made him despondent. Bancroft was really much more interested in the *idea* of vigilantism as a figure for understanding citizenship and national identity. In the simplest possible sense, vigilantism was good because it represented the possibility that any given group of citizen subjects could act in their best wisdom and free from the constraints of a possibly addled government. More generally, vigilantism represented the limit point of the relationship between the people and the state. This link between insurgency and American national identity was certainly not new, nor was Bancroft's fascination with the boundary between the democratic state and its (conditionally free) citizens. What was important was Bancroft's characterization of these questions as regionally western. In effect, Bancroft was making an early, albeit anemic, version of the argument that the American national character could be understood by looking to the western frontier. Frederick Jackson Turner's version of this idea, first appearing six years after the *Popular Tribunals* volumes, offered a much more sophisticated and compelling version of the same argument. Whereas Bancroft attempted to link American identity to the West through popular tribunals as representative of the citizenry's right to seize the reins of power from the state, Turner linked national identity to the West through the more appealing ideals of ambition, unified struggle, and the emergence of a composite national identity.[84]

In his attempt to identify vigilantism as a key to understanding something about the American nation and its people Bancroft was of one mind with another famous vigilante narrator: Ida B. Wells. A year before Bancroft's release of the *Popular Tribunals* volumes, Wells had released the first in a series of antilynching pamphlets: *Southern Horrors: Lynch Law in All Its Phases*.[85] Wells also suspected that lynching represented the limit point of the relationship between the people and the state, though her analysis proved to be nearly the opposite of Bancroft's in every other way.

It is almost axiomatic to assert that something about lynching changed in 1890. The overall number of lynchings per year went up, lynching became increasingly concentrated regionally in the South, and lynching victims became increasingly and disproportionately black. But even in the context of these well-documented changes, the stories *lynchers* told about their violent practices did not, in fact, depart dramatically from the idealized narrative deployed by frontier vigilantes. In fact, perhaps the most well known of all justificatory American lynching narratives, *Birth of a Nation* (or the lesser-well-known book on which the film is based, Thomas Dixon's *The Clansmen*) is little more than a reworking of the official vigilante history set in the Reconstruction South.[86] However, even if post-1890 southern lynchers continued to make recourse to the same ideal narrative to justify their violent practices, this period marked a central shift in the relationship between vigilante violence and vigilante narrative. In 1892, when Wells wrote the first of her antilynching pamphlets, she seized the power of narrative from the vigilantes.

# 4

# Narrative Revisions and
# the End of the Vigilante Ideal

This almost universal tendency to accept as true the slander
which the lynchers offer to civilization as an excuse for their
crime might be explained if the true facts were difficult to
obtain. But not the slightest difficulty intervenes.

—Ida B. Wells Barnett, "Lynching and the Excuse for It"

On May 21, 1892, Ida B. Wells's first major editorial on lynching, "Eight
Men Lynched," was published in the independent Negro newspaper
*Free Speech*.[1] Wells's incisive and aggressive critique of southern lynching
practices provoked a vehement response in Memphis.[2] On May 25, the white
newspaper the *Evening Semitar* ran a violent and hate-filled editorial rejoinder
to Wells's examination of the narrative justifications of lynchers, calling on the
public to "tie the wretch who utters these calumnies to a stake at the intersection of Main and Madison Sts., brand him in the forehead with a hot iron
and perform upon him a surgical operation with a pair of tailor's shears."[3] The
lynchers who gathered that evening in the cotton exchange building, while failing to enact the macabre scene described in the editorial, succeeded in running
Mr. Fleming (the co-owner and business manager of *Free Speech*) out of town,
bringing about the end of the paper. Wells, in New York at the time, escaped
harm but was unable to return home to Memphis because of the lingering
danger. "Not the slightest difficulty intervene[d]"[4] for Wells in her attempt
to dismantle the mythical southern lynching narrative of black male predators sexually assaulting white women, but intense difficulties arose as a result
of her success at doing so. Ida B. Wells effectively challenged lynchers in the
most powerful way possible—by dismantling the narratives used to justify and
define their violent practices.[5]

Less than six months later, Wells's editorial was republished as *Southern
Horrors: Lynch Law in All Its Phases*—a pamphlet that included an account
of the hostilities in Memphis. Two years later, she published *A Red Record:*

*Tabulated Statistics and Alleged Causes of Lynching in the United States, 1892–1893–1894*. In these two groundbreaking works, Wells confronted and dismantled the narrative of ideal vigilantism and succeeded in establishing a counternarrative wherein lynching and vigilantism were constituted as expressions of hatred, racism, and unmitigated brutality. Most famously, Wells refuted the myth of the black southern rapist—a myth that was a regional adaptation of the narrative of ideal vigilantism and one that was notoriously inaccurate and insidious. Indeed, all of the southern lynching narratives that Wells spoke out against—the newspapers and personal accounts—are recognizable as reworkings of the narrative of ideal vigilantism that had gained popularity throughout the nineteenth century. But these narratives changed dramatically as a result of Wells's campaign.

This chapter looks closely at Wells's *Southern Horrors* and *A Red Record* in order to trace the two central ways in which the frontier narrative of ideal vigilantism was rewritten in the South. The "Bible Belt pornography" of the southern lynching narrative was in essence a retelling of the frontier narrative of ideal vigilantism. As lynching became increasingly common in the South, this formerly broad narrative formula was reworked in ways that made it particularly compelling—if not necessarily more accurate—for white lynchers. So, for example, assertions of "uncontrolled criminal conditions" were reinscribed in a more specific way as allegations of rampant sexual assaults by black men on white women. This new, specifically southern vigilante narrative was of central concern to Wells and motivated her extended and painstaking attempts to "set the record straight." The chapter then turns to Wells's new lynching narrative—one that directly opposed Bancroft's nearly simultaneous attempt to associate vigilantism and an idealized American citizenship. Instead, Wells recast the vigilante narrative, creating an opposing set of associations wherein vigilantism was characterized as morally reprehensible and directly harmful to the reunifying nation. Insofar as lynching itself had always been constituted, produced, and defined by its associated narrative justifications, Wells's ability to intervene in the "web of relations" between violence and narrative justification had an important impact on the practice of lynching itself.[6]

My concern in this chapter is with the vigilante narrative formula as it was altered, affected, and changed by Wells. In that sense, my focus is neither on Wells herself nor on the broader scope of antilynching activism in the period—both of which have been extensively explored by other scholars. A number of recent biographies offer comprehensive considerations of Wells's activism, both during the period when Wells wrote the pamphlets I consider in this chapter as well as before and after.[7] This work offers a range of important insights about Wells's work on the pamphlets in the context of her own evolution as an activist as well as in relationship to larger social, cultural, and political conditions. It is useful to note here the widely accepted idea that the specific circumstances surrounding the Memphis lynching provoked Wells to recognize the ways that lynching was justified and legitimated through narrative claims and falsehoods. Wells writes in her autobiography that before the Memphis lynching, she "had accepted the idea meant to be conveyed—that although lynching was irregular and contrary to law and order, unreasoning anger over the terrible crime of rape led to the lynching; that perhaps the brute deserved death anyhow and the mob was justified in taking his life."[8] But the three men lynched in Memphis had not been accused of rape. One of the men, Thomas Moss, "was as good a friend as any Ida had in Memphis"[9] and is described by Paula Giddings as "the embodiment of the hard work, self-discipline, and clean living that Southern whites insisted African Americans lacked."[10] Moss's brutal and surprising death, Wells claimed, "opened [her] eyes to what lynching really was. An excuse to . . . keep the race terrorized."[11] Her realization about the rift between lynching narrative and lynching practice undoubtedly motivated her turn from other forms of activism to an antilynching crusade. Significantly, these circumstances framed her crusade as one of research and truth telling—in effect, as a campaign located substantially within the realm of narrative.[12] Because of this, her intervention was uniquely well positioned to intervene in the long entwined practices and narratives of the vigilantes.

## The Evolution of Vigilante Narrative

The vigilante narrative appeared as early as "A Sketch of Panic in Eastern Texas, during the Month of April, 1836" (written within a few years of the events in question) and Charles Summerfield's 1849 account of the 1842 Cane Hill Company and in areas ranging from southwestern Louisiana to Northern California. As outlined in Chapter 1, the narrative of ideal vigilantism was animated and amplified by related constructions about popular democracy, patriotic insurgency, and heroic violence. The narrative formula comprising the vigilante ideal was repeated in a variety of different regions and throughout the nineteenth century, showing that this story of "proper" vigilantism traveled through time and across regions. In some cases, such as the published and widely circulated accounts written by Thomas Dimsdale and Edward Bonney, it is easy to see how the glory of vigilantes in one community became an aspirational ideal for would-be vigilantes in other localities. There is even more evidence, however, that suggests that vigilante lore traveled via word of mouth, as populations and individuals moved between and among regions.

The Idaho vigilante chronicler William McConnell makes positive reference to Henry Plummer's execution in Montana and to an unspecified vigilance committee in Arkansas.[13] Alexander Barde, the Acadian vigilante and historian, was aware of multiple committees and lynchings in neighboring Texas.[14] The Montana committee's historian, Dimsdale, knew of vigilantes in California and Nevada.[15] In all of these cases, an awareness of the practices of vigilantes in other communities created a context for the developing committees by serving as either an example of "successful" vigilantism elsewhere or by illustrating an "improper" use of vigilantism against which the new committee's practices were antithetically constituted as ideal.[16] This is one of the broadest ways of thinking about the Foucauldian "web of relations" between vigilante violence and vigilante narrative—as a series of stories that circulated between and among regions and individuals conveying not only a violent practice but an ideal that defined and legitimized the violence in already familiar ways. This narrative accrual swept irregularly across regions and decades and, ultimately, reached its zenith in the South. Wells's intervention has to be understood as a characteristically distinct resistance to this cultural force. Unlike earlier critics of vigilantism, Wells engaged with lynching as a multiregional practice; from the outset, Wells understood that lynching could be best understood as an expression of large-scale cultural ideologies of racism rather than an expression of specific local conditions or circumstances. Her refutation of the supposed relationship between rape and lynching was effective precisely because she was able to detect and point out similarities between lynchings and lynching narratives in different localities and communities.[17] More importantly, however, Wells went straight to the heart of the justificatory narratives that lynchers used to idealize their violence and, as a result, significantly altered the location of lynching violence within the larger context of American social ideals. The antilynching movement that Wells inaugurated was, like Bancroft's work on vigilantism in the West, an expression of a much larger set of claims about the future of the South and its significance within the future of the nation as a whole. Just as Bancroft was arguing *for* the merits of vigilantism as the ideal regional representation of democratic citizen participation, Wells was arguing *against* lynching as the dystopic expression of "a regional culture gripped by white supremacy."[18]

Wells's essays, *Southern Horrors* and *A Red Record*, are largely similar in structure. Each text begins with Wells's brief theoretical commentary on the nature of lynching practices and narratives and then moves systematically through a series of particular case studies. In many of these case studies, Wells draws on published accounts of specific lynchings to allow her readers to see "the slander which the lynchers offer to civilization as an excuse for their crime"[19]—that is, the narratives that southern vigilantes used to legitimate and justify their actions. This section looks at Wells's examples of southern lynching narratives in order to highlight the ways in which these accounts made use of and reworked the features of the narrative of ideal vigilantism. According to this reading, the "southern lynch mob" is a particular regional variant of the American vigilante committee and one that is explicitly produced and defined by its historical predecessors.

A focus on narrative effectively locates southern lynching practices in a historical continuum that begins in the realm of frontier lynching practices and reveals important connections between the two regions. The question that dominated early scholarship on lynching—"Why did southern white people lynch southern black people in such staggering numbers?"—often led to explanations related to long-standing structures and ideologies of racial animus. In effect, southern lynching in this context is fittingly connected to a longer history of slavery and racial violence in the South (if not the larger nation). But to ask the question "Why did southern white people *lynch* southern black people?" foregrounds a different set of connections and emphasizes the connections between lynch mobs (vigilantes) in the late nineteenth-century South and lynch mobs (vigilantes) in earlier periods and other regions. It enables us to see that white people *lynched* Southern black people as a violent expression of racism *and* because it was a violent expression long justified and glorified as an expression of national heroism. Bay correctly points out that "what distinguishes lynchings from all other forms of murder is not any specific type of violence, but the lynchers' claims to justification and social legitimacy."[20] But this idea bears expansion. Vigilante claims to justification and legitimacy were centrally related to the usurpation of a form of violence—execution— from the state. Vigilantes weren't just *socially* legitimate, they were *nationally* legitimate—acting when the state would, or could, not. This construction had deep roots in the nation's earliest ideas about democratic citizen participation and popular organizing and decades of development in the hands of the vigilantes. In other words, lynching violence in the South was produced and supported by both racist ideologies and paradoxical claims to patriotism.

## Southern Lynchers and Ideal Vigilantism

An example of the relationship between the narrative of ideal vigilantism and southern lynching narratives can be found in the fifth chapter of *Southern Horrors*, "The Malicious and Untruthful Press." The chapter begins with Wells's extended citation of a May 17, 1892, article from the Memphis *Daily Commercial*. The article, "More Rapes, More Lynchings," relies on the familiar conventions of the narrative of ideal vigilantism. The article begins, like frontier vigilante histories, with a claim about the necessity of the narrative itself: "The lynching of three Negro scoundrels reported in our dispatches from Anniston, Ala., for a brutal outrage committed upon a white woman will be a text for much comment on 'southern barbarism' by Northern newspapers; but we fancy it will hardly prove effective for campaign purposes among intelligent people."[21] "Narrative necessity" here is framed by a regional/cultural conflict between North and South—an alleged misapprehension that the author claims no concern with and then aggressively seeks to mitigate throughout the remainder of the article. This opening salvo is followed by an extended explanation of, and justification for, the increasing number of black people's deaths at the hands of southern lynch mobs. The defense begins, of course, with an assertion of uncontrolled criminal conditions:

> The frequency of these lynchings calls attention to the frequency of the crimes which causes lynching. The "Southern barbarism" which deserves the serious attention of all people North and South, is the barbarism which preys upon weak and defenseless women. Nothing but the most prompt, speedy and extreme punishment can hold in check the horrible and beastial [*sic*] propensities of the Negro race.[22]

True to formula, this claim about criminal conditions makes hyperbolic reference to "horrible" and "bestial" crimes—crimes so hideous that any manner of response would be both justified and requisite. This particular version of the "criminal conditions" claim amplifies the necessity of the article's narration of the violence by foregrounding the relationships among violence, language, and perception. Initially, the phrase "southern barbarism" is used in the article to refer to northern perceptions of lynching violence; in the reworking, however, "southern barbarism" is redefined by the author to refer to the uncontrolled criminal behaviors of southern black men. This shift, of course, reveals the principal function of extended narrative justifications of lynching: to mark the line between *valorous* (vigilante) violence and *criminal* ("Negro") violence.

The article, like all vigilante narratives, offers an extended description of the uncontrolled criminal conditions facing beleaguered southern white women. The nefarious southern black criminals, like their frontier predecessors, enact their despicable deeds through intricate organizational practices. "In each case," the article asserts, "the crime was deliberately planned and perpetrated by several Negroes. They watched for an opportunity when the women were left without a protector. It was not a sudden yielding to a fit of passion, but the consummation of a devilish purpose which has been seeking and waiting for the opportunity."[23] Even more interesting is the article's corollary assertion about these premeditated assaults, insofar as the description borrows directly from the narrative scene of remote frontier communities. "This feature of the crime not only makes it the most fiendishly brutal, but it adds to the terror of the situation in the thinly settled country communities. No man can leave his family at night without the dread that some roving Negro ruffian is watching and waiting for this opportunity."[24] The "lawlessness" attributed to remoteness in the frontier is here amplified with racist overtones. "Remoteness" per se is made even more dangerous as the crisis of lawlessness is an effect of a southern racial chaos wherein "Negro ruffians" are roving uncontrolled throughout white society.

Having "established" the element of extraordinary criminal conditions, the article moves on to an assertion of the *failure of the state*. This familiar idea is interestingly reconfigured in this context as a further effect of unique, and distinctly racialized, criminal conditions. "The Negro as a political factor can be controlled," the article proudly asserts. "But neither laws nor lynchings can subdue his lusts."[25] The link, here, between the location of southern black men in politics and in the social order marks another uniquely southern version of the diffuse social condition of lawlessness. Rather than making (not wholly accurate) reference to a literal absence of civil structures, "lawlessness" here is defined as an effect of racial difference. Immune to the restraints of both civilization and force, the article asserts that blackness itself is constitutive of a kind of abject lawlessness.[26] But, of course, as the vigilante story always goes, these extraordinary conditions are met by their antithesis—*the valorous vigilante*. The article concludes, "What is to be done? The crime of rape is always horrible, but [for] the southern man there is nothing which so fills the soul with horror, loathing and fury as the outraging of a white woman by a Negro."[27] Embattled and threatened in his allegedly remote home, and witness to a parade of outrages against the women he feels obligated to protect, the southern white man does what must be done: he lynches.

Wells follows the *Daily Commercial* article with one from the June 4 *Evening Semitar*. This second article contains further examples of how the vigilante narrative was reworked in the Jim Crow South. For example, "orderliness" and "public popularity" are understood as distinctly white racial characteristics, as revealed in the assertion "The white people won't stand this sort of thing, and whether they be insulted as individuals are [*sic*] as a race, the response will be prompt and effectual."[28] "This sort of thing," of course, refers to "the violation of white women by Negroes, which is the outcropping of a bestial perversion of instinct."[29] Promptness and effectiveness here stand in for "orderliness" and are understood as exclusively white racial characteristics;

antithetically, "blackness" is cast as instinctual or, at its worst, *perversely* instinctual. This bifurcation of "whiteness" and "blackness" into two distinct
categories of being defined the racist (il)logic of the southern adaptation of
the narrative of ideal vigilantism. Notably, the article contains a concession of
the degree to which this formulation was underwritten by a conceptual, as opposed to actual, difference between southerners by acknowledging, "There are
well-bred Negroes among us, and it is truly unfortunate that they should have
to pay, even in part, the penalty of the offenses committed by the baser sort,
but this is the way of the world. The innocent must suffer for the guilty."[30] In
other words, the article admits, participation in the social and civic order of
the South was fundamentally defined and limited by race. Within this context, *public popularity* can be understood as standing in for the public sentiments of *white* southerners—for *black* southerners had neither access nor right
to public opinion as it was understood in these texts.

Given the well-documented sadism of many southern lynchings the article
ends on a particularly surprising note—when the author attempts to associate
violence itself with blackness and a constitutional moderation with whiteness,
including white criminality:

> The Caucasian blackguard simply obeys the promptings of a depraved
> disposition, and he is seldom deliberately rough or offensive toward
> strangers or unprotected women.
>
> The Negro tough, on the contrary, is given to just that kind of
> offending, and he almost invariably singles out white people as his
> victims.[31]

In yet another racialized distribution, violence is understood through the
juxtaposition of whiteness and blackness. "Blackness" here is characterized as
"given to" the worst and "most depraved" kind of violence—in other words,
violence against women. And in what may be the most disturbing narrative
mischaracterization on the vigilante record, this "violent black nature" is characterized as "racist," and southern white people are portrayed as the victims of
racial violence. Within this particular narrative universe, the white man does
what he has to do in violation of his own moderate nature.

Drawing on newspaper reports, and the words of revered southern politi-
cians, ministers, and businessmen, Wells's pamphlets document the repeated
deployments of this southern narrative of ideal vigilantism. These accounts
reveal numerous examples of southern lynchers' attempts to enact some of the
qualifying aspects of ideal vigilantism—orderliness and public popularity. An
account of a lynching in Wickliffe, Kentucky, for example, includes details

about an extended, though clearly illegitimate, trial proceeding. Reminiscent of the orderly but farcical practices detailed in Summerfield's account of the Cane Hill Company, the Kentucky lynchers traveled amid a series of towns aboard boats and trains, gathering "evidence" and "witness testimony" before executing their clearly innocent victim.[32] Offering further evidence that these southern lynchers attempted to engage in orderly practice, Wells notes, "In some of these cases the mob affects to believe in the Negro's guilt. *The world is told that the white woman in the case identifies him, or the prisoner 'confesses.'*"[33] Wells also tells the story of a lynch mob/vigilance committee in Shelby County, Tennessee, submitting the issue of execution to a public vote. Following an "investigation" of the circumstances surrounding a rape, "the committee returned and made its report, and the chairman put the question of guilt or innocence to a vote. All who thought the proof was strong enough to warrant execution were invited to cross over to the other side of the road. Everybody but four or five negroes [*sic*] crossed over."[34] This is a near perfect reenactment of the "public vote" taken by the Alder Gulch committee following the murder of Nicolas Tbalt and but one of the numerous examples of incidents in which the specific practices of southern lynchers mirrored those of vigilantes in the frontier.

In light of the degree to which white southerners lynched their black victims with impunity, it is striking that they bothered to extract "identifications" or "confessions" at all. Of course, this demonstration of *orderliness* served to constitute their violent practices in a particular way. Bothering to extract evidence or a confession, regardless of how bogus either might have been, served to mitigate the "barbarism" of their self-sanctioned violent practices. Indeed, this was a well-established vigilante conceit and practice. Readings of southern lynching that foreground the impunity enjoyed by many lynch mobs tend to underemphasize the strange and formal aspects of vigilante practice in this period and region. Paula Giddings notes that the Memphis lynching of Moss and the others was described by the *Appeal-Avalanche* as "one of the most orderly of its kind ever conducted," and Gail Bederman points out that newspapers in the North "frequently (if improbably) . . . depicted white lynch mobs as paragons of disciplined, self-restrained manliness."[35] Her observation, of course, is related to a broader and rich analysis of the relationship between constructions of manliness, race, and ideas about "civilization," and she is likely correct that the assertions of self-restraint were both exaggerated and made in the service of shoring up gendered and racial logics. But the northern descriptions of lynch mobs as "disciplined" and "self-restrained" were less improbable than inevitable. Orderliness was a crucial aspect of vigilante legitimation, in both narrative description and performance. The solemnity and orderliness that inhered in some vigilante and lynching practices, while no evidence of real moderation, were crucial aspects of the ritual and its attendant benefits.

Southern lynch mobs were markedly more violent than their frontier predecessors. Even so, however, it is notable that in many of the cases Wells cites (and she makes a point of citing the most shocking and horrifying cases she can find) extraordinarily perverse treatments of the body occurred only *after* the lynching victim was already dead. So, for example, while her case studies include numerous examples of burnings, dismemberment, and the taking of body trophies, often these extreme violent practices transpired in the hours of perverse public spectacle that followed relatively straightforward hangings. The occurrence of these bizarre public rituals, and the alarming frequency with which sadistic torture *was* enacted on individuals while they were still alive, makes it difficult to assert that southern lynch mobs prided themselves in their orderliness or self-control. But noting the degree to which southern lynch mobs commonly executed the accused men first in what was a historically acceptable mode does complicate the widely accepted axiom that southern lynch mobs were uniformly deranged and sadistic. In fact, the relationship between brutality in frontier and southern lynching can be more accurately understood as one of degree. Within the context of frontier lynching, extreme sadism (torture, burning) was relatively rare but not unheard of. These practices became more common in the South as the lynching *re*enactments of southerners increased in frequency and scale. These were not two unrelated sets of practices; rather, they were two qualitatively different versions of the same violent act.

The escalation of sadism in southern lynching was supported by a culture of violent racism that not only tolerated but encouraged unconscionable brutality. Even within this culture, however, there were individuals who spoke out against southern lynchers. These individuals, like their predecessors in the frontier, threatened the *public popularity* of the vigilantes and met with similar fates. Wells included a detailed account of a minister in Texas who was "ridden out of Paris on a rail because [he] was the only man in Lamar county [*sic*] to raise [his] voice against the lynching of Smith."[36] This incident is strikingly reminiscent of the "banishment" of vigilante detractors in the frontier. The white editor of the *Herald* in Montgomery, Alabama, was run out of town for questioning, five years *before* Wells wrote *Southern Horrors*, the veracity of the rape myth. His editorial queried, "Why is it that white women attract negro men now more than in former days? There is a secret to this thing, and we greatly suspect it is the growing appreciation of white Juliets for colored Romeos."[37] The dangerous suggestion that the sexual liaisons between black men and white women were, in fact, consensual, shattered the bedrock of the southern narrative of ideal vigilantism. Those who drew attention to this possibility were a direct and present danger to the legitimacy of southern lynching.

Like their predecessors in the frontier, southern lynchers did not, and could not, tolerate detractors. Wells includes an account of an incident in Virginia wherein "Mayor Trout, of Roanoke, Virginia, called out the militia in 1893, to protect a Negro prisoner, and in doing so nine men were killed and a number wounded."[38] The vehemence of the lynchers overwhelmed the mayor and militia and the attempt to save the prisoner's life was a failure. The following year an attempt to forestall a lynching in Ohio, while ultimately successful, involved even greater deadly force when "Governor McKinley, of Ohio . . . sent the militia to Washington Courthouse, in October 1894, and five men were killed and twenty wounded in maintaining the principle that the law must be upheld."[39] In fact, one of Wells's guiding insights about lynching was that *public popularity* played a central role in constituting and defining the violent practice. In *A Red Record*, she writes, "Public sentiment by its representatives has encouraged Lynch Law, and upon the revolution of this sentiment we must depend for its abolition."[40] It was with this central understanding in mind that Wells wrote against the narratives used by southern lynchers.

As the number of moderator movements in frontier regions suggests, vigilantes were never without their critics and opponents. However, few of these earlier challengers took up their battle as astutely as Wells did—in the realm of narrative. Beginning in the preface to *Southern Horrors* and continuing throughout *A Red Record*, Wells sought to achieve one principal goal—to delegitimate lynching. This singular ambition reveals that Wells understood what the vigilante historians had known first—that lynching practices have a unique and dependent relationship to and on lynching narratives. Knowing this, Wells understood that dismantling the practice of lynching would require dismantling the narrative justifications used to constitute and legitimate these violent acts. At the end of *Southern Horrors*, Wells outlined a number of political and civil actions that she believed would most directly contribute to an antilynching campaign. In addition to recommending large-scale labor strikes as well as boycotts of segregated modes of public transportation, Wells proposed the aggressive distribution of a new lynching narrative.

> The assertion has been substantiated throughout these pages that the press contains unreliable and doctored reports of lynchings, and one of the most necessary things for the race to do is to get these facts before the public. The people must know before they can act, and there is no educator to compare with the press.[41]

While southern lynching practices would not diminish, in frequency or sever-ity, until nearly two decades later, the meaning of lynching would undergo a radical shift beginning with this courageous woman's decision to speak the truth. As Paula Giddings aptly asserts in her biography of Wells, "The nation's first antilynching movement had begun."[42]

## Vigilante Violence: The New Southern Narrative

The cornerstone of Wells's antilynching campaign is a revised account of south-ern lynching, for she was convinced that southern lynchers were lying to justify their violent practices. She sought an antidote to this deception in a careful presentation of the "facts." Following the attack in Memphis on the *Free Speech* and its staff, Wells's motivation to publish a more accurate report on southern lynching redoubled: "Since my business has been destroyed and I am an exile from home because of that editorial, the issue has been forced, and as the writer of it I feel that the race and the public generally should have a statement of the facts as they exist."[43] Wells's sense of narrative necessity is familiar from earlier pro-vigilante accounts written by the committee historians: "It is with no plea-sure I have dipped my hands in the corruption here exposed. Somebody must show that the Afro-American race is more sinned against than sinning and it seems to have fallen upon me to do so."[44] By the time she wrote *A Red Record* two years later, Wells's understanding of the link between lynching violence and narrative had become even more well established.

> If the Southern people in defense of their lawlessness, would tell the truth and admit that colored men and women are lynched for almost any offense, from murder to a misdemeanor, there would not now be the necessity for this defense. But when they intentionally, maliciously and constantly belie the record and bolster up these falsehoods by the words of legislators, preachers, governors and bishops, then the Negro must give to the world his side of awful story.[45]

Wells was centrally fixated on the narrative justifications used by lynchers, but her battering assaults on these narratives were enriched by a complex under-standing of the functions served by these excuses. On lynching violence gener-ally, she wrote, "Naturally enough the commission of these crimes began to tell upon the public conscience, and the southern white man, as a tribute to the nineteenth century civilization, was in a manner compelled to give excuses for his barbarism."[46] Wells also understood why these excuses took on the particu-lar form of the rape myth:

Humanity abhors the assailant of womanhood, and this charge upon the Negro at once placed him beyond the pale of human sympathy. With such unanimity, earnestness and apparent candor was this charge made and reiterated that the world has accepted the story that the Negro is a monster which the Southern white man has painted him. And to-day, the Christian world feels, that while lynching is a crime, and lawlessness and anarchy the certain precursors of a nation's fall, it can not by word or deed, extend sympathy or help to a race of outlaws, who might mistake their plea for justice and deem it an excuse for their continued wrongs.[47]

As already noted, Wells herself was persuaded by the claims of lynchers until she bore firsthand witness to the falseness of these claims. Unquestionably, this prior misapprehension only strengthened Wells's sense of narrative necessity, offering a motivation equal to that of the vigilante historians who came before her. The vigilante historians were seeking to justify either their own actions or the actions of their associates, all through a narrative that they themselves largely believed. Wells, having arrived at a radically altered set of perceptions, produced "an incendiary critique of the interlocking sexual and racial myths that white Southerners used to justify [lynching]."[48]

Wells's reworking of the southern vigilante assertion of *uncontrolled criminal conditions* is one of the most trenchant and innovative aspects of her critique. The southern vigilante version, of course, alleges rampant and uncontrolled black assaults on white femininity. Wells unpacks and discredits this narrative construction through a complex analysis of the social relationships among white men, white women, black men, and black women in the South. Wells initiates her critique by granting that there were, in fact, sexual liaisons between black men and white women, but she is quick to point out that it was only the virulent racism of white southern men that mandated that these encounters be understood as "assaults." As Wells unequivocally states, "Hundreds of such cases might be cited, but enough have been given to prove the assertion that there are white women in the South who love the Afro-American's company even as there are white men notorious for their preference for Afro-American women."[49] By drawing attention to the interracial sexual proclivities of white men and white women, Wells effectively pulls attention *away* from the sexual conduct of black men. Thus, Wells establishes her first premise—while the basic circumstances surrounding certain lynching cases might be true, the interpretation of these circumstances through a racist lens inaccurately posited criminal behavior where none existed. In effect, she refutes the southern lynch mob's assertion about uncontrolled criminal conditions.

Circumventing the rape myth altogether, Wells goes on to argue that the southern lynching narrative, while commonly deployed, believed, and circulated, does not accurately reflect the majority of known lynching cases. Making a careful study of the *Chicago Tribune* lynching statistics, tabulated for the first time in the year she wrote *Southern Horrors,* Wells observes that rape was neither the exclusive nor the predominant cause of lynching.

> To palliate this record (which grows worse as the Afro-American becomes intelligent) and excuse some of the most heinous crimes that ever stained the history of a country, the South is shielding itself behind the plausible screen of defending the honor of its women. This, too, in the face of the fact that only *one-third* of the 728 victims to mobs have been *charged* with rape, to say nothing of those of that one-third who were innocent of the charge.[50]

And here, Wells captures the ambiguous power of vigilante narrative. By connecting specific lynchings and the attendant falsehoods used to justify the violence, Wells makes a sweeping assertion about the illegitimacy of lynching in general. Yet—and this is why Wells presents extensive proof of consensual sexual relationships between black men and white women—the "rape myth" permeated and affected both lynching practices and the broader culture of the South. This narrative was important, Wells tells us, not because it bore any actual relationship to real local circumstances or conditions but because it seemed believable and legitimizing to those who participated in lynching violence.

Ultimately, it was that *lynchers* were genuinely convinced of the righteousness of their own actions that made them so singularly dangerous. Wells writes:

> Nobody in this section of the country believes the old threadbare lie that Negro men rape white women. If Southern white men are not careful, they will over-reach themselves and public sentiment will have a reaction; a conclusion will then be reached which will be very damaging to the moral reputation of their women.[51]

And here, Wells goes even further in directing attention away from the sexual conduct of black men and toward southern white people. The "white woman" was the mythically constructed repository of sexual and racial purity within the racist logic of the Jim Crow South, but Wells was unwilling to allow this mythical construction to go unchallenged. As she dangerously points out in this passage, white women were potentially "impure" both sexually (in the sense that they both had and expressed sexual desires of their own) and racially (in that these desires were sometimes directed toward black southern men). In fact, as revealed in the newspaper accounts Wells cites in *Southern Horrors*, lynchers were distinctly invested in shoring up the myth of the sexually and racially pure white woman in order to produce a narrative context for their practices wherein their violence was both justified and righteous.[52]

The southern vigilante allegation of *the failure of the state* is also radically reconfigured in *Southern Horrors* and *A Red Record*. "Lawlessness," for Wells, was not the uncontrolled increase in sexual assaults on white women but "the black shadow of lawlessness in the form of lynch law . . . spreading its wings over the whole country."[53] She writes, "The South is brutalized to a degree not realized by its own inhabitants, and the very foundation of government, law and order, are imperilled [*sic*]."[54] In this skillful rearticulation, Wells turns the criminal chaos of the vigilante narrative inside out and draws attention to the inability or unwillingness of state-sanctioned legal structures to stop lynching. Wells notes, "The government which had made the Negro a citizen found itself unable to protect him. It gave him the right to vote, but denied him the protection which should have maintained that right."[55] Like the vigilante historians, Wells identifies the corruption of state-sanctioned legal structures as constitutive of lynching, though in her version, the corruption was made manifest as "the mockery of law and justice which disarmed men and locked them up in jails where they could be easily and safely reached by the mob."[56] By highlighting the criminality, lawlessness, and disorder of the vigilantes, Wells is able to invert the traditional vigilante claim that their practices, while illegal, were appropriately *extra*legal.

This strategy had been used against the vigilantes before, such as in the case of the Alder Gulch moderators who "insist[ed] on occasions, in season and out of season upon the sacred right of trial by the constitution and laws of the country qualified to discharge official duties."[57] But Wells's version of this critique is more successful for a number of reasons—in part, because the state was more conspicuously complicit in southern lynching violence, as evidenced by the growing number of failed prosecutions of lynchers. Equally as important, however, was that Wells makes this intervention in a much broader and effectively transregional way. While the specific circumstances of any given lynching were important in Wells's work—her well-chosen examples are presented in vivid and often graphic detail—her principal intent was to draw connections between lynching incidents across the South to reveal the ways that each of the violent events were connected. In identifying and engaging with these connections, Wells takes on the "web of relations" between lynching narratives and lynching events. This web of narrative constitution had legitimated and valorized over a century's worth of violence; rather than dispute any given example or incident, Wells confronts the entire structure.

There is no greater target in Wells's work than the allegedly *valorous vigilante* of the southern narrative. In a breathtakingly powerful and apt summary, she states:

> To justify their own barbarism they assume a chivalry which they do not possess. True chivalry respects all womanhood, and no one who reads the record, as it is written in the faces of the million mulattoes [*sic*] in the South, will for a minute conceive that the southern white man had a very chivalrous regard for the honor due the women of his own race or respect for the womanhood which circumstances placed in his power. That chivalry which is "most sensitive concerning the honor or women" can hope for but little respect from the civilized world, when it confines itself entirely to the women who happen to be white. Virtue knows no color line, and the chivalry which depends upon complexion of skin and texture of hair can command no honest respect.[58]

This passage, in addition to deliberately insulting the claimed chivalry of the white southern man, draws attention to the fourth figure in the racialized and gendered imaginary of the Jim Crow South—the black woman. Her reference to "the faces of the million mulattos in the South" challenged white southern men to account for decades of sexual violence done to black women. In so doing, Wells called attention to the mythical nature of the idealized social relationships between the races *and* the sexes. Her argument takes the following form: It was inarguable, she points out, that there had been sexual liaisons between the races. If relationships between black men and white women were culturally impossible under a logic that prohibited such liaisons, then she—and any logical reader—would be forced to conclude that these racially ambiguous faces were the result of sexual relationships between white men and black women. And here, Wells advances her own version of the argument that interracial sexual liaisons were categorically nonconsensual. In so doing, she relocates the black southern woman into the center of a logic of sexual protection and purity, "full and fully entitled subjects."[59] Within this revised arrangement, white men lacked not only the valor and chivalry they claimed to possess but the fundamental decency to protect the women over whom they had dominion.

Wells also had little tolerance for the orderly performances of southern vigilantes. She summarizes their attempts to legitimize their violence as follows:

In lynching, opportunity is not given the Negro to defend himself against the unsupported accusations of white men and women. The word of the accuser is held to be true and the excited bloodthirsty mob demands that the rule of law be reversed and instead of proving the accused to be guilty, the victim of their hate and revenge must prove himself innocent. No evidence he can offer will satisfy the mob; he is bound hand and foot and swung into eternity. Then to excuse its infamy, the mob almost invariably reports the monstrous falsehood that its victim made a full confession before he was hanged.[60]

In Wells's perception, those who lynched were by definition "mobs." Opposing earlier proponents of vigilantism (e.g., Summerfield and Bancroft), Wells takes the orderly behaviors of southern lynchers to be nothing other than further evidence of their blatant racial hatred and violent ill will. The lynchers in her examples are characterized as "wild with joy over the apprehension" of a victim, "infuriated" and "ferocious."[61] She borrows her most vivid description of the mob from Reverend King, the minister run out of Paris, Texas, for opposing a lynch mob. The description of the crowd follows King's detailed and deeply disturbing account of the tortures enacted on Henry Smith.

No one was himself now. Every man, woman and child in that awful crowd was worked up to a greater frenzy than that which actuated Smith's horrible crime. The people were capable of any new atrocity now, and as Smith's yells became more and more frequent, it was difficult to hold the crowd back, so anxious were the savages to participate in the sickening tortures.[62]

This passage captures the image of the lynch mob that Wells is intent on presenting. The term "savages" here, while originally Reverend King's, accurately captures one of Wells's central ideas about the lynch mob. Much of her criticism of vigilantism and lynching relies on a sharp juxtaposition between civility and anarchy. "Civility," for Wells, was an ideal—a political aspiration for the South that motivated and inspired her activist writings. As Bederman notes, the very idea of "civilization" was central to late nineteenth-century constructions of race and gender, and "discourses about lynching reinforced the way the discourse of civilization linked powerful manliness to whiteness."[63] In Wells's version of the "New South," the racial violence and inequality of the conditions under which she wrote would be replaced by political, judicial, and social equality between the races. She makes frequent recourse to "anarchy" as a descriptor for the social conditions against which she writes. In the anarchic South about which Wells writes, black men were killed brutally, publicly, and with the apparent complicity of the state. In other words, lynching had to be stopped for the good of the nation.

Within the context of the southern vigilante narrative, *public popularity* was constructed in exclusively white racial terms. Wells challenges this idea by suggesting a range of protest actions that could, and should, be taken up by the black public. She draws on an example from Memphis to make this argument. When local authorities failed to prosecute those who had lynched three men,

> the black men left the city by thousands, bringing about great stagna-
> tion in every branch of business. Those who remained so injured the
> business of the street car company by staying off the cars, that the
> superintendent, manager and treasurer called personally on the editor
> of the "Free Speech," [and] asked them to urge our people to give them
> their patronage again.[64]

For Wells, this suggested a larger and more important possibility:

> To Northern capital and Afro-American labor the South owes its re-
> habilitation. If labor is withdrawn capital will not remain. The Afro-
> American is thus the backbone of the South. A thorough knowledge
> and judicious exercise of this power in lynching localities could many
> times effect a bloodless revolution. The white man's dollar is his god,
> and to stop this will be to stop outrages in many localities.[65]

Wells was keenly aware of the necessity of changing public perceptions of lynching by both dismantling the unjust narratives lynchers used to justify their actions and awakening the courage of "the men and women in the South who disapprove of lynching and remain silent on the perpetration of such outrages."[66] But these were Wells's ideas about how to intervene in the public perceptions of white southerners. She was also arguing for an aggressive activism from the black public—an activism that would find its most direct and acute version in her suggestion that "a Winchester rifle should have a place of honor in every black home."[67] In prescribing a "thorough knowledge and judicious exercise of power," Wells explicitly makes a claim for access to the public sphere on behalf of southern black people.

Through these narrative reworkings, Wells changes the location of lynching and vigilantism within the context of American cultural ideals. In its most modest form, she presents this argument in the name of the South; in the section of *A Red Record* titled "A Friendly Warning," she details one English businessman's unwillingness to do business with a socially anarchic and violent South.[68] But her most sweeping and powerful rhetoric is reserved for the nation as a whole.

> Since the crusade against lynching was started, however, governors of states, newspapers, senators and representatives and bishops of churches have all been compelled to take cognizance of the prevalence of this crime and to speak in one way or another in defense of the charge against this barbarism in the United States. This has not been because there was any latent spirit of justice voluntarily asserting itself, especially in those who do the lynching, but because the entire American people now feel, both North and South, that they are objects in the gaze of the civilized world and that for every lynching humanity asks that America render its account to civilization and itself.[69]

To understand the significance of this passage, its helps to compare it to Hubert Howe Bancroft's reflections on popular tribunals at the end of his second volume on the topic:

> For some few centuries yet the iron-bound dogmatism of ancient societies will continue to condemn the action and principles of popular tribunals. . . .
>
> But the time will come when intelligent men everywhere will acknowledge the superiority of this principle. When laws intended to regulate intemperance, and the moral ideal shall have attained a higher plane, it will then be seen that government is most stable which is founded on rectitude and independence, which relies for its support on the will of a virtue-loving people, and not on tradition or inexorable law. It will then be seen, more clearly than now, that all power vests in the people, whether they choose to use it or to remain bound by superstitious veneration of shadow, that even after law is made and execution provided, the executive has no power except such as is daily and hourly continued to him by the people.[70]

Both of these passages suggest that lynching and vigilantism define the American nation and its citizens. This is the crux of how Wells changed vigilante narrative. For Bancroft and for the myriad vigilantes and vigilante supporters that preceded and succeeded him, vigilantism was an American *ideal*. For Wells, her fellow activists, and increasing numbers of individuals in the century following her pamphlets, vigilantism became an American *problem*.

## Narrative Inversions: The "Exportation" of Southern Lynching

To a notable degree, *Southern Horrors* and *A Red Record*, written a mere two years apart, advance the same argument; use overlapping evidence; and in some cases, include precisely the same phrases. While considerably longer, *A Red Record* does not depart from *Southern Horrors* in any significant way. I understand this repetition in the two texts to be indicative of Wells's particular and nuanced understanding of the relationship between lynching narratives and lynching violence. In the twelve months following the publication of *Southern Horrors*, 159 people died at the hands of lynch mobs. In *A Red Record*, Wells carefully lists the names of these individuals (when known), the dates of their deaths, and the alleged crimes for which they were executed.[71] During this same period, and in conjunction with many of these violent events, the "southern lynching narrative" was told and heard many times. The narrative of vigilante justification worked, as it always had, because it was so oft repeated that it accrued a kind of legitimacy and truth-value. And so Wells posited and repeated her own antilynching narrative construction: *Mobs of white, sadistic racists gathered and enacted unspeakable violence on southern African American men for the exclusive purpose of expressing their social power, and neither the state nor a cowardly public did anything to stop them.*

In chapter 5 of *Southern Horrors*, "The South's Position," Wells considers the dangers of lynching as a predominant feature of the South's reputation in both the rest of the United States and abroad. The violence of lynching, she asserts, is symbolic of the larger social inequities of Jim Crow segregation, such that "there is little difference between the Ante-bellum South and the New South. The result is a growing disregard of human life. Lynch law has spread its insiduous [*sic*] influence till men in New York State, Pennsylvania and on the free Western plains feel they can take the law in their own hands with impunity."[72] And here, Wells's consideration of lynching dovetails with Mark Twain's work in his essay "On Lynching," discussed in the Introduction. In both cases, these authors allow the virulence and extremity of southern lynching to underwrite a temporal and regional reordering of the practice itself. Lynching did not, as Twain claimed, newly reach the western states after the turn of the century. Nor did lynching, as Wells suggests, "spread" from the South to "the free western plains." In fact, lynching practices and the narratives used to constitute and justify these practices began in the western plains and only later became a gruesome and spectacular aspect of southern segregationist culture. But in part because of Wells's activism, southern lynching came to stand in for all lynching, and its actual historical predecessor receded into an often-overlooked past.

Though Wells's achievements are variously described, there is little dispute about the significance of her work. In Giddings's assessment, Wells wrote "the first comprehensive study of [lynching] that spoke to its true motives, meaning, and how it reflected not the moral failings of blacks but that of a culture gripped by white supremacy."[73] Bay argues that "Wells-Barnett single-handedly transformed lynching into a women's issue."[74] And Bederman correctly asserts, while "Wells could not force white Americans to *oppose* lynching . . . in 1894, they could no longer *ignore* lynching."[75] To these arguably correct assessments, I would add that Wells effectively altered the *narrative* character of a set of violent practices—the once heroic practice of vigilantism came to be widely regarded as wholly distinct from the *un*heroic practice of lynching. This revised reputation ultimately contributed to a decline in both the prevalence of vigilantism and the number of lynchings in the South and the remainder of the United States. Indeed, I argue that Wells is principally responsible for the decline of lynching in the South after World War I and virtual nonexistence after World War II. So thoroughgoing was Wells's reworking of the lynching narrative that lynching became synonymous with racial hatred and violence more broadly, leading to assertions such as John Markovitz's that the antilynching movement made it "possible to see lynching as a metaphor for racism."[76] Perhaps the greatest evidence of Wells's success is found in the way her narrative reworking effectively erased the traces of its own production. Wells's narrative reworking—*mobs of white, sadistic racists gathered and enacted unspeakable violence on southern African American men for the exclusive purpose of expressing their social power, and neither the state nor a cowardly public did anything to stop them*—doesn't seem like a narrative construction at all; it simply seems descriptive. But the formulation *was* a narrative construction insofar as it took account of and directly reworked the earlier narrative formulae that had enabled vigilantes to enact and legitimate violence for the better part of a century.

Of course, the narrative *is* true: Vigilantism, as it was practiced during the early Jim Crow decades in the southern United States, *was* largely a means of enforcing racial difference and disadvantage. But these lynching practices were only ever a dominant subset of a larger body of violent practices. The larger set of violent practices included and began with the significant number of vigilante committees operating in frontier regions in both the South and the West. It is considerably less common for present-day Americans to make recourse to vigilantism as a means of taking control over ruptures in the social order than it was in the nineteenth century. Less common, however, does not mean that vigilantism has disappeared altogether. And here, I mean literally that in a variety of very specific localities, Americans continue to convene under self-conceived authority in order to prosecute and even sometimes "execute" alleged criminals. In other words, though Wells's narrative came to dominate our cultural understanding of vigilantism and lynching, it didn't entirely replace the earlier narrative in which vigilantism and even lynching are characterized as heroic. It is necessary to see that Bancroft and Wells wrote simultaneously about vigilantism, lynching, and the American character in two such opposite ways in order to understand how American culture supports two diametrically opposed understandings of vigilantism in the present day.

# Conclusion

*Living in, and with, the Past*

When I teach undergraduates about the history of vigilantism and lynching in the United States, I include a question on the final that asks them to compare two songs. The first song is Abel Meeropol's (a.k.a. Lewis Allen's) "Strange Fruit"—most famously recorded by Billie Holiday.[1] The second song, written and performed by Toby Keith, is the pro-vigilante anthem "Beer for my Horses."[2] I use the songs because they represent America's two, nominally unrelated, lynching pasts. *An ideal vigilance committee convened and acted in an organized and evenhanded manner in response to uncontrolled criminal conditions and was roundly supported and applauded by its community for doing so.* This American lynching past persists in a song like "Beer for my Horses" and in the Vigilante Parade in Helena, Montana. *Mobs of white, sadistic racists gathered and enacted unspeakable violence on southern African American men for the exclusive purpose of expressing their social power, and neither the state nor a cowardly public did anything to stop them.* This American lynching past is represented by Meeropol's "Strange Fruit" and in the *Without Sanctuary* collection.

I spend much of the course laying out the central claim of this book—that these two pasts may not be as different as we have come to believe. I demonstrate to my students that southern lynch mobs thought of themselves as expressing something ideal in their vigilante practices—even if we cannot quite imagine today how racial lynching could be explained or understood in this way. I show my students how those who lynched in the frontier grossly exaggerated levels of criminality, the failures of state-sanctioned law and order, and their own valor. My syllabus incorporates the documents of vigilantes in both regions in order to help my students see that all of these lynchers were deeply invested in making themselves appear orderly, popular, and occasionally even moderate—regardless of whether they actually were any of these things. I want my students to learn that the disjuncture between these two narrative descriptions of vigilantism and lynching has less to do with the actual differences between past events than it does with historiographical conventions of period and region and the effects of centralizing race as a category of historical analysis. The goal of the exam question—indeed, of the entire class as well as this book—is to muddy seemingly clear historical waters.

I have numerous motivations for believing this reconsideration of the history of lynching and vigilantism is fruitful. First, I am motivated by the often-unchecked persistence of the heroic and idealized version of vigilantism—a version of vigilantism that, à la Bancroft, remains tied to an idealized but paradoxical patriotism. We need to be fully able to name and understand the construction of this past in order to engage with its "heroically" continuing presence. Second, I am committed to highlighting Wells's work as an example of the potential of narrative intervention as a way of making change. While Wells's work did not put an immediate end to lynching violence or, clearly, to the possibility of engaging in vigilantism, her work shifted the meaning of the practice in significant and indelible ways. This is significant not only in the context of understanding how lynching and vigilante narratives have and have not changed through time but so that we may more fully conceptualize how violence is fundamentally legitimated and constituted through narrative practices. Because if we can see this, as Wells did, we become able to intervene and act against violence.

## Historical Motivations: Party Hangings and Border Vigilantes

Encountering the Vigilante Parade in present-day Montana while doing my research surprised me, but meeting a group of vigilante reenactors surprised me even more. Such a group, however, does exist—the "Tombstone Vigilantes" in Tombstone, Arizona. Founded in 1948 and incorporated in 1954, this civic organization specializes in frontier reenactment (e.g., gunfights), raises money for local charities, and works to preserve and publicize Tombstone history. In large part the organization raises money because its members are extremely successful at reenactment competitions—but they also raise funds by staging "mock hangings." The Tombstone Vigilantes can be hired for events to arrive in period western wear and to wrestle a designated "victim" over to a gallows and into a noose. As their website whimsically asserts, "We . . . do mock hangin's on request!"[3] Within the hypersimulated environment of Tombstone, Arizona—a town that is locked in a kind of perpetual reenactment—these seemingly odd practices are oddly at home. And the vigilantes themselves are a dedicated bunch, working tirelessly to perfect the gun battles with which they compete and entertain tourists. They avowedly and convincingly claim to be devoted to the preservation of the local past.[4] Notwithstanding the detail of their dress and the quality of their gun battles, this claim makes the least sense with respect to vigilantism. Vigilantism was virtually unheard of in Tombstone, and this particular aspect of their reenactment bears little resemblance to the actual local past.

In 2001, a kindergarten teacher from Los Angeles moved to Tombstone in an effort to escape urban decay. He initially found work as a gunfight reenactor at the O.K. Corral and with the local paper—the *Tombstone Tumbleweed*. This young man, Chris Simcox, also became a vigilante. By this, I do not mean that he joined the Tombstone Vigilantes and became a recreational reenactor; I mean that he quite literally began to patrol the desert landscape around Tombstone in search of illegal immigrants. In his own assessment, during those early patrols he "encounter[ed] thousands of migrants and apprehend[ed] over 500."[5] In 2002, Simcox founded "Civil Homeland Defense," an organization (like others of its kind) focused specifically on stemming what the group argues is an uncontrolled tide of illegal immigration.[6] Three years later, Simcox and Jim Gilchrist founded the more widely known Minuteman Civil Defense Corps (MCDC).[7]

Like vigilantes throughout the past two centuries, Simcox perceived uncontrolled criminal conditions and a failure of state-sanctioned law and order and felt a valorous obligation to do something about it. His sense of the relationship between criminality and illegal immigration began long before he arrived in Arizona:

> I've lived in Manhattan and I have lived in Chicago and I've lived in Los Angeles. Those people don't come here to work. They come here to rob and deal drugs.
>
> Oh Jesus, it is unbelievable. I mean, we need the National Guard to clean out all our cities and round them up. They are hard-core criminals. They have no problem slitting your throat and taking your money or selling drugs to your kids or raping your daughters and they are evil people.[8]

Having left Los Angeles to escape the "evilness" of these uncontrolled criminal conditions, Simcox arrived in Arizona to discover that he had been relocated to the epicenter of these very issues. He decided, as the saying goes, "to take the law into his own hands." Dipping into the historical reservoir of vigilante justification, Simcox decided that vigilantism could, as Bancroft had written over a century earlier, "strip from law its trammels, its hypocrisy, humbug, and technical chicanery"; or, as Simcox himself stated less poetically, "We actually have more freedom to tackle the problem than the government and law enforcement agencies that are bogged down in the quagmire of laws and restrictions."[9] His organizations hold scheduled desert patrols, during which the border-crossers they encounter are captured and, they insist, held safely pending the arrival of the Arizona border patrol. Lest Simcox seem like a lone-wolf extremist, it should be noted that each of his vigilante organizations has received widespread support. Most notably, the MCDC now has chapters in states and cities across the United States.[10]

Simcox is not a member of the Tombstone Vigilantes—they explicitly disavow any association with his anti-immigration endeavors. These are two unrelated, yet oddly coexistent, reenactments of the same vigilante ideal. In both cases the narrative frame is the same—*An ideal vigilance committee convened and acted in an organized and evenhanded manner in response to uncontrolled criminal conditions and was roundly supported and applauded by its community for doing so.* It is certainly not insignificant that in the case of the Tombstone Vigilantes the reenactment is a mere simulation; in the case of Simcox's organizations the reenactments are entirely real. The rumors surrounding the violence done by border-vigilante groups in the Arizona desert abound. As stated by Bob Moser of the Southern Poverty Law Center, "Crimes against border-crossers are hard to detect in the lonely Arizona Desert—but suspicious incidents keep cropping up."[11] Admittedly, no specific violence has been attributed to either Simcox or the MCDC at this time. Nonetheless, encountering a group of vigilante pranksters at a birthday party is not the same thing as encountering a group of armed vigilantes in the middle of the night in the Arizona desert.

That both of these two groups are reenacting the same vigilante narrative cannot be overlooked. The fact is, in some corners the narrative of ideal vigilantism remains an ideal. It remains an ideal for the Tombstone Vigilantes, symbolizing frontier heroism, a glorious past, and masculinist courage. For Simcox, the narrative also remains an ideal, symbolizing present-day heroism, a glorious future, and masculinist courage. These two idealized understandings of vigilantism cannot be disentangled from one another. In the case of Chris Simcox, the simulated performance of frontier heroism at the O.K. Corral bled rather easily into the actual practice of vigilantism in the Arizona desert. It's fairly easy to see how this might have happened. And undoubtedly,

Chris Simcox and his minuteman colleagues genuinely believe in the valor of their undertaking. After all, there's a two-hundred-year-old tradition supporting their belief in this kind of valor.

It may well be that as long as there are those who glorify this past—through parades, reenactments, and country-western songs—there will be those who will seek to relive it. This is partially what Ida B. Wells meant when she referred to the "almost universal tendency to accept as true the slander which the lynchers offer to civilization as an excuse for their crime."[12] If we accept the narrative of ideal vigilantism as "true," we implicitly accept the possibility of its deployment. If the vast history of lynching—its multiple local adaptations and adoptions, its ability to act in the service of larger systems of social inequality and difference, its vulnerability to distortion and sadistic expression—teaches us anything, it's that this "ideal" is a dangerous one indeed. But our way out of and away from this past requires that we understand the makeup of its appeal—how and why a man like Chris Simcox came to believe that he was serving and saving the nation after 9/11 by taking to the desert night with a sidearm. We need to understand how and why the young people of Helena, Montana, feel civic pride in their vigilante forefathers and commemorative costumes. These people aren't simply naive or wrong—they're products of a history we all share.

## Historiographical Motivations: Narrative and Change

Just as an overly romanticized and idealized version of our vigilante past underwrites continued recourse to vigilantism as an expression of patriotism, our understanding of Jim Crow era racial lynching underwrites something about our present as well. The vast majority of work on southern lynching is organized centrally around race. In historiographical terms—which I use here to refer to the ways we make conscious use of the past for political ends—this foregrounding of race has enabled a number of different and important political possibilities. Leon Litwack describes the lynching images in the *Without Sanctuary* collection as "some of the bleakest examples of violence and dehumanization in the history of humankind."[13] At the least, we study and remember these images to reckon with some of the darkest corners of our national past. And indeed, this reckoning may be long overdue. In response to the original showing of *Without Sanctuary* in 2000, Patricia Williams wrote that "lynching is one of the more complicated public secrets of this nation's past. Everyone claims to know about lynching, yet there is virtually nothing about it in history or social science books."[14] Unquestionably, the extensive work published over the course of the past decade about lynching and race in the Jim Crow

South has served to ameliorate this ignorance and to memorialize the victims of this violent past. The idea that lynching expresses this nation's deepest and most unchecked racial animus enables comparisons between racial violence in the Jim Crow South and contemporary racial violence. In strictly political-historiographical terms, these have all been useful and fruitful achievements.

My interest in relocating southern Jim Crow lynching and Wells's anti-lynching activism in a temporally longer and regionally broader framework seeks a slightly different historiographical-political end. I write in Chapter 4 that Wells's narrative reworking—*mobs of white, sadistic racists gathered and enacted unspeakable violence on southern African American men for the exclusive purpose of expressing their social power, and neither the state nor a cowardly public did anything to stop them*—doesn't seem like a narrative construction at all; it simply seems true. But this familiar story *was* a narrative reworking—one for which Wells must be given much of the credit. As Paula Giddings points out in her recent biography of Wells, Wells has been too often overlooked in histories of rights movement in the South. Giddings suggests that this undoubtedly has to do with some combination of her personality—what Giddings calls her "difficult" nature—and her ideology. She writes:

> I concluded that Wells's legacy was the victim of those same progressive movements of which she was a part. Predominately white reform organizations could never subscribe to her views about race; those with race-based agendas, such as the NAACP, the NACW, and to a lesser extent the Urban League, could not accommodate her views regarding leadership and class.[15]

All of these reasons amplified, surely, by gender discrimination among black male activists, racial discrimination among white female activists, and the fact that Wells "spent her life largely outside the folds of any enduring organization."[16] Betwixt and between both ideologically and subjectively, Wells became "a restless ghost . . . seek[ing] its rightful place in history."[17]

For these reasons alone, we need to foreground and highlight Wells's remarkable achievements. One way to do this, of course, is a project like Giddings's biography that focuses on Wells's life and activist evolution within the context of the Jim Crow South. But in addition to this, and to see some of what Wells accomplished, we need to locate her work within a longer history of lynching and vigilantism. It wasn't that nobody before Wells wanted to stop vigilantism; it was that nobody before Wells figured out how to do it so successfully. Wells was inarguably a singular and remarkable spokesperson for the human rights of southern black people, but she was also—and this is considerably less visible given conventions of region and period—the first transregional opponent of vigilantism who understood how lynching narrative and lynching violence were intertwined.

In addition to remembering Wells specifically, there's a larger issue at stake here concerning the relationship between narrative, violence, and political change. All too often, histories of lynching in the South emphasize the victimization of southern black people without making any mention of the successes of antilynching activists. While I understand the rhetorical power inherent in an analogy of a Jim Crow era lynching to a contemporary act of racial violence (or, with increasing frequency, to any contemporary hate crime), these analogies occur in a timeless, changeless space wherein it is all but impossible to locate changes made by Wells and others. We are unable to see how devastatingly powerful narrative intervention can be as a form of change making. It is significant, in this respect, not only *that* Wells succeeded but *how* she succeeded. This is ultimately, I think, the greatest lesson to be learned from America's lynching past. Vigilantes succeeded in large part because they understood that the power to justify and legitimate their actions lay in their power to tell stories. Bancroft understood that the making of a region and its past lay in the power of storytelling as well. And Wells understood that the power to change the Jim Crow South and the course of history lay in telling old stories in new ways. When we say the world is made of language, that it is "discursively constructed," we are saying something that is not only theoretical but deeply material as well. The knowledge of the material effects of narrative—knowledge made crystal clear through the history of vigilantism and lynching—comes with a real responsibility. If I can impress one thing on my students by the end of the course on vigilantism and lynching, it is this very lesson about *our* abiding narrative obligations.

# Appendix A

## *Official Vigilante Histories*

| Author | Narrative Title | Status of Narrative | Vigilance Committee | Location | Dates of Committee |
|---|---|---|---|---|---|
| Levi Ashcraft | "Thrilling Scenes in Texas" | Never published | Shelby County Moderators | Shelby County, Texas | 1840–1844 |
| Eph Daggett | "Recollections of the War of the Moderators and Regulators" | Never published | Shelby County Regulators | Shelby County, Texas | 1840–1844 |
| John Middleton | *History of the Regulators and Moderators and the Shelby County War in 1841 and 1842 in the Republic of Texas* | Published in 1883 | Shelby County Regulators | Shelby County, Texas | 1840–1844 |
| Anonymous | *The Banditti of the Rocky Mountains and Vigilance Committee in Idaho* | Published in 1856 | Alder Gulch vigilantes | Bannack/Virginia City, Montana (Idaho Territory) | 1863–1864 |
| Thomas Dimsdale | *The Vigilantes of Montana or Popular Justice in the Rocky Mountains: Being a Correct and Impartial Narrative of the Chase, Trial, Capture and Execution of Henry Plummer's Notorious Road Agent Band* | Published in newspaper in 1865, as book in 1866 | Alder Gulch vigilantes | Bannack/Virginia City, Montana (Idaho Territory) | 1863–1864 |
| Nathaniel Langford | *Vigilante Days and Ways* | Published in 1890 | Alder Gulch vigilantes | Bannack/Virginia City, Montana (Idaho Territory) | 1863–1864 |
| Edward Bonney | *The Banditti of the Prairies or, The Murderer's Doom!! A Tale of the Mississippi Valley* | Published in 1850 | Bonney, acting alone | LaSalle County, Illinois | 1840s |
| Alexander Barde | *Histoire des Comites de Vigilance aux Attakapas* | Published in 1861 (in French) | Fourteen-plus assorted vigilance committees | Southwestern Louisiana | 1859 |
| Charles Summerfield (Alfred Arrington) | *Illustrated Lives of the Desperadoes of the New World* | Published in 1849 | Cane Hill Company | Northwest Arkansas | 1842 |
| William McConnell | *Frontier Law: A Story of Vigilante Days* | Published in 1924 | Payette and Idaho City vigilance committees | Western Idaho | 1864 |
| Asa Shinn Mercer | *The Banditti of the Plains or the Cattlemen's Invasion of Wyoming in 1892 (The Crowning Infamy of the Ages)* | Published in 1894 | Stock growers association and local ranchers | Powder River Region, North Central Wyoming | 1892 |
| Almarin Paul | "The Sixty Day Rule in San Francisco of the Vigilance Committee of 1856, by an Eye-Witness, Almarin Paul" | Never published | San Francisco Committee of Vigilance of 1856 | Northern California | 1856 |

# Appendix B

## The Works of Hubert Howe Bancroft

Volume 1: *The Native Races, Volume 1: Wild Tribes*
Volume 2: *The Native Races, Volume 2: Civilized Nations*
Volume 3: *The Native Races, Volume 3: Myths and Languages*
Volume 4: *The Native Races, Volume 4: Antiquities*
Volume 5: *The Native Races, Volume 5: Primitive History*
Volume 6: *History of Central America, Volume 1: 1501–1530*
Volume 7: *History of Central America, Volume 2: 1530–1800*
Volume 8: *History of Central America, Volume 3: 1801–1887*
Volume 9: *History of Mexico, Volume 1: 1516–1521*
Volume 10: *History of Mexico, Volume 2: 1521–1600*
Volume 11: *History of Mexico, Volume 3: 1600–1803*
Volume 12: *History of Mexico, Volume 4: 1804–1824*
Volume 13: *History of Mexico, Volume 5: 1824–1861*
Volume 14: *History of Mexico, Volume 6: 1861–1887*
Volume 15: *History of the North Mexican States and Texas, Volume 1: 1531–1800*
Volume 16: *History of the North Mexican States and Texas, Volume 2: 1801–1889*
Volume 17: *History of Arizona and New Mexico, 1530–1888*
Volume 18: *History of California, Volume 1: 1542–1800*
Volume 19: *History of California, Volume 2: 1801–1824*
Volume 20: *History of California, Volume 3: 1825–1840*
Volume 21: *History of California, Volume 4: 1840–1845*
Volume 22: *History of California, Volume 5: 1846–1848*
Volume 23: *History of California, Volume 6: 1848–1859*
Volume 24: *History of California, Volume 7: 1860–1890*
Volume 25: *History of Nevada, Colorado, and Wyoming, 1540–1888*
Volume 26: *History of Utah, 1540–1886*
Volume 27: *History of the Northwest Coast, Part One: 1543–1800*

Volume 28: *History of the Northwest Coast, Part Two: 1800–1846*
Volume 29: *History of Oregon, Part One: 1834–1848*
Volume 30: *History of Oregon, Part Two: 1848–1888*
Volume 31: *History of Washington, Idaho and Montana, 1845–1889*
Volume 32: *History of British Columbia, 1792–1887*
Volume 33: *History of Alaska, 1730–1885*
Volume 34: *California Pastoral, 1769–1848*
Volume 35: *California Inter Pocula*
Volume 36: *Popular Tribunals, Volume 1*
Volume 37: *Popular Tribunals, Volume 2*
Volume 38: *Essays and Miscellany*
Volume 39: *Literary Industries*

# Appendix C

*Vigilance Committee Interviews*

*All interviews and accounts are taken from the California Biographical Manuscripts collection, C-D, Reel 21, ms 179 through Reel 24, ms 203, Bancroft Library, University of California, Berkeley.*

1. Statement of Isaac Bluxome, "33 Secretary"
2. Statement of Dr. R. Beverly Cole on Vigilance Committees in San Francisco (1877)
3. Statement of William T. Coleman
4. Statement of H. P. Coons
5. Statement of Oliver B. Crary on Vigilance Committees in San Francisco
6. Statement of Clancy John Dempster
7. Statement of James Dows on Vigilance Committees in San Francisco
8. Statement of John L. Durkee on Vigilance Committees in San Francisco
9. Statement of James D. Farwell on Vigilance Committees in San Francisco
10. Statement of George W. Frink
11. *The Early Days of San Francisco*, by James R. Garniss
12. Statement of Charles V. Gillespie
13. *Acts of the Manilas: Lawlessness at San Juan n 1856*, by Michael Kraszewski
14. Statement of John P. Manrow on Vigilance Committees in San Francisco
15. Visit to Monterey by R. J. Maxwell
16. Statement of James Neall
17. Statement of General James N. Olney
18. Statement of Gerritt W. Ryckman
19. Statement of Capt. W. T. Sayward
20. Statement of George E. Schenck on the Vigilance Committee (1856)
21. Statement of Thomas J. L. Smiley on Vigilance Committee and Early Times in San Francisco

22. Statement of William F. Swasey
23. Statement of Miers F. Truett
24. Vigilance Committees in San Francisco Miscellany—including statements on the subject by Aaron M. Burns, Dr. J.D.B. Stillman, Dr. William H. Rogers, Hall McAlister, Rev. Dr. Sylvester Woodbridge, James C. L. Wadworth (Asa M. Bowen), A. M. Comstock
25. Statement of William B. Watkins on Vigilance Committees in San Francisco

# Notes

## INTRODUCTION

1. Michel Foucault, *Discipline and Punish: The Birth of the Prison*, trans. Alan Sheridan (New York: Vintage Books, 1995).

2. James Allen, *Without Sanctuary: Lynching Photography in America* (Santa Fe, NM: Twin Palms, 2000). See also http://www.withoutsanctuary.org/main.html. The collection was shown initially in January and early February 2000 at the Ruth Horowitz Gallery in New York under the title *Witness*. Additional objects at the New York exhibit included newspaper accounts of the lynching of Leo Frank, a wall commemorating well-known antilynching activists, and items such as a cane with a handle sculpted to look like a hanged, or lynched, Chinese male.

3. The Vigilante Parade in Helena, Montana, began as a high school tradition in 1924 when then-principal Albert J. Roberts was looking for a new tradition to replace what he considered to be violent and dangerous student-generated annual events (such as a fight between the senior and junior classes). The seventy-fifth version of this parade that I attended in 2002 retained much of its original format. The parade is composed of student floats and entries from Helena's two public high schools; participation is voluntary, but entries must be related in some way to either Helena or Montana history. In any given year, parade entries might have little to do with the specific events surrounding Montana's seven or so vigilance movements.

4. Crucial texts in the field include Jacqueline Dowd Hall, *Revolt against Chivalry: Jessie Daniel Ames and the Women's Campaign against Lynching* (New York: Columbia University Press, 1993); Robyn Wiegman, *American Anatomies: Theorizing Race and Gender* (Durham, NC: Duke University Press, 1995); Jacqueline Goldsby, *A Spectacular Secret: Lynching in American Life and Literature* (Chicago: University of Chicago Press, 2006); W. Fitzhugh Brundage, *Lynching in the New South: Georgia and Virginia, 1880–1930* (Urbana: University of Illinois Press, 1993); W. Fitzhugh Brundage, ed., *Under Sentence of Death: Lynching in the New South* (Chapel Hill: University of North Carolina Press, 1997); Stewart Tolnay and E. M. Beck, *A Festival of Violence: An Analysis of Southern Lynchings, 1882–1930* (Urbana: University of Illinois Press, 1995); Bernd Beck and Timothy Clark, "Strangers, Community Miscreants, or Locals," *Historical Methods* 35, no. 2 (2002): 77–83; Sandra Gunning, *Race, Rape, and Lynching: The Red Record of American Literature, 1890–1912* (New York: Oxford University Press,

1996); and Jonathan Markovitz, *Legacies of Lynching: Racial Violence and Memory* (Minneapolis: University of Minnesota Press, 2004).

5. Her collected works are published in Ida B. Wells, *On Lynchings* (Manchester: Ayer, 1987). The collection contains *Southern Horrors: Lynch Law in All Its Phases* (1892); *A Red Record: Tabulated Statistics and Alleged Causes of Lynchings in the United States, 1892–1893–1894* (1894); and *Mob Rule in New Orleans: Robert Charles and His Fight to the Death* (1900). Unless noted otherwise, citations refer to the Ayer edition (in which each pamphlet retains its original and separate pagination).

6. Michael Pfeifer, *The Roots of Rough Justice: Origins of American Lynching* (Urbana: University of Illinois Press, 2011); Ken Gonzalez-Day, *Lynching in the West, 1850–1935* (Durham, NC: Duke University Press, 2006). Richard Slotkin draws attention to the function of the mythologized vigilante figure in each of the three periods he studies: *Regeneration through Violence: The Mythology of the American Frontier, 1600–1860* (Norman: University of Oklahoma Press, 2000); *The Fatal Environment: The Myth of the Frontier in the Age of Industrialization, 1800–1890* (Norman: University of Oklahoma Press, 1994), 126–137; and *Gunfighter Nation: The Myth of the Frontier in the Twentieth-Century America* (Norman: University of Oklahoma Press, 1998), 169–193.

7. Susan Sontag, *Regarding the Pain of Others* (New York: Picadour, 2003), 91–94.

8. Ibid., 85–86.

9. Ibid., 86.

10. We can understand these practices as an exemplary of what Roy Rosenzweig and David Thelen describe as the American tendency to "personalize the public past" (*The Presence of the Past: Popular Uses of History in American Life* [New York: Columbia University Press, 1998], 115). By locating unrelated events in a the context of contemporary, relevant ones, Americans are able to create trajectories and timelines that not only explain past events but that illuminate present-day contexts *and* potentially forecast future outcomes (73, 77).

11. This argument was made first by James Elbert Cutler in *Lynch-Law: An Investigation into the History of Lynching in the United States* (New York: Longman's, Green, 1905). Cutler's explicitly racist justification of southern lynching is cited surprisingly often by subsequent scholars. Richard Maxwell Brown, an authority on the subject of American vigilantism, distinguishes between "productive" and "destructive" forms of vigilantism, a distinction that becomes operationally synonymous with region in his book *Strain of Violence: Historical Studies of American Violence and Vigilantism* (Oxford: Oxford University Press, 1975). Similarly, Norton Moses's multiregional work on vigilante practice accords functional legitimacy to western vigilantism and an unrelated racial animus to southern lynching; see Norton Moses, *Lynching and Vigilantism in the United States: An Annotated Bibliography* (Westport, CT: Greenwood, 1997); Norton Moses, "Lynching: Attitudes as Predeterminants of Brutality" (unpublished essay, n.d.).

12. Gonzalez-Day's *Lynching in the West* is part of a larger body of work that seeks to apply the insights of southern lynching scholarship to vigilantism in the West by identifying the ways in which frontier vigilantism was, like its southern counterpart, an expression of racial exclusion and violence. See Mike Davis, "'What Is a Vigilante Man?' White Violence in California History," in *No One Is Illegal: Fighting Violence and State Repression on the U.S.-Mexico Border*, ed. Justin Akers Chacón and Mike Davis (Chicago: Haymarket Books, 2006); Craig Foster, "Myth v. Reality in the Burt Murder and Harvey Lynching," *Journal of the West* 43, no. 4 (2004): 49–57; William Carrigan, *The Making of a Lynching Culture: Violence and Vigilantism in Central Texas, 1836–1916* (Urbana: University of Illinois Press, 2004); and William Carrigan and Clive Webb, "The Lynching of Persons of Mexican Origin or Descent in the United States, 1848 to 1982," *Journal of Social History* 37, no. 2 (2003): 411–438.

13. Christopher Waldrep, *The Many Faces of Judge Lynch: Extralegal Violence and Punishment in America* (New York: Palgrave, 2002). Waldrep's edited collection of texts about lynch-

ing is organized in a similar vein; see *Lynching in America: A History in Documents* (New York: New York University Press, 2006).

14. Pfeifer, *Roots of Rough Justice*; Michael Pfeifer, *Rough Justice: Lynching and American Society 1874–1947* (Champaign: University of Illinois Press, 2004). See also Manfred Berg, *Popular Justice: A History of Lynching in America* (Chicago: Rowman and Littlefield, 2011).

15. Waldrep, *Many Faces*, 56–66.

16. Mark Twain, *Roughing It* (1872; repr., New York: Penguin Books, 1980), 75–76. Unless noted otherwise, citations refer to the Penguin edition.

17. Mark Twain to Hezekiah Hosmer, September 15, 1870, Hezekiah L. Hosmer Papers, SC 104, Montana Historical Society Archives, Helena.

18. Orion Clemens to Samuel L. Clemens, March 11, 1871. This letter is reprinted in the critical edition of *Roughing It* published by the University of California Press in 1993 (see pp. 778–781). The original letter is held at the Bancroft Library at the University of California, Berkeley.

19. Twain, *Roughing It*, 780 (erasure in original).

20. Mark Twain to Hezekiah Hosmer, September 15, 1870.

21. Thomas Dimsdale, *The Vigilantes of Montana or Popular Justice in the Rocky Mountains: Being a Correct and Impartial Narrative of the Chase, Trial, Capture, and Execution of Henry Plummer's Road Agent Band* (Norman: University of Oklahoma Press, 1953). Dimsdale's account, notwithstanding its claim to be an "impartial narrative," is actually an "official history" of the Montana vigilante movement. As such, it is part of a genre of similar texts—"official histories" of specific vigilante movements written shortly after uprisings in a number of different localities. These histories were written, in virtually all cases, by individuals who either had personally participated in or had close personal association with those who had participated in the vigilante movements in question. I address the structure and function of these "official histories" at length in the next two chapters.

22. Twain, *Roughing It*, 70.

23. Ibid., 72.

24. Ibid., 71, 77.

25. Ibid., 78.

26. Ibid.

27. Ibid., 79.

28. Ibid.

29. Ibid.

30. Ibid., 80.

31. Ibid., 83. Undoubtedly, one could also do an excellent reading of the two Slades within the context of Twain's obsession with twins and doubles; see Forrest G. Robinson, "Mark Twain 1835–1910: A Brief Biography," in *Historical Guide to Mark Twain*, ed. Shelly Fisher Fishkin (New York: Oxford University Press, 2002), 17–18.

32. Mark Twain, "The United States of Lyncherdom," in *Huck Finn; Pudd'nhead Wilson; No. 44, The Mysterious Stranger; and Other Writings* (New York: Penguin Putnam, 2000), 756.

33. Twain, "United States of Lyncherdom," 754.

34. It is illuminating to think about the evolution of Twain's work more broadly during the period between *Roughing It* in 1870 and "The United States of Lyncherdom" in 1901. According to Shelly Fisher Fishkin, Twain's later work reveals his evolution from youthful "knee-jerk racis[m]" to being "a writer . . . profoundly engaged by the conundrum of racism" (*Historical Guide*, 154). This suggestion is importantly amplified by what Robinson refers to as "the increasing gravity of [Twain's] disenchantment with himself and the world" (*Historical Guide*, 19). "The United States of Lyncherdom" resonates with either or both of these observations, though it would be too simplistic to locate Twain's opposition to lynching exclusively in his later work. It is highly probable that Twain wrote the equally vehement antilynching screed

"Only a Nigger" in 1869 and his expressed desire to write a book about lynching in 1901 suggests more than an ephemeral interest in the topic (Fisher Fishkin, *Historical Guide*, 134, 151).

35. For an extensive study of the Pierce City lynching, see Kimberly Harper, *White Man's Heaven: The Lynching and Expulsion of Blacks in the Southern Ozarks, 1894–1909* (Fayetteville: University of Arkansas Press, 2010).

36. Twain, "United States of Lyncherdom," 754–745.

37. Ibid., 755.

38. Harper, *White Man's Heaven*, 47, 52. A contemporary account can be found in Ralph Ginzburg's *100 Years of Lynching* (Baltimore, MD: Black Classic Press, 1962), 42, which contains a reprinted August 21, 1901, article from the *Chicago Record-Herald*.

39. Harper, *White Man's Heaven*, 42.

40. Ibid., 24. Harper notes that the young women had already reported an alleged attack roughly six months earlier but had reported only attempted robbery rather than sexual assault.

41. Hall, *Revolt against Chivalry*, 150.

42. Ibid., 149.

43. Wells, *A Red Record*, in *On Lynchings*, 13.

44. For a concise and informative review of some of the issues attendant to these discussions, see Hayden White's essay "The Question of Narrative in Contemporary Historical Theory," in *The Content of the Form: Narrative Discourse and Historical Representation* (Baltimore, MD: Johns Hopkins University Press, 1987). For a more general review, see Geoffrey Robert, ed., *The History and Narrative Reader* (London: Routledge, 2001). Of interest also is Gabrielle Spiegel's 2009 presidential address to the American Historical Association in which Spiegel asserts that the impact of the linguistic turn on historical study has "run its course" (available online at http://www.historians.org/info/AHA_History/spiegel.cfm).

45. White's extensive oeuvre of work on this topic includes *Metahistory: The Historical Imagination in Nineteenth-Century Europe* (Baltimore, MD: Johns Hopkins University Press, 1973); *Figural Realism: Studies in the Mimesis Effect* (Baltimore, MD: Johns Hopkins University Press, 1999); *Tropics of Discourse: Essays in Cultural Criticism* (Baltimore, MD: Johns Hopkins University Press, 1978); and *The Content of the Form: Narrative Discourse and Historical Imagination Narrative Discourse and Historical Representation* (Baltimore, MD: Johns Hopkins University Press, 1987).

46. White, *Figural Realism*, 3.

47. Ibid., 18.

48. Michel-Rolph Trouillot, *Silencing the Past: Power and the Production of History* (Boston: Beacon, 1995), 13 (italics in original).

49. For a related methodological approach, see Carroll Smith-Rosenberg, *This Violent Empire: The Birth of an American National Identity* (Chapel Hill: University of North Carolina Press, 2010), wherein she describes her turn to "literary critical practices (close readings, rhetorical analysis) and to post-structural and postcolonial theory" when she found "traditional historical narrative structures and forms of evidence insufficient to the task" (xiii).

50. Ann Fabian, *The Unvarnished Truth: Personal Narratives in Nineteenth-Century America* (Berkeley: University of California Press, 2000), 4.

51. Hans Ulrich Gumbrecht, *In 1926: Living at the Edge of Time* (Cambridge, MA: Harvard University Press, 1997), 430. The book is an experimental, nonnarrative study of the year 1926 designed to explore Gumbrecht's notion of "simultaneity"—a possible solution to the conundrum of "how to write history" in the wake of the failures of communism, constructivism, and new-historicism.

52. For examples of how some recent scholars have engaged with this definitional challenge, see Waldrep, *Many Faces*, 2; Berg, *Popular Justice*, ix–x; and Gonzalez-Day, *Lynching in the West*, 11.

53. Ida B. Wells, *Southern Horrors and Other Writings: The Anti-Lynching Campaign of Ida B. Wells, 1892–1900* (Boston: Bedford/St. Martin's, 1997), 51.

54. Ibid.

55. Ibid.

## CHAPTER 1

1. Thomas Dimsdale, *The Vigilantes of Montana or Popular Justice in the Rocky Mountains: Being a Correct and Impartial Narrative of the Chase, Trial, Capture, and Execution of Henry Plummer's Road Agent Band* (1866; repr., Norman: University of Oklahoma Press, 1953), 27.

2. Dimsdale, *Vigilantes of Montana*, 24.

3. Michel Foucault, "Tales of Murder," in *I, Pierre Rivière, Having Slaughtered My Mother, My Sister, and My Brother: A Case of Parricide in the 19th Century*, trans. Frank Jellinek (Lincoln: University of Nebraska Press, 1987), 205.

4. See the data tables in Richard Maxwell Brown, *Strain of Violence: Historical Studies of American Violence and Vigilantism* (Oxford: Oxford University Press, 1975), 305–319.

5. These accounts are notably similar to a body of colonial texts described by Richard Slotkin:

> These accounts purport to be first- or second-hand reports of day-to-day events and topography in the new world. The authors usually had ulterior motives in publishing them—a desire to explain or justify, through imaginative reconstruction of events, a course of action they had taken or their right to possess the land; or simply an attempt to persuade potential European settlers of the beauties and wealth of the strange new world.

See *Regeneration through Violence: The Mythology of the American Frontier, 1600–1860* (Norman: University of Oklahoma Press, 2000), 18.

6. Brown, *Strain of Violence*, 305–319.

7. See Marjoleine Kars, *Breaking Loose Together: The Regulator Rebellion in Pre-Revolutionary North Carolina* (Chapel Hill: University of North Carolina, 2002); Leonard L. Richards, *Shays's Rebellion: The American Revolution's Final Battle* (Philadelphia: University of Pennsylvania, 2003); Thomas Slaughter, *The Whiskey Rebellion: Frontier Epilogue to the American Revolution* (Oxford: Oxford University, 1988); and Paul Douglas Newman, *Fries's Rebellion: The Enduring Struggle for the American Revolution* (Philadelphia: University of Pennsylvania, 2005). For a consideration of the relationship between vigilantism and regulator movements, see Manfred Berg, *Popular Justice: A History of Lynching in America* (Chicago: Rowman and Littlefield, 2011), 14–18.

8. Richard Maxwell Brown, *The South Carolina Regulators* (Cambridge: Belknap, 1963).

9. Kars, *Breaking Loose Together*, 2.

10. Ibid., 219n2.

11. Ibid., 167.

12. Ibid., 109–110.

13. Brown, *Strain of Violence*, 44, 56.

14. Peter Silver, *Our Savage Neighbors: How Indian War Transformed Early America* (New York: Norton, 2008), xxv. See also Carroll Smith-Rosenberg, "Rebellious Dandies and Political Fictions," in *This Violent Empire: The Birth of an American National Identity* (Chapel Hill: University of North Carolina Press, 2010), 92–101.

15. On the intensely symbolic nature of southern lynching, see Ida B. Wells, *Southern Horrors and Other Writings: The Anti-Lynching Campaign of Ida B. Wells, 1892–1900* (Boston: Bedford/St. Martin's, 1997); Robyn Wiegman, "The Anatomy of Lynching," in *American*

*Anatomies: Theorizing Race and Gender* (Durham, NC: Duke University Press, 1995); Jacqueline Goldsby, *A Spectacular Secret: Lynching in American Life and Literature* (Chicago: University of Chicago Press, 2006); W. Fitzhugh Brundage, *Lynching in the New South: Georgia and Virginia, 1880–1930* (Urbana: University of Illinois Press, 1993); and Jonathan Markovitz, *Legacies of Lynching: Racial Violence and Memory* (Minneapolis: University of Minnesota Press, 2004).

16. Brown, *Strain of Violence*, 103.

17. Ibid., 102. As noted in Chapter 2, the 1856 San Francisco committee is central to Brown's argument about the historical shift from classical to neo-vigilantism.

18. For a related argument about narrative and war, see Jill Lepore, *In the Name of War: King Philip's War and the Origins of American Identity* (New York: Vintage Books, 1999), ix–xxiii.

19. Just as vigilantism was an expression of a more general form of proto and early nationalism, the vigilante narratives were part of a larger set of historical circumstances. Extensive scholarship on narrative forms from colonial America into the nineteenth century charts the many ways in which public culture was increasingly linked to the production and circulation of narrative and textual forms. In addition to Lepore, see Silver, *Our Savage Neighbors*; Ann Fabian, *The Unvarnished Truth: Personal Narratives in Nineteenth-Century America* (Berkeley: University of California Press, 2000); and Shelly Streeby, *American Sensations: Class, Empire, and the Production of Popular Culture* (Berkeley: University of California Press, 2002).

20. Foucault, "Tales of Murder," 200. The Rivière collection, as its extended title indicates, concerns a nineteenth-century case of parricide and includes a "dossier" of documents relating to the crime and trial as well as critical essays, or "notes," by eight scholars. Foucault's commentary is specifically concerned with the confessional narrative produced by Rivière at the behest of the judge during the course of the trial.

21. Foucault, "Tales of Murder," 206.

22. A fascinating corollary argument can be found in Dave Tell's essay "The 'Shocking Story' of Emmett Till and the Politics of Public Confession," *Quarterly Journal of Speech* 94, no. 2 (2008): 156–178. Tell argues that the famous *Look* magazine interview with Emmett Till's killers "'push[ed] aside' competing accounts . . . provid[ing] definitive answers to once-contested questions, and, ultimately . . . dictat[ing] the terms of Till's circulation" (158).

23. Archival examples abound. Middleton makes reference to an "exactly fair and true narrative" written by Watt Moorman, the leader of the Shelby County Regulators, that had been already "destroyed, or lost," by 1883. John Middleton, *History of the Regulators and Moderators and the Shelby County War in 1841 and 1842 in the Republic of Texas* (1883; repr., Fort Worth: Loving, 1983), 5. See also "A Sketch of the Panic of Eastern Texas, during the Month of April, 1836," Ragout Collection, Briscoe Center for American History, University of Texas, Austin; and Charles Summerfield, *The Rangers and the Regulators of the Tenaha; or, Life among the Lawless: A Tale of the Republic of Texas* (New York: Robert M. DeWitt, 1856). But even more broadly, I could claim that wherever one finds vigilantism, either historically or representationally, one will also encounter the formulaic narrative of vigilante justification.

24. Hayden White, *Figural Realism: Studies in the Mimesis Effect* (Baltimore, MD: Johns Hopkins University Press, 1999), 18.

25. The indeterminacy of these histories has been far more of a lure than a deterrent for both professional and amateur historians. Attempts to establish "what really happened" during particular vigilante uprisings and/or relating to specific lynching incidents abound. A few examples of scholarly work are James H. Madison, *A Lynching in the Heartland: Race and Memory in America* (New York: Palgrave, 2001); Yohuru Williams, "Anatomy of an Untruth: The Controversy of 'Picnic' and the True Cause of Lynching," *Black History Bulletin* 65/66, no. 4 (2002/2003): 1–4, 9–10; Yohuru Williams, "Permission to Hate: Delaware, Lynching, and the Culture of Violence in America," *Journal of Black Studies* 32, no. 1 (2001): 3–29; and

Tom Smith, *Crescent City Lynchings: The Murder of Chief Hennessy, the New Orleans "Mafia" Trials, and the Parish Prison Mob* (New York: Lyons Press, 2007). Additionally, there have been a significant number of new projects written by amateur and/or local historians, such as Cynthia Carr, *Our Town: A Heartland Lynching, a Haunted Town, and the Hidden History of White America* (New York: Crown, 2006); Gary B. Border, *A Hanging in Nacogdoches: Murder, Race, Politics, and Polemics in Texas's Oldest Town, 1870–1916* (Austin: University of Texas Press, 2006); Timothy Cole, *The Forest City Lynching of 1900: Populism, Racism, and White Supremacy in Rutherford County, North Carolina* (Jefferson, NC: McFarland, 2003); Michael Fedo, *The Lynchings in Duluth* (St. Paul: Minnesota Historical Society, 2000); and Michael Fedo, *Trial by Mob* (Duluth, MN: Norshor, 1993).

26. The Shelby County created by the new republic in 1836 included the present-day Penola and Harrison Counties.

27. Bill O'Neil, *War in East Texas: Regulators and Moderators* (Nacogdoches: East Texas Historical Association, n.d.), 24–25.

28. Ibid., 25.

29. Terry Jordan, "Population Origins in Texas, 1850," *Geographical Review* 59, no. 1 (1969): 87.

30. Ibid.

31. Levi Henderson Ashcraft, "Thrilling Scenes in Texas" (unpublished manuscript, n.d., ca. 1850s), Samuel E. Asbury Papers, East Texas Research Center, Stephen F. Austin State University, Nacogdoches.

32. Eph Daggett, "Recollections of the War of the Moderators and Regulators," Shelby County Texas Collection, Briscoe Center for American History, University of Texas, Austin.

33. Middleton, *History of the Regulators and Moderators.*

34. For further information, see C. L. Sonnichsen, *Ten Texas Feuds* (Albuquerque: University of New Mexico Press, 1957); Lela Rhodes Neill, "Episodes in the Early History of Shelby County" (master's thesis, Stephen F. Austin State University); and the Samuel E. Asbury Papers, Briscoe Center for American History, University of Texas, Austin.

35. Leonard J. Arrington, *History of Idaho: Volume One* (Moscow: University of Idaho Press, 1994), 188. See also Benjamin Thomas, "The Historical Geography of Idaho Counties," *Oregon Historical Quarterly* 50, no. 3 (1949): 193–194.

36. Kent Curtis, "Producing a Gold Rush: National Ambitions and the Northern Rocky Mountains, 1853–1863," *Western Historical Quarterly* 40, no. 3 (2009): 279–281.

37. Stanley Davison and Dale Tash, "Confederate Backwash in Montana Territory," *Montana: The Magazine of Western History* 17, no. 4 (1967): 50–58.

38. Curtis, "Producing a Gold Rush," 286–294.

39. Anonymous, *The Banditti of the Rocky Mountains and Vigilance Committee in Idaho* (1865; repr., Minneapolis, MN: Ross and Haines, 1964).

40. Nathaniel Langford, *Vigilante Days and Ways* (Helena, MT: American and World Geographic, 1996). There are an unusually large number of published materials concerning this group, the most recent of which is Frederick Allen, *A Decent Orderly Lynching: The Montana Vigilantes* (Norman: University of Oklahoma Press, 2004). For further pro-vigilante accounts, see Birney Hoffman, "Vigilante," *Saturday Evening Post*, February 23, 1929, 3–5, 86, 88, 89, 92; March 2, 1929, 33, 35, 107, 108, 111; March 9, 1929, 24, 25, 149, 150, 152, 154; March 16, 1929, 20, 21, 65, 66, 69; March 23, 1929, 37, 40, 110, 114, 119; Birney Hoffman, *Vigilantes: A Chronicle of the Rise and Fall of the Plummer Gang of Outlaws in and about Virginia City Montana in the Early '60's* (New York: Grosset and Dunlap, 1929); and Helen Fitzgerald Sanders, *X Beidler: Vigilante* (Norman: University of Oklahoma Press, 1957). More critical interpretations can be found in R. E. Mather and F. E. Boswell, *Hanging the Sheriff: A Biography of Henry Plummer* (Missoula: Historical Montana, 1998); R. E. Mather and F. E. Boswell, *Vigilante Victims: Montana's 1864 Hanging Spree* (San Jose: History West,

1991); R. E. Mather and F. E. Boswell, *The Bannack Gallows* (San Jose: History West, 1998); and Frank Bird Linderman, *Henry Plummer: A Novel* (Lincoln: University of Nebraska Press, 2000). There are also a wealth of unpublished manuscripts held at the Montana Historical Society, including Matt Alderson's "X. Beidler: Evangelist to the Montana Road Agents," and John K. Standish's "Captain James Williams Was Fearless Leader of Montana Vigilantes; No Mention Made of Activities by Early Historians."

41. Langford, *Vigilante Days and Ways*, 7.

42. I follow Dimsdale's record of the total number of executions.

43. Edward Bonney, *The Banditti of the Prairies or, The Murderer's Doom!! A Tale of the Mississippi Valley* (Norman: University of Oklahoma Press, 1963), xviii.

44. Elmer Baldwin, *History of La Salle County Illinois* (Chicago: Rand McNally, 1877), 374–381; Michael Cyprian O'Byrne, *History of La Salle County Illinois* (Chicago: Lewis, 1924), 108–109.

45. Baldwin, *History*, 145–146.

46. Bonney, *Banditti of the Prairies*, xi.

47. Frank Prassel, *The Great American Outlaw: A Legacy of Fact and Fiction* (Norman: University of Oklahoma Press, 1993), 82. Bonney's career, and account, is complicated by intense anti-Mormonism and an ambiguous relationship to the Danite Band. For further information, see Prassel, *Great American Outlaw*, 81–85; and Philip Jordon, introduction to *The Banditti of the Prairies or, The Murderer's Doom!! A Tale of the Mississippi Valley*, by Edward Bonney (Norman: University of Oklahoma Press, 1963).

48. The area included the parishes of Acadia, Allen, Calcasieu, Cameron, Jeff Davis, Evangeline, Iberia, Lafayette, southern St. Landry, St. Martin, St. Mary, and Vermillion, and is now called Acadiana. See Alexander Barde, *The Vigilante Committees of the Attakapas: An Eyewitness Account of Banditry and Backlash in Southwestern Louisiana* (Lafayette: Acadiana Press, 1981), 271.

49. Harry Lewis Griffin, *The Attakapas Country: A History of Lafayette Parish, Louisiana* (Gretna, LA: Firebird, 1999), 11. See also Jacqueline Voorhies, "The Attakapas Post: The First Acadian Settlement," *Louisiana History: The Journal of the Louisiana Historical Association* 17, no. 1 (1976): 91–96.

50. Sarah Russell, "Ethnicity, Commerce, and Community on Lower Louisiana's Plantation Frontier, 1803–1828," *Louisiana History: The Journal of the Louisiana Historical Association* 40, no. 4 (1999): 389–405.

51. William Arceneaux, *Acadian General: Alfred Mouton and the Civil War* (Lafayette: Center for Louisiana Studies, 1981), 31. Areceneaux's book is held by the Williams Research Center, New Orleans, Louisiana.

52. Russell, "Ethnicity, Commerce, and Community."

53. Ibid., 405. See also Sarah Russell, "Intermarriage and Intermingling: Constructing the Planter Class in Louisiana's Sugar Parishes, 1803–1850," *Louisiana History: The Journal of the Louisiana Historical Association* 46, no. 4 (2005): 407–434.

54. Griffin, *Attakapas Country*, 176–177.

55. "Louisiana," *Daily Delta*, September 13, 1859.

56. Alexander Barde, *Historie des comites de vigilance aux Attakapas* (Shreveport: Centenary College of Louisiana Press, 2007). Barde's book is held by the Louisiana State Historical Society, New Orleans. The narrative was translated into English in 1936 by Henrietta Guilbeua Rogers as a master's thesis project and was published for the first time in translation in 1981 by the Acadiana Press. The narrative has recently been republished in French as part of a Louisiana history series.

57. Barde, *Historie*, 209.

58. Ibid., 245, 250.

59. The total number of committees remains unclear. Barde writes separate chapters on the seven central committees, makes specific reference to eight others (*Historie*, 97, 225, 237), and then regretfully concedes that there are as many as ten committees he has left out of the narrative altogether (254).

60. Charles Summerfield, *Illustrated Lives of the Desperadoes of the New World* (Philadelphia: T. B. Peterson, 1849). Summerfield text is held by the Briscoe Center for American History, University of Texas, Austin.

61. Interestingly, Arrington also wrote a narrative about the Shelby County Regulator/Moderator War but claimed he was forced to fictionalize the events. He explains in the preface that "many of the actors in those stormy scenes which find a place in the sequel are still living, while the others now no more, have friends and relatives who would be pained to a profound degree by revelations of so special a character. I was compelled, therefore, by motives of humanity, to exhibit the facts in the shape of a tale or story" (vii). This account, *The Rangers and the Regulators of the Tenaha; or, Life among the Lawless: A Tale of the Republic of Texas*, was first published in 1856 under Summerfield's name and then published a second time in 1892, when it was posthumously, and peculiarly, included in the Captain Mayne Reid adventure series.

62. Ted R. Worley, "The Story of Alfred W. Arrington," *Arkansas Historical Quarterly* 14, no. 1 (1955): 320–323.

63. Margie Daniels, *History of Benton, Washington, Carroll, Madison, Crawford, Franklin, and Sebastian Counties, Arkansas* (Chicago: Goodspeed, 1889, 143–147.

64. Daniels, *History*, 143.

65. See Brian Walton, "The Second Party System in Arkansas, 1836–1848," *Arkansas Historical Quarterly* 28, no. 2 (1969): 120–155. While Wilson does lay out the two economic and cultural systems present in the Arkansas Territory, he also challenges assumptions about what these differences produced in terms of party affiliation and voting patterns.

66. Worley, "Story of Alfred W. Arrington," 318.

67. William McConnell, *Frontier Law: A Story of Vigilante Days* (Yonkers-on-Hudson: World Book, 1924). McConnell's book is held by the Idaho State Historical Society, Boise.

68. Ibid., 138, 146–151.

69. Ibid., 170–171.

70. Ibid., 194–195.

71. Benjamin Thomas, "The Historical Geography of Idaho Counties," *Oregon Historical Quarterly* 50, no. 3 (1949): 186.

72. Leonard Arrington, *History of Idaho*, vol. 1 (Moscow: University of Idaho Press, 1994), 188. See also Thomas, "Historical Geography," 188.

73. Carlos Schwantes, *In Mountain Shadows: A History of Idaho* (Lincoln: University of Nebraska Press, 1991), 111–112. See also Arrington, *History of Idaho*, 195–196.

74. August Bolino, "The Role of Mining in the Economic Development of Idaho Territory," *Oregon Historical Quarterly* 59, no. 2 (1958): 132–133. Remarkably, the mines were even profitable for Chinese miners, who faced not only thievery and violence but "alien" miners' taxes. See Arrington, *History of Idaho*, 254, 220.

75. Schwantes, *In Mountain Shadows*, 66. See also Arrington, *History of Idaho*, 213, 225.

76. For a ten-month span in 1863, the newly formed territory technically had *no* criminal code when the area fell into an administrative vacuum between territorial administrations. See Schwantes, *In Mountain Shadows*, 69.

77. Ibid., 64.

78. Arrington, *History of Idaho*, 225.

79. Asa Shinn Mercer, *The Banditti of the Plains, or the Cattlemen's Invasion of Wyoming in 1892 (The Crowning Infamy of the Ages)* (San Francisco: Grabhorn Press, 1935).

80. C. Lewis Gould, *Wyoming, from Territory to Statehood* (Worland, WY: High Plaines, 1989), 9.

81. Ibid., 10, 63.

82. Ibid., 63–64.

83. Ibid., 64–65.

84. W. Turrentine Jackson, "The Wyoming Stock Growers' Association Political Power in Wyoming Territory, 1873-1890," *Mississippi Valley Historical Review* 33, no. 4 (1947): 261.

85. James Winton Eaton, "The Wyoming Stock Growers' Association's Treatment of Nonmember Cattlemen during the 1880's," *Agricultural History* 58, no. 1 (1984): 71.

86. As an example, Eaton defends the WSGA against charges of exclusion, paying particular attention to their "inclusive" membership policies before, during, and after the period of the Maverick law, whereas Gould focuses on the wealth of the Wyoming cattle speculators, noting that many of them were "wealthy denizens of British clubs and eastern society" ("Wyoming Stock Growers' Association's Treatment," 71–73).

87. Ibid., 72; Jackson, "Wyoming Stock Growers' Association Political Power," 266.

88. Gould, *Wyoming*, 50, 101–107, 132.

89. Helena Huntington Smith, *The War on the Powder River: The History of an Insurrection* (Lincoln: University of Nebraska Press, 1966), 224–225, 272. See Smith for both an extended biography of Mercer and a thorough study of the conflict. George Hufsmith, *The Wyoming Lynching of Cattle Kate 1889* (Glendo, WY: High Planes Press, 1993) is also concerned with the Wyoming vigilantes, although primarily with the events surrounding the July 1889 vigilante execution of James Averell and Ellen Watson. For a history of the movement itself, see John W. Davis, *Goodbye, Judge Lynch: The End of a Lawless Era in Wyoming's Big Horn Basin* (Norman: University of Oklahoma Press, 2005).

90. The California gold rush is indisputably the most well known, and mythologized, event of its type. Recent scholars have begun to challenge both the centrality of this event within larger historical processes and communities as well as the way that the events have been characterized in terms of economic and community development. Regarding the former, see Ramón Gutiérrez and Richard Orsi, eds., *Contested Eden: California before the Gold Rush* (Berkeley: University of California Press, 1998); regarding the latter, see Susan Lee Johnson, *Roaring Camp: The Social World of the California Gold Rush* (New York: W. W. Norton, 2000).

91. Johnson, *Roaring Camp*, 12; Julie Cooley Altrocchi, "Paradox Town: San Francisco in 1851," *California Historical Quarterly* 28, no. 1 (1949): 31–33.

92. Barbara Berglund, *Making San Francisco American: Cultural Frontiers in the Urban West, 1846–1906* (Lawrence: University of Kansas Press, 2010), 4.

93. Altrocchi, "Paradox Town," 31; Berglund, *Making San Francisco American*, 4.

94. Berglund, *Making San Francisco American*, 5–6.

95. Ibid., 11.

96. Brown, *Strain of Violence*, 135.

97. Almarin Paul, "The Sixty Day Rule in San Francisco of the Vigilance Committee of 1856, by an Eye-Witness, Almarin Paul," North Baker Research Center, California Historical Society, San Francisco.

98. Arrington, *History of Idaho*, 240.

99. David Johnson, "Vigilance and the Law: The Moral Authority of Popular Justice in the Far West," *American Quarterly* 33, no. 5 (Winter 1981): 579. It also bears noting that both the 1851 and 1856 San Francisco committees made extensive, copious records of their proceedings and practices—all of which can now be studied in detail in a number of different archives, such as the Bancroft Library (University of California, Berkeley), the Huntington Library (San Marino), the California Historical Society Library (San Francisco), and the California State Library (Sacramento).

100. Paul, "Sixty Day Rule," 1.

101. In addition to Richard Maxwell Brown's work on the San Francisco committees (chapter 5 in *Strain of Violence*), see Michelle Jolly, "The Price of Vigilance: Gender, Politics, and the Press in Early San Francisco," *Pacific Historical Review* 73, no. 4 (2004): 541–579; Robert M. Senkewicz, *Vigilantes in Gold Rush San Francisco* (Palo Alto, CA: Stanford University Press, 1985); John Boessenecker, *Gold Dust and Gunsmoke: Tales of Gold Rush Outlaws, Gunfighters, Lawmen, and Vigilantes* (New York: Wiley and Sons, 1999); and Clare V. McKanna, "Enclaves of Violence in Nineteenth-Century California," *Pacific Historical Review* 73, no. 3 (2004): 391–423.

102. Michael Pfeifer, *Rough Justice: Lynching and American Society 1874–1947* (Urbana: University of Illinois Press, 2006), 11.

103. Karen Halttunen, *Confidence Men and Painted Women: A Study of Middle Class Culture in America, 1830–1870* (New Haven, CT: Yale University Press, 1982), 25.

104. Richard Maxwell Brown, *Strain of Violence: Historical Studies of American Violence and Vigilantism* (Oxford: Oxford University Press, 1975), 93; Ken Gonzalez-Day, *Lynching in the West: 1850–1935* (Durham, NC: Duke University Press, 2006), 12.

105. Curtis, "Producing a Gold Rush," 278.

106. Barde, *Historie*, 252.

107. Anonymous, *Banditti of the Rocky Mountains*, 27.

108. Bonney, *Banditti of the Prairies*, 3. These passages are so similar as to suggest that the anonymously written 1865 history borrowed more than the "banditti" title from Bonney's work. Interestingly, this remarkable repetition is not noted in either twentieth-century republication. In 1963, the University of Oklahoma Press reissued Bonney's account and, consistent with common interpretations of frontier vigilantism, engaged with the account on its own terms, questioning only whether or not some or all of the narrative had been ghostwritten. Philip Jordan, in a critical introduction to the book, concludes, "No evidence was set forth to substantiate the implication" (xix). A year later, the anonymous Rocky Mountain account was republished by Ross and Haines. The editor's preface (written by Jerome Peltier) draws attention to the fact that the anonymous account predates Dimsdale's and exists in slightly different archived versions, but there is no mention of the uncanny similarity to Bonney's text. The two intertwined accounts are read separately as what they claim to be, "real and true," albeit retrospectively problematic, windows to past events.

109. The unpleasant obligations of the vigilante narrators is quite similar to the sort of distress Jill Lepore attributes to narrators of King Philip's War in *Name of War*, 64.

110. Dimsdale, *Vigilantes of Montana*, 53.

111. Summerfield, *Illustrated Lives*, 9.

112. Barde, *Historie*, 219. Barde's proximity to the "facts" of the Attakapas vigilantes is asserted throughout the narrative as he records his attempts to obtain information directly from the individual committees' leaders (97, 140, 216). The narrative is unique in this regard, as Barde's research is woven into the narrative and almost seems to take place concurrently with the vigilantes' actions. While all of these narrators are explicitly conscious of their relationships to the accounts and their placement within the events and stories, Barde is an extreme case in point. His certification of the authenticity of his account, based on the idea that it will be read by others familiar with the events in question, is somewhat ambiguous. Earlier in the narrative, he elects not to list the two hundred members of the Vermillionville committee, stating, " I shall perhaps have space to list [the names] elsewhere in full, and which I would cite especially with eagerness if I thought that these pages were destined to live" (198). As revealed in the new edition's book flap, Barde's concerns were legitimate: "So controversial was this book when first published that most of the original copies were purchased and destroyed by irate relatives, friends and even descendents of those whom Barde identified as villains."

113. Mercer, *Banditti of the Plains*, 1.

114. Middleton, *History of the Regulators*, 3.

115. See also Barde, *Historie*, 4; Dimsdale, *Vigilantes of Montana*, 53; Anonymous, *Banditti of the Rocky Mountains*, 31–32, 33; Langford, *Vigilante Days and Ways*, 11, 253; Mercer, *Banditti of the Plains*, 19–20; Paul, "Sixty Day Rule," 1; Ashcraft, "Thrilling Scenes in Texas," 12; and Middleton, *History of the Regulators*, 5, 15.

116. Summerfield, *Illustrated Lives*, 60.

117. Langford, *Vigilante Days and Ways*, 11.

118. Barde, *Historie*, 4.

119. Pfeifer, *Rough Justice*, 101.

120. Dimsdale, *Vigilantes of Montana*, 27.

121. Ibid., 22.

122. Ibid., 22, 25, and 70. For similar accounts of the intricate organization of the Alder Gulch road agents, see Anonymous, *Banditti of the Rocky Mountains*, 85, 122, 123; and Langford, *Vigilante Days and Ways*, 108, 195.

123. Anonymous, *Banditti of the Rocky Mountains*, 123; Langford, *Vigilante Days and Ways*, 195.

124. Dimsdale, *Vigilantes of Montana*, 22.

125. Barde, *Historie*, 2.

126. Barde, *Historie*, 2. Descriptions of intricately organized outlaw gangs can also be found in McConnell, *Frontier Law*, 197; Bonney, *Banditti of the Prairies*, 6–7; Ashcraft, "Thrilling Scenes in Texas," 2.

127. Barde, *Historie*, 2.

128. Ibid., 3.

129. Mercer, *Banditti of the Plains*, 19.

130. Bonney, *Banditti of the Prairies*, 61.

131. Ibid., 5.

132. Langford, *Vigilante Days and Ways*, 11.

133. See also McConnell, *Frontier Law*, 106, 114–115; Summerfield, *Illustrated Lives*, 12, 13, 21; Barde, *Historie*, 96–97, 197; Anonymous, *Banditti of the Rocky Mountains*, 34, 99, 100; Dimsdale, *Vigilantes of Montana*, 26–35 and 47–53; Paul, "Sixty Day Rule," 21, 22; Ashcraft, "Thrilling Scenes in Texas," 29; and Middleton, *History of the Regulators*, 8.

134. Silver, *Our Savage Neighbors*, 47.

135. Ashcraft, "Thrilling Scenes in Texas," 2.

136. While the allegation of state absence may have been overstated in many of the vigilante narratives, the construction is hardly surprising. The equation of vulnerability with the remote and unsettled had already developed currency earlier, during mid-eighteenth-century and late eighteenth-century conflicts with indigenous people; see Silver, *Our Savage Neighbors*, 42–43.

137. Ashcraft, "Thrilling Scenes in Texas," 2.

138. Ibid., 3.

139. Daggett, "Recollections of the War," 16.

140. Ibid.

141. Wayne Gard, *Frontier Justice* (Norman: University of Oklahoma Press, 1949) offers such an explanation of vigilantism. But it bears noting that his argument, for example, in the chapter "Without Benefit of Blackstone," relies on sources such as Ashcraft and Hubert Howe Bancroft (a legendary supporter of the vigilantes). I follow legal historian Lawrence Friedman's counterassertion that the lawlessness of the frontier has been much exaggerated and that "vigilantes were also reacting to a code that was simply not to their liking" (*A History of American Law* [New York: Simon and Schuster, 1985], 160, 368). See also David Grimsted's review of Brown's *Strain of Violence*, "Making Violence Relevant," *Reviews in American History* 4, no. 3 (September 1976): 331–338, regarding the dangers of relying on vigilante accounts for historical study.

142. Langford, *Vigilante Days and Ways*, 253.

143. McConnell, *Frontier Law*, 106.

144. Ibid., 115.

145. Ibid., 116.

146. Ibid., 118.

147. Ibid.

148. In the next chapter, I look closely at the expression of juridical critique through pantomimed court room proceedings. Here, I would just note that these narratives all describe, and attempt to articulate the position of the vigilantes against, extant juridical structures. For examples, see McConnell, *Frontier Law*, 146–147, 164, 168; Barde, *Historie*, 13, 28–30, 43–45; Dimsdale, *Vigilantes of Montana*, 101, 195–205; Anonymous, *Banditti of the Rocky Mountains*, 138–139; Langford, *Vigilante Days and Ways*, 186, 227, 287–289; Mercer, *Banditti of the Plains*, 12, 14, 21, 22, 28–30, 53–55, 60–61, 99; Paul, "Sixty Day Rule," 8, 19–22; Bonney, *Banditti of the Prairies*, 24; Ashcraft, "Thrilling Scenes in Texas," 8, 12, 21, 28–29, 31; Middleton, *History of the Regulators*, 8–9, 16–21, 25–27; and Daggett, "Recollections of the War," 8–10, 16–19, 25, 32.

149. Barde, *Historie*, 4.

150. Summerfield, *Illustrated Lives*, 16.

151. See also Barde, *Historie*, 35, 56, 96, 112–113, 197; Dimsdale, *Vigilantes of Montana*, 5–16, 46, 76, 142; *Banditti of the Rocky Mountains*, 69–70; Langford, *Vigilante Days and Ways*, 9, 10, 138, 182; Mercer, *Banditti of the Plains*, 22, 74; Paul, "Sixty Day Rule," 2, 21, 22; and Bonney, *Banditti of the Prairies*, 20–21, 56, 113, 136.

152. Hubert Howe Bancroft, "Committees of Vigilance and Popular Tribunals" (chapter draft) Records of the Library and Publishing Companies, OS Box 19, folder 5, BANC MSS B-C 7, Bancroft Library, University of California, Berkeley, 18.

153. Summerfield, *Illustrated Lives*, 21; emphasis in original.

154. Dimsdale, *Vigilantes of Montana*, 6–7.

155. The valorous vigilante emerged in a context that rendered his actions both familiar and laudable. As Shelly Streeby points out, by the mid nineteenth-century, "the 'volunteer'— the virtuous citizen soldier who defended the nation out of a love for this native land—was often championed as a manly ideal and as a symbol of the United States in the popular press" (82).

156. Paul, "Sixty Day Rule," 6–7.

157. Barde, *Historie*, 7–8.

158. Ibid., 143–144.

159. Ashcraft, "Thrilling Scenes in Texas," 240.

160. Ibid., 31.

161. Summerfield, *Illustrated Lives*, 21.

162. Paul, "Sixty Day Rule," 22–23.

163. Ibid.

164. Langford, *Vigilante Days and Ways*, 179.

165. Ibid., 191.

166. Ibid., 227.

167. Foucault, "Tales of Murder," 206.

168. Barde, *Historie*, 183.

169. Dimsdale, *Vigilantes of Montana*, 154–155.

## CHAPTER 2

1. The idea of "Bible Belt pornography" is borrowed from Jacquelyn Dowd Hall, *Revolt against Chivalry: Jessie Daniel Ames and the Women's Campaign against Lynching* (New York:

Columbia University Press, 1993), 150. The entire formulation reads, "Rape and rumors of rape became a kind of acceptable folk pornography in the Bible Belt."

2.　Charles Summerfield, *Illustrated Lives of the Desperadoes of the New World: Containing an Account of the Different Modes of Lynching; the Cane Hill Murders; the Victims; the Execution; the Justification, etc.* . . . (Philadelphia: T. B. Peterson, 1849).

3.　This opportunity was notably seized first by Montana historians R. E. Mather and F. E. Boswell. In a series of books on the Alder Gulch committee, written between 1987 and 1998, Mather and Boswell systematically dismantle the heroic narratives associated with this committee and replace them with accounts that are highly critical of the vigilantes. See *Hanging the Sheriff: A Biography of Henry Plummer* (Missoula: Historic Montana, 1998); *Vigilante Victims: Montana's 1864 Hanging Spree* (San Jose: History West, 1991); and *The Bannack Gallows* (Oklahoma City, OK: History West, 1998).

4.　Michel Foucault, "Tales of Murder," in *I, Pierre Rivière, Having Slaughtered My Mother, My Sister, and My Brother: A Case of Parricide in the 19th Century,* trans. Frank Jellinek (Lincoln: University of Nebraska Press, 1987), 199–212.

5.　Ibid., 210.

6.　Ibid., 203.

7.　Richard Slotkin locates the circulation of another important American fable, the "Boone myth," within the larger context of book trade between Europe and the United States and among various regions within the United States; see *Regeneration through Violence: The Mythology of the American Frontier, 1600–1860* (Norman: University of Oklahoma Press, 2000), 398. It is likely the published vigilante narratives traveled many of these same routes.

8.　Ralph Ginzburg, *One Hundred Years of Lynching* (1962; repr., Baltimore: Black Classic Press, 1988), 42.

9.　Mark Twain, "The United States of Lyncherdom," in *Huck Finn; Pudd'nhead Wilson; No. 44, The Mysterious Stranger; and Other Writings* (New York: Penguin Putnam, 2000).

10.　Ida B. Wells, *A Red Record,* in *On Lynchings* (Manchester: Ayers, 1987), 12–13; Hall, *Revolt against Chivalry,* 150; Foucault, "Tales of Murder, 201.

11.　Ted R. Worley, "The Story of Alfred W. Arrington," *Arkansas Historical Quarterly* 14, no. 4 (1955): 320–322.

12.　This account is based on Summerfield, *Illustrated Lives.* I borrow the phrase in heading above from Mark Twain's tale of the ship captain Ned Blakely in *Roughing It* (1872; repr., New York: Penguin Books, 1980), 265–270.

13.　Ibid., 24.

14.　Ibid., 25.

15.　Ibid., 28; emphasis in original.

16.　Ibid.; emphasis in original.

17.　Ibid.

18.　Ibid.; emphasis in original.

19.　Ibid., 30.

20.　Irregularities in punctuation appear exactly as in Summerfield's version; however, some of his descriptive asides have been omitted.

21.　According to Summerfield, Rev. A. "Uncle Buck" Buchanan was a leading member of the committee and, like the majority of the members, a minister. Summerfield describes him as an "ultra-Calvinist" who "fixed his eye with so steady a stare on the stern features of the law, that he forgot the milder, angel-face of the gospel." See *Illustrated Lives,* 16.

22.　Ibid., 32.

23.　Ibid., 32–33.

24.　Ibid., 33.

25.　Ibid., 34.

26.　Ibid., 40.

27. The third guilty man, another brother, was already dead by this time. See ibid., 59.

28. The allegation that the vigilantes threatened the trial witnesses is strikingly reminiscent of allegations made in the official histories. Levi Ashcraft, for example, notes the mysterious disappearance of witnesses as evidence of the failure of law and order and a factor leading to the formation of the vigilance committee in Shelby County; see "Thrilling Scenes in Texas."

29. Summerfield, *Illustrated Lives*, 60.

30. Michael Pfeifer's extended analysis of the relationship between lynching practices and the formal aspects of state criminal justice procedures offers an important perspective on this issue, drawing attention to regional variance instead of transregional similarity, as I do here; see *Rough Justice: Lynching and American Society, 1874–1947* (Urbana: University of Illinois Press, 2004).

31. Lawrence M. Friedman, *A History of American Law* (New York: Simon and Schuster, 1985), 367.

32. There is some possibility that these particular men were doomed all along. Summerfield suggests that the five men may have been singled out initially because they were neither supporters of nor participants in the vigilante company; see *Illustrated Lives*, 25.

33. Ibid., 36.

34. Ibid., 38.

35. Ibid., 24.

36. Ibid., 25.

37. Ibid., 37.

38. Ibid., 25.

39. Ibid., 38.

40. Ibid., 40.

41. Ibid., 38–40; second italics added.

42. Ibid., 11.

43. Ibid., 16.

44. Ibid., 21.

45. Carroll Smith-Rosenberg, *This Violent Empire: The Birth of American National Identity* (Chapel Hill: University of North Carolina Press, 2010), 3: "How popular could popular sovereignty become before anarchy ensued?" See also Marjoleine Kars, *Breaking Loose Together: The Regulator Rebellion in Pre-Revolutionary North Carolina* (Chapel Hill: University of North Carolina, 2002), 134.

46. Hubert Howe Bancroft, *Popular Tribunals*, vol. 1, vol. 36of *The Works of Hubert Howe Bancroft* (San Francisco: History Company, 1887), 12–13.

47. Friedman, *History of American Law*, 369.

48. Notably, Richard Maxwell Brown also identifies organization as one of the two defining features of vigilantism in *Strain of Violence: Historical Studies of American Violence and Vigilantism* (Oxford: Oxford University Press, 1975). He asserts, "Vigilante movements (as distinguished from ephemeral lynch mobs) are thus identifiable as the two main characteristics of (1) regular (although illegal) organization and (2) existence for a definite (often short) period of time" (97).

49. Ibid., 144–179.

50. Ibid., 146.

51. On the development of the laws of evidence in the period from 1776–1830, see Friedman, *History of American Law*, 152–156.

52. The swearing in of the star witness was particularly horrifying to Summerfield: "As for myself, though by no means an *ascetic*, I must confess I felt a cold shudder creep over me when 'Romping Ann,' as she was commonly called, kissed the Bible, with a loud smack, and commenced her narration, with an air at once pert and pompously ludicrous" (*Illustrated Lives*, 40).

53. Bancroft, *Popular Tribunals*, vol. 1, 15.

54. Friedman's characterization of law practices in territorial regions suggests that vigilantes actually behaved much as state-sanctioned bodies did, drawing on a combination of borrowed legal forms and statutes and contingent practices developed in response to local conditions; see *History of American Law*, 166.

55. Extensive evidence of such proceedings is included in the committee records held at the Bancroft Library. In the case of Thomas Burns, for example, the records include a June 17, 1851, letter from Burns to the committee attesting to his innocence, requesting clarification of the charges against him, and imploring the committee to give him more time to comply with the banishment order (Box 1, folder 23); a June 19, 1851, letter submitted by two restaurant proprietors, Fordham and Hunting, asserting Burns's "good character" (Box 1, folder 28); and a record of the renewed expulsion order issued against Burns (Box 1, folder 39). Additional documents pertaining to Burns's trial can be found in Box 1, folders 29, 30, 45, 46–49, 66, 102, and Box 2, folder 158. The 1851 San Francisco Committee of Vigilance demonstrated at least nominal equity when they decided, at the July 6, 1851, general meeting, to adopt a procedural policy that all accused men had the right to plead guilty or not guilty as well as the right to defend themselves before the committee. Many of the proceedings, however, continued to take place as Burns's trial had—with testimony and character statements submitted either via letter or in the absence of the accused.

56. Regarding this trial, McConnell asserts, "One man, a member of the notorious Picket Corral gang, was named and proved by the testimony of many present, to have passed different amounts of bogus gold dust at various roadhouses. Accordingly it was suggested that a beginning might as well be made by giving the bogus-dust operator twenty-four hours to leave the country." *Frontier Law: A Story of Vigilante Days* (Yonkers-on-Hudson: World Book, 1924), 139–140.

57. Owen Hoge, the son of an early Wyoming rancher, offers this recollection of the committee's proceeding: "The first action taken was to decide just what characters should be disposed of and in what manner. A formal and impartial trial was held, and the vigilance committee condemned six of the worst men of the town to death. Forty others whose misdeeds were not so flagrant were let off with orders to leave town. If they resisted the order, however, other punishment was in store for them." "Bringing the Law to Laramie City," WPA file 854, Wyoming State Historical Society, Helena, 4.

58. Bancroft, *Popular Tribunals*, vol. 1, 661.

59. Alexander Barde, *The Vigilante Committees of the Attakapas: An Eyewitness Account of Banditry and Backlash in Southwestern Louisiana* (Lafayette: Acadiana Press, 1981), 50.

60. Nathaniel Langford, *Vigilante Days and Ways* (Helena, MT: American and World Geographic, 1996), 180.

61. It is likely that these various "trial" strategies also drew on more widely held cultural beliefs that under particular circumstances (execution, imprisonment, returning to the crime scene) criminals were virtually guaranteed to speak the truth. See Ann Fabian, *The Unvarnished Truth: Personal Narratives in Nineteenth-Century America* (Berkeley: University of California Press, 2000), 49–78.

62. This story can be found in chapters 29 and 30 of Langford's *Vigilante Days and Ways*; chapter 15 of Thomas Dimsdale's *The Vigilantes of Montana or Popular Justice in the Rocky Mountains: Being a Correct and Impartial Narrative of the Chase, Trail, Capture, and Execution of Henry Plummer's Road Agent Band* (1866; repr., Norman: University of Oklahoma Press, 1953); chapter 2 of Lew Callaway's *Montana's Righteous Hangmen: The Vigilantes in Action* (Norman: University of Oklahoma Press, 1997); and in Henry Fisk Sanders's "Organization of the Vigilance Committee" and "Trial and Execution of George Ives," Montana Historical Society, MC53, Box 5, folders 1 and 2. I draw on Dimsdale, Langford, and Sanders in compiling this account, with specific citations noted. The name Tbalt (Sanders's spelling) appears in other records as Tiebalt. The phrase quoted in the heading above comes from an April 28,

1866, editorial published in the Carson, Nevada, *Appeal*. The extended passage reads, "It don't change the real state of facts to charge the vigilants [*sic*] with the commission of the same crime of which their victims were guilty." The crime was, in this case, murder. Article quoted in Bancroft, *Popular Tribunals*, vol. 1, 668.

63. Langford, *Vigilante Days and Ways*, 179.

64. This posse preexisted the actual organization of the vigilance committee but already embodied many of the central figures of the organization (such as Sanders, who acted as a prosecutor at the ensuing trial and the subsequent vigilante proceedings) and the general vigilante dynamic of taking over criminal prosecution from the sanctioned authorities. The official committee, with its founding constitution, regulations and bylaws, and signed members, was organized in the week following the trial.

65. By Sanders's own admission, the miners' court was not equipped to conduct a criminal trial. He asserts, in "Organization of the Vigilance Committee," "The miners' courts were able to deal with the lesser misdemeanors when they could be detected with reasonable success" (1). Sanders, "Organization of the Vigilance Committee," MC53, Box 5, folder 1, Montana Historical Society, Helena. The formation of the vigilance committee in Nevada City indicates the perception that neither civil nor miners' authorities were equipped to deal with crime. The general function of miners' courts was to navigate disputes between miners, such as claims disputes. For further on the Alder Gulch miners' court, see Henry Fisk Sanders, "Early Judiciary of Montana," Montana State Historical Society, MC53, Box 5, folder 3, 1–4. For mining courts in general, see Wayne Gard, *Frontier Justice* (Norman: University of Oklahoma Press, 1949), 150–151.

66. Sanders, "Trial and Execution," 1.

67. According to Dimsdale, the dispute about the trial was in a dead heat until Gibbons's vote was rejected on the basis of his "mixed blood." *Vigilantes of Montana*, 103–104.

68. The crowd estimate comes from Langford, *Vigilante Days and Ways*, 184; the strategy of filling the crowd with Gibbons's supporters is recorded in Dimsdale, *Vigilantes of Montana*, 104.

69. An impressively detailed, and critical, reading of the trial can be found in R. E. Mather and F. E. Boswell, "Alder Gulch Mines: The Story of George Ives," in *Gold Camp Desperadoes: Violence, Crime, and Punishment on the Mining Frontier* (Norman: University of Oklahoma Press, 1993),123–152.

70. Sanders, "Trial and Execution," 7.

71. Sanders, "Organization," 16.

72. Sanders, "Trial and Execution," 9.

73. Ibid., 4.

74. Sanders, "Organization," 6.

75. Friedman, *History of American Law*, 369.

76. Richard Slotkin, *The Fatal Environment: The Myth of the Frontier in the Age of Industrialization, 1800–1890* (1985; repr., Norman: University of Oklahoma Press, 1994), 136–137.

77. It is important to note, as Stanley Davison and Dale Tash observe, that the significant pro-Confederacy population in the territories "led to Jim Crow laws and other discrimination against non-whites." "Confederate Backwash in Montana Territory," *Montana: The Magazine of Western History* 17, no. 4 (1967): 52.

78. Mather and Boswell, "Alder Gulch Mines," 144.

79. Ibid., 142.

80. Slotkin, *The Fatal Environment*, 136–137.

81. Bancroft, *Popular Tribunals*, vol. 1, 679.

82. Brown asserts that "self-preservation" and "the right of revolution" are the two other, less central, components of the doctrine of vigilance; see *Strain of Violence*, 115. According to Brown:

> In the nineteenth century the doctrine of "vigilance" suffused America in a way that had not been the case before or since. To be vigilant in regard to all manner of things was an idea that increasingly commanded Americans as the decades passed. The doctrine of vigilance provided a powerful intellectual foundation for the burgeoning vigilante movements, and, in turn, vigilante movements reinforced the doctrine of vigilance. (114)

Brown's assertion on this point helps to explain how and why vigilantism became and remained popular throughout the century. A useful account of related phenomena in the emerging urban environment can be found in Karen Halttunen's *Confidence Men and Painted Women: A Study of Middle Class Culture in America, 1830–1870* (New Haven, CT: Yale University Press, 1982).

83. Brown, *Strain of Violence*, 118.

84. Ibid.

85. I address Slade's execution extensively in the Introduction. Sanders's characterization of his "crime" appears in "Organization," 16.

86. The man, Steve "Big Steve" Young, attended the hanging of three other desperadoes and fatally challenged the vigilantes by asserting that no "strangling sons of bitches" could force him out of town. Apparently, he was mistaken, as "finding him thus obstinate, the Vigilantes seized him, dragged him to the foot of B Street, at the railway track, where they hung him to a telegraph pole" ("The Laramie Outbreak," *Cheyenne Leader*, October 20, 1868). See also Charles Coutant, "Early History of Laramie City," Coutant Collection, Box 8, folder 85, Wyoming State Historical Society, Cheyenne, 7.

87. Regarding this incident, McConnell states, "As there had been no charges preferred against any of their number, it was not contemplated by the Vigilance Committee to interfere with them" (146). Once challenged, however, the vigilantes found cause to try the men and decreed that their challenge was tantamount to "a declaration of their sympathy and affiliation with the lawless characters who the Payette Vigilance Committee is organized to suppress" (156). Two of the men were sentenced to hang, one was banished, and the rest were released. McConnell, unpleasantly surprised by the verdict, helped the men to escape. Ultimately, the men were not executed but were forced to leave Payette. See *Frontier Law*, 146–171.

88. Charles Coutant, untitled manuscript, Coutant Collection, "Wyoming—Early Settlement, 1867–ca. 1904," Box 8, folder 86, Wyoming State Historical Society, Cheyenne, 3.

89. Charles Coutant, "Laramie Co.," Coutant Collection, "Wyoming—Early Settlement, 1867–ca. 1904," Box 8, folder 85, Wyoming State Historical Society, 5.

90. Ibid., 5–6.

91. "About Vigilantes," *Cheyenne Leader*, January 13, 1868.

92. Ibid., 5–6.

93. "Vigilantes Again—Two Men Hung," *Cheyenne Leader*, March 21, 1868. According to this article, a jury convened by the coroner issued a finding that the men's deaths had been "occasioned by strangulation" by "perpetrators unknown."

94. Coutant, "Laramie Co.," 7–8.


## CHAPTER 3

1. Michel Foucault, "Tales of Murder," in *I, Pierre Rivière, Having Slaughtered My Mother, My Sister, and My Brother: A Case of Parricide in the 19th Century*, trans. Frank Jellinek (Lincoln: University of Nebraska Press, 1987), 205.

2. Richard Slotkin, *Regeneration through Violence: The Mythology of the American Frontier, 1600–1860* (Norman: University of Oklahoma Press, 2000), 397.

3. For a useful and related consideration of archive building, archive usage, and western colonial expansion, see Antoinette Burton, "Thinking beyond the Boundaries: Empire, Femi-

nism and the Domains of History," *Social History* 26, no. 1 (2001): 60–71. Burton draws attention to the ways that archive building and historical production are not merely coincidental to the consolidation of power but intrinsic to its mechanisms (68).

4. Hubert Howe Bancroft, "Vigilance in Northern California," OS BOX 14:14, Hubert Howe Bancroft: Records of the Library and Publishing Companies, BANC MSS B-C 7, the Bancroft Library, University of California, Berkeley, 18–19. Though the Bancroft archivists have noted that this chapter was unpublished, a few of the individual stories in this deleted chapter do actually appear in the first *Popular Tribunals* volume. See Hubert Howe Bancroft, *Popular Tribunals*, vol. 1, vol. 36 of *The Works of Hubert Howe Bancroft* (San Francisco: History Company, 1887).

5. For book-length biographies of Bancroft, see John William Caughey, *Hubert Howe Bancroft: Historian of the West* (Berkeley: University of California Press, 1946); and Harry Clark, *A Venture in History: The Production, Publication, and Sale of the* Works *of Hubert Howe Bancroft* (Berkeley: University of California Press, 1973).

6. Caughey, *Hubert Howe Bancroft*, 90.

7. Hubert Howe Bancroft, *The Native Races*, vol. 1, vol. 1 of *The Works of Hubert Howe Bancroft* (San Francisco: History Company, 1887), vii.

8. Hubert Howe Bancroft, *Literary Industries*, vol. 39 of *The Works of Hubert Howe Bancroft* (New York: Harper and Brothers, 1891), 363–364.

9. Bancroft, *Literary Industries*, 363.

10. Bancroft's use of "popular tribunals" as the category term for vigilance practices is revealing. Vigilance committees in the West were not universally "popular," either in terms of their public support or in terms of their representation of public interests. As I argue in the previous chapter, vigilance committees went to great lengths to create the *appearance* of public support as this support was a requisite component of justification.

11. Caughey, *Hubert Howe Bancroft*, 262–263. Caughey's table is based on the combined assessments of Henry Oaks, William Nemos, Thomas Savage, and Frances Fuller Victor (see 261n11).

12. Clark, *Venture in History*, 24–36.

13. These assessments of Bancroft's achievements can also be found in James Barnes, "A Review of *A Venture in History*: The Production, Publication, and Sale of the Works of Hubert Howe Bancroft," *History and Theory* 15, no. 2 (976): 212–225; Willa Klug Baum, "Oral History: A Revived Tradition at the Bancroft Library," *Pacific Northwest Quarterly* 58, no. 2 (1967): 57–64; and, regarding the history of vigilantism is particular, Richard Maxwell Brown, *Strain of Violence: Historical Studies of American Violence and Vigilantism* (New York: Oxford University Press, 1977).

14. For a listing of the release year and production order of the series, see Clark, *Venture in History*, 59.

15. Richard White, "The Gold Rush: Consequences and Contingencies," *California History* (Spring 1998): 44.

16. Bancroft, *Literary Industries*, 363–364.

17. Caughey suggests Bancroft may have received some assistance from his wife and daughter on the first *Popular Tribunals* volume; see *Hubert Howe Bancroft*, 262–263.

18. Bancroft, *Literary Industries*, 365; Hubert Howe Bancroft, "Committees of Vigilance and Popular Tribunals" (chapter draft), Records of the Library and Publishing Companies, OS Box 19, folder 5, 7, BANC MSS B-C 7, Bancroft Library, University of California, Berkeley.

19. Bancroft, "Committees of Vigilance," 7.

20. Ibid.

21. Bancroft, *Popular Tribunals*, vol. 1, 7.

22. Hubert Howe Bancroft, *Popular Tribunals*, vol. 2, vol. 37 of *The Works of Hubert Howe Bancroft* (San Francisco: History Company, 1887), iii.

23. Bancroft, *Popular Tribunals*, vol. 1, vii.

24. I argue in Chapters 1 and 2 that the narratives of justification deployed by vigilantes relied on abstract features—criminality, valor, popularity—that were easily cast in localized terms.

25. Brown, *Strain of Violence*, 96.

26. Ibid., 305–319.

27. This fact is crystal clear in historical retrospect, since the equivalent documents for, say, the Alder Gulch committee were as carefully guarded by local interests as those of the San Francisco committees.

28. Bancroft, *Literary Industries*, 365.

29. California Biographical Manuscripts collection, C-D, Reel 21, ms 179 through Reel 24, ms 203, Bancroft Library, University of California, Berkeley.

30. John S. Hittell, *A History of San Francisco and Incidentally of the State of California* (San Francisco: Bancroft, 1878). Hittell was also the editor of the pro-vigilante *Alta California* during the rise of the 1856 committee. The paper's endorsement of the committee was reciprocated, as noted in Richard Beverly Cole's interview with Bancroft: "The morning after Casey's attempt at King a large meeting was held [on] Sacramento St. between Weidesdorff and Sansome Sts—at which meeting it was decided that merchants and auctioneers withdraw their patronage from [the] *Herald* and give it to [the] *Alta* which favored the movement whilst [the] *Herald* undermined it." "Volume 264, Vigilance Committee, 1856—San Francisco," Bancroft reference notes, BANC MSS 97/31, Bancroft Library, University of California, Berkeley.

31. Bancroft reference notes, BANC MSS 97/31, Bancroft Library, University of California, Berkeley.

32. A few scattered references such as "according to a resident in relation to recent affairs in Montana" are intriguing but frustrating as there is presently no way to trace the reference to anything else in Bancroft's documents.

33. Among Bancroft's manuscripts, one finds the handwritten chapter drafts for all of the volumes of the Pacific states' history series. A meticulous archivist at the Bancroft has correctly catalogued the documents, noting their ultimate (and often changed) order of appearance in the two volumes along with marking certain chapters as either deleted or relegated to a different part of the series.

34. In addition to Richard Maxwell Brown's work on the San Francisco committees, see Michelle Jolly, "The Price of Vigilance: Gender, Politics, and the Press in Early San Francisco," *Pacific Historical Review* 73, no. 4 (2004): 541–579; Robert M. Senkewicz, *Vigilantes in Gold Rush San Francisco* (Palo Alto, CA: Stanford University Press, 1985); John Boessenecker, *Gold Dust and Gunsmoke: Tales of Gold Rush Outlaws, Gunfighters, Lawmen, and Vigilantes* (New York: John Wiley and Sons, 1999); and Claire V. McKanna, "Enclaves of Violence in Nineteenth-Century California," *Pacific Historical Review* 73, no. 3 (2004): 391–423.

35. Bancroft, "Committees of Vigilance," 24.

36. Ibid.

37. Bancroft, *Popular Tribunals*, vol. 1, vii.

38. Bancroft, *Literary Industries*, 371; emphasis added.

39. Bancroft, "Committees of Vigilance," 18.

40. Ibid., 19.

41. An unusually good example of Bancroft's suspicion of the expanding state comes in a chapter titled "The Crusade against Foreigners." While I address this chapter's central concern with race and vigilantism shortly, here it is useful to note Bancroft's *extensive* treatment of the foreign miners' tax. In effect, Bancroft argues that this capriciously adopted tax law not only unfairly targeted immigrant mine laborers but also produced tensions (and sometimes outright chaos) in the mining camps north of San Francisco. In other words, it was governmental incompetence and lack of forethought, rather than the ill intentions of

white, American-born miners, that led to the harassment of and violence against mine workers perceived as foreign—a group that included, but was not limited to, those of Chinese, Mexican, and French descent.

42. Bancroft, *Popular Tribunals*, vol. 2, 670.

43. See Bancroft, "Committees of Vigilance," 25, 18.

44. Bancroft, *Literary Industries*, 371–372.

45. Frederick Jackson Turner, "The Significance of the Frontier in American History," in *The Frontier in American History* (New York: Henry Holt, 1920), 1–38.

46. Bancroft, "Committees of Vigilance," 21–22.

47. Dempster, Clancey John, "The Vigilance Committee of 1856," California Biographical Manuscripts, C-D, Reel 22, 184, Bancroft Library, University of California, Berkeley, mss 3–4.

48. Ibid., ms 10.

49. Ibid., mss 9–10.

50. Bancroft, *Popular Tribunals*, vol. 2, 73.

51. On vice presidency, see Bancroft, *Popular Tribunals*, vol. 2, 86; on custodianship, see Bancroft, "Committees of Vigilance," 13; on editing, see "Committees of Vigilance," 16¼–16½.

52. Manrow, John P., "Statement . . . on Vigilance Committees in San Francisco. 1878," California Biographical Manuscripts, C-D, Reel 23, 192, Bancroft Library, University of California, Berkeley, ms 417½; emphasis added.

53. Ibid., mss 419½–420.

54. Dempster, "The Vigilance Committee of 1856," ms 1.

55. Hubert Howe Bancroft, "The Fruits of Vigilance," in *Popular Tribunals*, vol. 2, 639–663.

56. Hubert Howe Bancroft, "Crusade against Foreigners," Records of the Library and Publishing Companies, OS Box 16, folder 19, BANC MSS B-C 7, Bancroft Library, University of California, Berkeley.

57. See in particular Ken Gonzalez-Day, *Lynching in the West: 1850–1935* (Durham, NC: Duke University Press, 2006). Gonzalez-Day asserts, "Racial bias may be as integral to the study of Western lynching as it has been to the study of lynching nationwide" (12). While I believe the documents demonstrate a genuine disparity concerning the centrality of racial and ethnic difference in the nineteenth-century vigilance movements in the western territories and states, Bancroft's conspicuous erasures of racial violence confirm Gonzales-Day's suspicion that previous inattention to these issues may not accurately address the significance of race in this period and region.

58. Bancroft, "Vigilance." The folder containing the unpublished chapter "Vigilance in Northern California" (OS Box 14, folder 14) contains a variety of such stories; see in particular pages 5, 13, 16, and 31. Of the thirty-four stories of vigilante violence in the chapter, only two make it into Bancroft's published history.

59. Hubert Howe Bancroft, *California Inter Pocula*, vol. 38 of *The Works of Hubert Howe Bancroft* (New York: Harper and Brothers, 1891), 562.

60. Bancroft, "Crusade against Foreigners," 10.

61. Ibid., 26.

62. Bancroft, *Popular Tribunals*, vol. 2, 662.

63. Ibid., 668.

64. Ibid., 665.

65. This issue is most directly considered in an essay by Norton Moses, "Lynching: Attitudes as Predeterminants of Brutality" (unpublished essay, n.d.).

66. Undated article, quoted in Lela Rhodes Neill, "Episodes in the Early History of Shelby County" (master's thesis, Stephen F. Austin State University).

67. Levi Henderson Ashcraft, "Thrilling Scenes in Texas" (unpublished manuscript, n.d., ca. 1850s), Samuel E. Asbury Papers, East Texas Research Center, Stephen F. Austin State University, Nacogdoches, 5.

68. Ibid.

69. Ibid.

70. Thomas Dimsdale, *The Vigilantes of Montana or Popular Justice in the Rocky Mountains: Being a Correct and Impartial Narrative of the Chase, Trail, Capture, and Execution of Henry Plummer's Road Agent Band* (Norman: University of Oklahoma Press, 1953), 154.

71. The gruesome display of bodies did not originate with the vigilantes. Peter Silver documents the centrality of body displays in the context of eighteenth-century Indian wars: "Producing tableaus of devastation—like the scalped and cut-up . . . body left propped in a tree—was not incidental to such attacks, but one of their basic motives." *Our Savage Neighbors: How Indian War Transformed Early America* (New York: Norton, 2008), 42. Silver also documents the prevalence of "post-mortem abuse" in the period—a practice later common to lynching in the frontier and, as is well documented, in the South (58–59). The taking of body trophies was also drawn from an earlier period. For example, Jill Lepore writes, "From the earliest months of the war, mementos of the enemy, mainly body parts but also bits of clothing, had been cherished by Indians and colonists alike." *In the Name of War: King Philip's War and the Origins of American Identity* (New York: Vintage Books, 1999), 178; see also 173–175, 179–180. Though these perverse practices had clear origins, they were increasingly anachronistic and (presumably) disturbing given that by the early nineteenth century, even relatively tame public executions enacted by the state were less common. See Ann Fabian, *The Unvarnished Truth: Personal Narratives in Nineteenth-Century America* (Berkeley: University of California Press, 2000), 53.

72. Owen Hoge, "Life on the Early Frontier," *Republican-Boomerang*, June 1928, 8. There is a second, slightly different version of this account titled "Pioneer Recreates Life of Early Frontier," WPA file 1168, Wyoming State Historical Society, Helena.

73. Dimsdale, *Vigilantes of Montana*, 153–154.

74. This description of their execution comes from the stereographic image of the men's charred remains in James Allen, *Without Sanctuary: Lynching Photography in America* (Santa Fe, NM: Twin Palms, 2000), plates 69 and 70.

75. Brown, *Strain of Violence*, 155. In fact, the death mask and skin shoes remain on display to this day; they are currently held at the Carbon County Museum in Rawlins, Wyoming.

76. James Elbert Cutler, *Lynch-Law: An Investigation into the History of Lynching in the United States* (New York: Longman's, Green, 1905).

77. The note here is reproduced as it appeared in the January 11, 1868, *Cheyenne Leader* on the morning after the men were found. See also T. A. Larsen, *History of Wyoming* (Lincoln: University of Nebraska Press, 1978), 47.

78. Virginia Toole, *Vigilante Women* (South Brunswick, NJ: A. S. Barnes, 1966), 27. John "X" Beidler was soon to be an active member of the vigilance committee and often served as the group's executioner.

79. Ashcraft, "Thrilling Scenes in Texas," 5.

80. David Johnson, "Vigilance and the Law: The Moral Authority of Popular Justice in the Far West," *American Quarterly* 33, no. 5 (Winter 1981): 579.

81. Brown, *Strain of Violence*, 134–143; Christopher Waldrep, *The Many Faces of Judge Lynch: Extralegal Violence and Punishment in America* (New York: Palgrave, 2002).

82. The Montana committee hung twenty-nine men in the period from December 1863 to February 1864, executed one man by shooting, and banished a number of others. I have taken these numbers from Dimsdale's *Vigilantes of Montana*. In comparison, the San Francisco committee of 1856 hung two men, ostensibly drove one man to commit suicide, and banished

thirteen others (*Petaluma Argus*, January 14, 1856, as cited in Bancroft reference notes, BANC MSS 97/31 c, Bancroft Library, University of California, Berkeley, vol. 265, 8).

83. Foucault, "Tales of Murder," 205.

84. Turner, "Significance of the Frontier," 2, 15, 22, 24.

85. Ida B. Wells, *On Lynchings* (Salem: Ayer, 1987).

86. *Birth of a Nation*, directed by D. W. Griffith, Epoch Film, 1915; Thomas Dixon Jr., *The Clansmen: A Historical Romance of the Ku Klux Klan* (1905; repr., Lexington: University Press of Kentucky, 1970).

## CHAPTER 4

1. Wells married Ferdinand Barnett in 1895, after which she published under her married name, Wells-Barnett. In the interest of consistency, I use "Wells" throughout this chapter.

2. Wells describes these events in the first chapter of the October 1892 publication of the essay as the pamphlet "Southern Lynch Law in All Its Phases," republished in *On Lynchings* (Salem: Ayer, 1987).

3. Ida B. Wells, *Southern Horrors and Other Writings* (Boston: Bedford/St. Martin's, 1997), 52.

4. Ida B. Wells, "Lynching and the Excuse for It," *The Independent*, May 16, 1901.

5. Wells wrote *Southern Horrors* after three men were lynched in her hometown of Memphis, Tennessee—an incident widely known as "the lynching at the curve." Detailed accounts of the events leading up to the lynching and Wells's response can be found in Paula J. Giddings, *Ida, A Sword among Lions: Ida B. Wells and the Campaign against Lynching* (New York: HarperCollins, 2008); Mia Bay, *To Tell the Truth Freely: The Life of Ida B. Wells* (New York: Hill and Wang, 2009); James West Davidson, *"They Say": Ida B. Wells and the Reconstruction of Race* (New York: Oxford University Press, 2009); and Wells's autobiography, *Crusade for Justice: The Autobiography of Ida B. Wells*, ed. Alfreda Duster (Chicago: University of Chicago Press, 1970).

6. I use "web of relations" here in the Foucauldian sense and in the sense of the particular application of the term to lynching narratives that I describe in Chapter 1. See Michel Foucault, ed., *I, Pierre Rivière, Having Slaughtered My Mother, My Sister, and My Brother: A Case of Parricide in the 19th Century*, trans. Frank Jellinek (Lincoln: University of Nebraska Press, 1987).

7. See Linda McMurry, *To Keep the Waters Troubled: The Life of Ida B. Wells* (Oxford: Oxford University Press, 1998); Giddings, *Ida*; Davidson, *They Say*; and Bay, *To Tell the Truth*. Gail Bederman, *Manliness and Civilization: A Cultural History of Gender and Race in the United States, 1880–1917* (Chicago: University of Chicago Press, 1995), also includes an excellent chapter on the ideological context and impact of Wells's work.

8. Wells, *Crusade for Justice*, 64.

9. Davidson, *They Say*, 137.

10. Giddings, *Ida*, 88. Mia Bay further attributes Wells's ability and inclination to write the pamphlets to "her own experience with rumor and character defamation," both of which were crucial to the larger governing logic of racist lynching as it was legitimated by Victorian sexual and "scientific" ideologies (*To Tell the Truth*, 100, 98). See also Giddings, *Ida*, 207–208.

11. Wells, *Crusade for Justice*, 64.

12. Wells's campaign was by no means limited to a narrative context. She also deployed a "variety of economic pressure tactics" including a streetcar boycott and lending her support to the substantial out-migration to Oklahoma (Bederman, *Manliness and Civilization*, 55).

13. William McConnell, *Frontier Law: A Story of Vigilante Days* (Yonkers-on-Hudson: World Book, 1924), 115, 138.

14. Alexander Barde, *The Vigilante Committees of the Attakapas: An Eyewitness Account of Banditry and Backlash in Southwestern Louisiana* (Lafayette: Acadiana Press, 1981), 44, 105, 106, 249.

15. Thomas Dimsdale, *The Vigilantes of Montana or Popular Justice in the Rocky Mountains: Being a Correct and Impartial Narrative of the Chase, Trial, Capture, and Execution of Henry Plummer's Road Agent Band* (1866; repr., Norman: University of Oklahoma Press, 1953), 38, 93, 120.

16. For further evidence of the intricate relationships between and among vigilantes and vigilante committees, see Charles Summerfield, *Illustrated Lives of the Desperadoes of the New World* (Philadelphia: T. B. Peterson, 1849), 17; Anonymous, *The Banditti of the Rocky Mountains and Vigilance Committee in Idaho* (Minneapolis: Ross and Haines, 1964), 32, 66; Nathaniel Langford, *Vigilante Days and Ways* (Helena, MT: American and World Geographic, 1996), 255, 262; Asa Shinn Mercer, *The Banditti of the Plains, or the Cattlemen's Invasion of Wyoming in 1892 (The Crowning Infamy of the Ages)* (San Francisco: Grabhorn Press, 1935), 23, 25, 72, 105; Barde, *Vigilante Committees*, 44, 105, 106, 249; Almarin Paul, "The Sixty Day Rule in San Francisco of the Vigilance Committee of 1856, by an Eye-Witness Almarin Paul," North Baker Research Center, California Historical Society, San Francisco, 1, 22–23; Edward Bonney, *The Banditti of the Prairies or, The Murderer's Doom!! A Tale of the Mississippi Valley* (Norman: University of Oklahoma Press, 1963), xviii. There is also ample evidence of newspaper coverage of both local and remote vigilantism in the latter half of the nineteenth century. Press accounts, like those in the official histories, ranged from those that "glorified" vigilantism both locally and elsewhere, to more critical interpretations of "other" vigilantes in comparison to local committees.

17. Wells, *Crusade for Justice*, 65, 84; Giddings, *Ida*, 221, 223–226; Bay, *To Tell the Truth*, 101–103.

18. Giddings, *Ida*, 221.

19. Wells, "Lynching and the Excuse for It."

20. Bay, *To Tell the Truth*, 96.

21. Wells, *Southern Horrors*, 62.

22. Ibid.

23. Ibid.

24. Ibid.

25. Ibid., 63.

26. This is, in effect, the argument that James Elbert Cutler made in *Lynch-Law: An Investigation into the History of Lynching in the United States* (New York: Longman's, Green, 1905) and the reason I question the frequent citations of his work by antiracist scholars (see the Introduction, note 11).

27. Wells, *Southern Horrors*, 63.

28. Ibid., 64.

29. Ibid., 63.

30. Ibid., 64.

31. Ibid.

32. Wells, *A Red Record*, in *Southern Horrors*, 101–106.

33. Ibid., 117; emphasis added.

34. Ibid., 124.

35. Giddings, *Ida*, 183; Bederman, *Manliness and Civilization*, 50.

36. Wells, *A Red Record*, in *Southern Horrors*, 96.

37. Cited in Wells, *Southern Horrors*, 53.

38. Wells, *A Red Record*, in *Southern Horrors*, 153.

39. Ibid., 154.

40. Ibid.

41. Wells, *Southern Horrors*, 70.

42. Giddings, *Ida*, 189.

43. Wells, *Southern Horrors*, 53.

44. Ibid., 50.

45. Wells, *A Red Record*, in *Southern Horrors*, 78.

46. Ibid., 76.

47. Ibid., 78.

48. Bay, *To Tell the Truth*, 103.

49. Wells, *Southern Horrors*, 58.

50. Ibid., 61 (a slightly reworded version of this statement also appears on page 87 of *A Red Record*).

51. Wells, *A Red Record*, in *Southern Horrors*, 79.

52. Wells also challenged the veracity of the rape myth on the basis that "during all the years of slavery, no such charge was ever made, not even during the dark days of the rebellion, when the white man, following the fortunes of war went to do battle for the maintenance of slavery" (ibid.).

53. Wells, *Southern Horrors*, 61.

54. Ibid., 66.

55. Wells, *A Red Record*, in *Southern Horrors*, 77.

56. Wells, *Southern Horrors*, 65.

57. Henry Fisk Sanders, "Trial and Execution of George Ives," Montana Historical Society, MC53, Box 5, folder 2, 9.

58. Wells, *A Red Record*, in *Southern Horrors*, 80.

59. Giddings, *Ida*, 224. See also Bederman, *Manliness and Civilization*, 57; Bay, *To Tell the Truth*, 104. In addition to amplifying the fundamentally racist illogic of white male claims to chivalry, Wells was intent on halting the growing public perception that lynchers were exclusively men from the lower economic echelon. Citing an article from the *Appeal-Avalanche* in Memphis, Wells drew attention to "the personnel of the mob" wherein "men in all walks of life figured as leaders."

60. Wells, *A Red Record*, in *Southern Horrors*, 153.

61. Ibid., 93, 94, 99.

62. Ibid., 97.

63. Bederman, *Manliness and Civilization*, 52.

64. Wells, *Southern Horrors*, 68.

65. Ibid.

66. Ibid.

67. Ibid., 70.

68. Wells, *A Red Record*, in *Southern Horrors*, 136–138.

69. Ibid., 131–132.

70. Hubert Howe Bancroft, *Popular Tribunals*, vol. 2, vol. 37 of *The Works of Hubert Howe Bancroft* (San Francisco: History Company, 1887), 670–671.

71. Wells, *Southern Horrors*, 148–152.

72. Ibid., 66.

73. Giddings, *Ida*, 221.

74. Bay, *To Tell the Truth*, 317.

75. Bederman, *Manliness and Civilization*, 70. Even Christopher Waldrep, who argues that Wells "may have claimed too much" about her success in making white Americans think more critically about lynching and race, uses Wells's work in the 1890s to locate an essential shift in the centralization of race in narrative accounts of lynching; see *The Many Faces of Judge Lynch: Extralegal Violence and Punishment in America* (New York: Palgrave, 2002), 122.

76. Jonathan Markovitz, *Legacies of Lynching: Racial Violence and Memory* (Minneapolis: University of Minnesota Press, 2004), xxix.

## CONCLUSION

1. See also *Strange Fruit*, directed by Joel Katz, PBS/Independent Lens, 2002.

2. Keith cowrote the song with Scotty Emerick and performed it with Willie Nelson. In addition to the song, Keith starred in a 2008 film of the same title.

3. See http://www.tombstonevigilantes.com/shows.html (accessed February 10, 2012).

4. They take particular pride in their perfection of the Earp-Clanton gun battle—a battle, they are quick to point out, that did not actually transpire at the O.K. Corral. They compare the historical accuracy of their each and every dodge, gunshot, and fall to the less accurate reenactments of the "outsiders" who have arrived in Tombstone to work for the corporate-run O.K. Corral.

5. Bob Moser, "Open Season," *Intelligence Report*, no. 109 (Spring 2003): 4.

6. Anti-illegal immigration vigilante organizations sprang up along the Arizona border following federal crackdowns on the California and Texas borders. Increased border enforcement both east and west of Arizona shifted flows of would-be immigrants into this new and much more deadly desert terrain. One of the earliest and most widely publicized of these groups was founded in 1999 in Cochise County, Arizona, by Roger Barnett. He and his brother became more commonly known—in their vigilante guise—as "the Barnett Boys." For further information, see Rachel Ochoa "Vigilante Border Patrol Stays Active," *Hispanic* 13, no. 9 (2000): 16; Justin Akers Chacon and Mike Davis, *No One Is Illegal: Fighting Violence and State Repression on the U.S.-Mexico Border* (Chicago: Haymarket Books, 2006); and Susy Buchanan and David Holthouse, "Locked and Loaded," *The Nation* 283, no. 6 (2006): 29–32.

7. Paradoxically, after nearly a decade of vigilante organizing, Simcox has become widely known as a spokesperson for the far right and ran against John McCain in the 2010 Senate primary.

8. Moser, "Open Season," 4.

9. Ibid., 1.

10. See http://www.minutemanhq.com/hq/ (accessed February 10, 2012).

11. Bob Moser, "Vigilante Violence," *Intelligence Report*, no. 109 (Spring 2003): 1–4.

12. Ida B. Wells, "Lynching and the Excuse for It," *The Independent*, May 16, 1901, reprinted in Bettina Aptheker, ed., "Lynching and Rape: An Exchange of Views," Occasional Paper No. 25 (New York: American Institute for Marxist Studies, 1977).

13. James Allen, *Without Sanctuary: Lynching Photography in America* (Santa Fe, NM: Twin Palms, 2000), 33.

14. Patricia Williams, "Diary of a Mad Law Professor: Without Sanctuary," *The Nation*, February 14, 2000, 9.

15. Paula J. Giddings, *Ida, A Sword among Lions: Ida B. Wells and the Campaign against Lynching* (New York: HarperCollins, 2008), 7.

16. Mia Bay, *To Tell the Truth Freely: The Life of Ida B. Wells* (New York: Hill and Wang, 2009), 322.

17. Giddings, *Ida*, 7.

# Bibliography

"About Vigilantes." *Cheyenne Leader*, January 13, 1868.

Alderson, Matt. "X. Beidler: Evangelist to the Montana Road Agents." SC 115, Montana Historical Society, Helena.

Allen, Frederick. *A Decent Orderly Lynching: The Montana Vigilantes*. Norman: University of Oklahoma Press, 2004.

Allen, James. *Without Sanctuary: Lynching Photography in America*. Santa Fe, NM: Twin Palms, 2000.

Altrocchi, Julie Cooley. "Paradox Town: San Francisco in 1851." *California Historical Quarterly* 28, no. 1 (1949): 31–33.

Anonymous. *The Banditti of the Rocky Mountains and Vigilance Committee in Idaho*. 1865. Reprint, Minneapolis, MN: Ross and Haines, 1964.

Aptheker, Bettina, ed. "Lynching and Rape: An Exchange of Views." Occasional Paper No. 25, American Institute for Marxist Studies, 1977.

Arceneaux, William. *Acadian General: Alfred Mouton and the Civil War*. Lafayette: Center for Louisiana Studies, 1981.

Arrington, Alfred W. *The Rangers and the Regulators of the Tenaha; or, Life among the Lawless: A Tale of the Republic of Texas*. New York: Robert M. DeWitt, 1892.

Arrington, Leonard J. *History of Idaho*. Vol. 1. Moscow: University of Idaho Press, 1994.

Ashcraft, Levi Henderson. "Thrilling Scenes in Texas." Unpublished manuscript, n.d., ca. 1850s, Samuel E. Asbury Papers, East Texas Research Center, Stephen F. Austin State University, Nacogdoches.

Baldwin, Elmer. *History of La Salle County Illinois*. Chicago: Rand McNally, 1877.

Bancroft, Hubert Howe. *California Inter Pocula*. Vol. 35 of *The Works of Hubert Howe Bancroft*. New York: Harper and Brothers, 1891.

———. "Committees of Vigilance and Popular Tribunals." Chapter draft. Records of the Library and Publishing Companies, OS Box 19, folder 5, BANC MSS B-C 7, Bancroft Library, University of California, Berkeley.

————. "Crusade against Foreigners." Records of the Library and Publishing Companies, OS Box 16, folder 19, BANC MSS B-C 7, Bancroft Library, University of California, Berkeley.

————. "The Fruits of Vigilance." In *Popular Tribunals*, vol.2. Vol. 37 of *The Works of Hubert Howe Bancroft*. San Francisco: History Company, 1887.

————. *Literary Industries*. Vol. 39 of *The Works of Hubert Howe Bancroft*. New York: Harper and Brothers, 1891.

————. *The Native Races*, vol. 1. Vol. 1 of *The Works of Hubert Howe Bancroft*. San Francisco: History Company, 1887.

————. *Popular Tribunals*, vols. 1 and 2. Vols. 36 and 37 of *The Works of Hubert Howe Bancroft*. San Francisco: History Company, 1887.

————. "Vigilance in Northern California." Records of the Library and Publishing Companies, BANC MSS B-C 7, Bancroft Library, University of California, Berkeley.

Bancroft reference notes. BANC MSS 97/31, Bancroft Library, University of California, Berkeley.

Barde, Alexander. *Historie des comites de vigilance aux Attakapas*. Shreveport: Centenary College of Louisiana Press, 2007.

————. *The Vigilante Committees of the Attakapas: An Eyewitness Account of Banditry and Backlash in Southwestern Louisiana*. Lafayette: Acadiana Press, 1981.

Barnes, James. "A Review of *A Venture in History*: The Production, Publication, and Sale of the Works of Hubert Howe Bancroft." *History and Theory* 15, no. 2 (1976): 212–225.

Baum, Willa Klung. "Oral History: A Revived Tradition at the Bancroft Library." *Pacific Northwest Quarterly* 58, no. 2 (1967): 57–64.

Bay, Mia. *To Tell the Truth Freely: The Life of Ida B. Wells*. New York: Hill and Wang, 2009.

Beck, Bernd, and Timothy Clark. "Strangers, Community Miscreants, or Locals." *Historical Methods* 35, no. 2 (2002): 77–83.

Bederman, Gail. *Manliness and Civilization: A Cultural History of Gender and Race in the United States, 1880–1917*. Chicago: University of Chicago Press, 1995.

Berg, Manfred. *Popular Justice: A History of Lynching in America*. Chicago: Rowman and Littlefield, 2011.

Berglund, Barbara. *Making San Francisco American: Cultural Frontiers in the Urban West, 1846–1906*. Lawrence: University of Kansas Press, 2010.

*Birth of a Nation*. DVD. Directed by D. W. Griffith. Epoch Film, 1915.

Boessenecker, John. *Gold Dust and Gunsmoke: Tales of Gold Rush Outlaws, Gunfighters, Lawmen, and Vigilantes*. New York: Wiley and Sons, 1999.

Bolino, August. "The Role of Mining in the Economic Development of Idaho Territory." *Oregon Historical Quarterly* 59, no. 2 (1958): 132–133.

Bonney, Edward. *The Banditti of the Prairies or, The Murderer's Doom!! A Tale of the Mississippi Valley*. Norman: University of Oklahoma Press, 1963.

Border, Gary B. *A Hanging in Nacogdoches: Murder, Race, Politics, and Polemics in Texas's Oldest Town, 1870–1916*. Austin: University of Texas Press, 2006.

Brown, Richard Maxwell. *The South Carolina Regulators*. Cambridge: Belknap, 1963.

————. *Strain of Violence: Historical Studies of American Violence and Vigilantism*. Oxford: Oxford University Press, 1975.

Brundage, W. Fitzhugh. *Lynching in the New South: Georgia and Virginia, 1180–1930*. Urbana: University of Illinois Press, 1993.

————, ed. *Under Sentence of Death: Lynching in the New South.* Chapel Hill: University of North Carolina Press, 1997.

Buchanan, Susy, and David Holthouse. "Locked and Loaded." *The Nation* 283, no. 6 (2006): 29–32.

Burns, Thomas. "Letter to Committee June 17, 1851." Box 1, folder 23, Records of the Library and Publishing Companies, Bancroft Library, University of California, Berkeley.

Burton, Antoinette. "Thinking beyond the Boundaries: Empire, Feminism, and the Domains of History." *Social History* 26, no. 1. (2001): 60–71.

California Biographical Manuscripts collection. C-D Reel 21, ms 179–Reel 24, ms 203, Bancroft Library, University of California, Berkeley.

Callaway, Lew. *Montana's Righteous Hangmen: The Vigilantes in Action.* Norman: University of Oklahoma Press, 1997.

Carr, Cynthia. *Our Town: A Heartland Lynching, a Haunted Town, and the Hidden History of White America.* New York: Crown, 2006.

Carrigan, William. *The Making of a Lynching Culture: Violence and Vigilantism in Central Texas, 1836–1916.* Urbana: University of Illinois Press, 2004.

Carrigan, William, and Clive Webb. "The Lynching of Persons of Mexican Origin or Descent in the United States, 1848 to 1982." *Journal of Social History* 37, no. 2 (2003): 411–438.

Caughey, John William. *Hubert Howe Bancroft: Historian of the West.* Berkeley: University of California Press, 1946.

Chacon, Justin Akers, and Mike Davis. *No One is Illegal: Fighting Violence and State Repression on the U.S.-Mexico Border.* Chicago: Haymarket Books, 2006.

Clark, Harry. *A Venture in History: The Production, Publication, and Sale of the Works of Hubert Howe Bancroft.* Berkeley: University of California Press, 1973.

Cole, Richard Beverly. "Volume 264, Vigilance Committee, 1856—San Francisco." Bancroft reference notes, BANC MSS 97/31, Bancroft Library, University of California, Berkeley.

Cole, Timothy. *The Forest City Lynching of 1900: Populism, Racism, and White Supremacy in Rutherford County, North Carolina.* Jefferson, NC: McFarland, 2003.

Coutant, Charles. "Laramie Co." Coutant Collection, "Wyoming—Early Settlement, 1867–ca. 1904," Box 8, folder 85, Wyoming State Historical Society, Cheyenne.

————. Untitled manuscript. Coutant Collection, "Wyoming—Early Settlement, 1867–ca. 1904," Box 8, folder 86, Wyoming State Historical Society, Cheyenne.

Curtis, Kent. "Producing a Gold Rush: National Ambitions and the Northern Rocky Mountains, 1853–1863." *Western Historical Quarterly* 40, no. 3 (2009): 275–297.

Cutler, James Elbert. *Lynch-Law: An Investigation into the History of Lynching in the United States.* New York: Longman's, Green, 1905.

Daggett, Eph. "Recollections of the War of the Moderators and Regulators." Shelby County Texas Collection, Briscoe Center for American History, University of Texas, Austin.

Daniels, Margie. *History of Benton, Washington, Carroll, Madison, Crawford, Franklin, and Sebastian Counties, Arkansas.* Chicago: Goodspeed, 1889.

Davidson, James West. *"They Say": Ida B. Wells and the Reconstruction of Race.* New York: Oxford University Press, 2009.

Davidson, Stanley, and Dale Tash. "Confederate Backwash in Montana Territory." *Montana: The Magazine of Western History* 17, no. 4 (1967): 50–58.

Davis, John W. *Goodbye, Judge Lynch: The End of a Lawless Era in Wyoming's Big Horn Basin*. Norman: University of Oklahoma Press, 2005.

Davis, Mike. "'What Is a Vigilante Man?' White Violence in California History." In *No One Is Illegal: Fighting Violence and State Repression on the U.S.-Mexico Border*, edited by Justin Akers Chacón and Mike Davis, 11–88. Chicago: Haymarket Books, 2006.

Dempster, Clancey John. "The Vigilance Committee of 1856." California Biographical Manuscripts, C-D, Reel 22, 184, Bancroft Library, University of California, Berkeley.

Dimsdale, Thomas. *The Vigilantes of Montana or Popular Justice in the Rocky Mountains: Being a Correct and Impartial Narrative of the Chase, Trail, Capture, and Execution of Henry Plummer's Road Agent Band*. 1866. Reprint, Norman: University of Oklahoma Press, 1953.

Dixon, Thomas, Jr. *The Clansmen: A Historical Romance of the Ku Klux Klan*. 1905. Reprint, Lexington: University Press of Kentucky, 1970.

Eaton, James Winton. "The Wyoming Stock Growers' Association's Treatment of Nonmember Cattlemen during the 1880's." *Agricultural History* 58, no. 1 (1984): 70–80.

Fabian, Ann. *The Unvarnished Truth: Personal Narratives in Nineteenth-Century America*. Berkeley: University of California Press, 2000.

Fedo, Michael. *The Lynchings in Duluth*. St. Paul: Minnesota Historical Society, 2000.

———. *Trial by Mob*. Duluth, MN: Norshor, 1993.

Fisher Fishkin, Shelly, ed. *Historical Guide to Mark Twain*. New York: Oxford University Press, 2002.

Foster, Craig. "Myth v. Reality in the Burt Murder and Harvey Lynching." *Journal of the West* 43, no. 4 (2004): 49–57.

Foucault, Michel. *Discipline and Punish: The Birth of the Prison*. Translated by Alan Sheridan. New York: Vintage Books, 1995.

———. *I, Pierre Rivière, Having Slaughtered My Mother, My Sister, and My Brother: A Case of Parricide in the 19th Century*. Translated by Frank Jellinek. Lincoln: University of Nebraska Press, 1987.

———. "Tales of Murder." In *I, Pierre Rivière, Having Slaughtered My Mother, My Sister, and My Brother: A Case of Parricide in the 19th Century*, translated by Frank Jellinek, 199–211. Lincoln: University of Nebraska Press, 1987.

Friedman, Lawrence. *A History of American Law*. New York: Simon and Schuster, 1985.

Gard, Wayne. *Frontier Justice*. Norman: University of Oklahoma Press, 1949.

Giddings, Paula J. *Ida, A Sword among Lions: Ida B. Wells and the Campaign against Lynching*. New York: HarperCollins, 2008.

Ginzburg, Ralph. *100 Years of Lynching*. 1962. Reprint, Baltimore: Black Classic Press, 1988.

Goldsby, Jacqueline. *A Spectacular Secret: Lynching in American Life and Literature*. Chicago: University of Chicago Press, 2006.

Gonzalez-Day, Ken. *Lynching in the West, 1850–1935*. Durham, NC: Duke University Press, 2006.

Gould, C. Lewis. *Wyoming, from Territory to Statehood*. Worland, WY: High Plains, 1989.

Griffin, Harry Lewis. *The Attakapas Country: A History of Lafayette Parish, Louisiana*. Gretna, LA: Firebird, 1999.

Grimsted, David. "Making Violence Relevant." *Reviews in American History* 4, no. 3 (1976): 331–338.

Gumbrecht, Hans Ulrich. *In 1926: Living at the Edge of Time*. Cambridge, MA: Harvard University Press, 1997.

Gunning, Sandra. *Race, Rape, and Lynching: The Red Record of American Literature, 1890–1912*. New York: Oxford University Press, 1996.

Gutierréz, Ramón, and Richard Orsi, eds. *Contested Eden: California before the Gold Rush*. Berkeley: University of California Press, 1998.

Hall, Jacqueline Dowd. *Revolt against Chivalry: Jessie Daniel Ames and the Women's Campaign against Lynching*. New York: Columbia University Press, 1993.

Halttunen, Karen. *Confidence Men and Painted Women: A Study of Middle Class Culture in America, 1830–1870*. New Haven, CT: Yale University Press, 1982.

Harper, Kimberly. *White Man's Heaven: The Lynching and Expulsion of Blacks in the Southern Ozarks, 1894–1909*. Fayetteville: University of Arkansas Press, 2010.

Hittell, John S. *A History of San Francisco and Incidentally of the State of California; and, A Guidebook to San Francisco*. San Francisco: Bancroft, 1878.

Hoffman, Birney. "Vigilante." *Saturday Evening Post*, February 23, 1929, 3–5, 86, 88, 89, 92; March 2, 1929, 33, 35, 107, 108, 111; March 9, 1929, 24, 25, 149, 150, 152, 154; March 16, 1929, 20, 21, 65, 66, 69; March 23, 1929, 37, 40, 110, 114, 119.

———. *Vigilantes: A Chronicle of the Rise and Fall of the Plummer Gang of Outlaws in and about Virginia City Montana in the Early '60's*. New York: Grosset and Dunlap, 1929.

Hoge, Owen. "Bringing the Law to Laramie City." WPA file 854, Wyoming State Historical Society, Helena.

———. "Life on the Early Frontier." *Republican-Boomerang*, June 1928.

———. "Pioneer Recreates Life of Early Frontier," WPA file 1168, Wyoming State Historical Society, Helena.

Hufsmith, George. *The Wyoming Lynching of Cattle Kate 1889*. Glendo, WY: High Plains Press, 1993.

Jackson, W. Turrentine. "The Wyoming Stock Growers' Association: Its Years of Temporary Decline, 1886–1890." *Agricultural History* 22, no. 4 (1948): 260–270.

———. "The Wyoming Stock Growers' Association Political Power in Wyoming Territory, 1873–1890." *Mississippi Valley Historical Review* 33, no. 4 (1947): 571–594.

Johnson, David. "Vigilance and the Law: The Moral Authority of Popular Justice in the Far West." *American Quarterly* 33, no. 5 (1981): 558–586.

Johnson, Susan Lee. *Roaring Camp: The Social World of the California Gold Rush*. New York: W. W. Norton, 2000.

Jolly, Michelle. "The Price of Vigilance: Gender, Politics, and the Press in Early San Francisco." *Pacific Historical Review* 73, no. 4 (2004): 541–579.

Jordon, Philip. Introduction to *The Banditti of the Prairies or, The Murderer's Doom!! A Tale of the Mississippi Valley*, by Edward Bonney, vii–xxi. Norman: University of Oklahoma Press, 1963.

Jordon, Terry. "Population Origins in Texas, 1850." *Geographical Review* 59, no. 1 (1969): 87.

Kars, Marjoleine. *Breaking Loose Together: The Regulator Rebellion in Pre-Revolutionary North Carolina*. Chapel Hill: University of North Carolina, 2002.

Langford, Nathaniel. *Vigilante Days and Ways*. Helena, MT: American and World Geographic, 1996.

"The Laramie Outbreak." *Cheyenne Leader*, October 20, 1868.

Larsen, T. A. *History of Wyoming*. Lincoln: University of Nebraska Press, 1978.

Lepore, Jill. *In the Name of War: King Philip's War and the Origins of American Identity*. New York: Vintage Books, 1999.

Linderman, Frank Bird. *Henry Plummer: A Novel*. Lincoln: University of Nebraska Press, 2000.

"Louisiana." *Daily Delta*, September 13, 1859.

Madison, James H. *A Lynching in the Heartland: Race and Memory in America*. New York: Palgrave, 2001.

Manrow, John P. "Statement . . . on Vigilance Committees in San Francisco, 1878." California Biographical Manuscripts, C-D, Reel 23, 192, Bancroft Library, University of California, Berkeley.

Markovitz, Jonathan. *Legacies of Lynching: Racial Violence and Memory*. Minneapolis: University of Minnesota Press, 2004.

Mather, R. E., and F. E. Boswell. "Alder Gulch Mines: The Story of George Ives." In *Gold Camp Desperadoes: Violence, Crime, and Punishment on the Mining Frontier*, 123–152. Norman: University of Oklahoma Press, 1993.

———. *The Bannack Gallows*. Oklahoma City, OK: History West, 1998.

———. *Hanging the Sheriff: A Biography of Henry Plummer*. Missoula: Historical Montana, 1998.

———. *Vigilante Victims: Montana's 1864 Hanging Spree*. San Jose: History West, 1991.

McConnell, William. *Frontier Law: A Story of Vigilante Days*. Yonkers-on-Hudson: World Book, 1924.

McKanna, Claire V. "Enclaves of Violence in Nineteenth-Century California." *Pacific Historical Review* 73, no. 3 (2004): 391–423.

McMurry, Linda. *To Keep the Waters Troubled: The Life of Ida B. Wells*. Oxford: Oxford University Press, 1998.

Mercer, Asa Shinn. *The Banditti of the Plains, or the Cattlemen's Invasion of Wyoming in 1892 (The Crowning Infamy of the Ages)*. San Francisco: Grabhorn Press, 1935.

Middleton, John. *History of the Regulators and Moderators and the Shelby County War in 1841 and 1842 in the Republic of Texas*. 1883. Reprint, Fort Worth: Loving Publishing Company, 1983.

Moser, Bob. "Open Season." *Intelligence Report*, no. 109 (Spring 2003): 1–4.

———. "Vigilante Violence." *Intelligence Report*, no. 109 (Spring 2003): 1–4.

Moses, Norton. "Lynching: Attitudes as Predeterminants of Brutality." Unpublished manuscript in possession of the author, n.d.

———. *Lynching and Vigilantism in the United States: An Annotated Bibliography*. Westport, CT: Greenwood, 1997.

Neill, Lela Rhodes. "Episodes in the Early History of Shelby County." Master's thesis, Stephen F. Austin State University, 1950.

Newman, Paul Douglas. *Fries's Rebellion: The Enduring Struggle for the American Revolution*. Philadelphia: University of Pennsylvania, 2005.

Oak, Henry Lebbeus. *"Literary Industries" in a New Light*. San Francisco: Bacon Printing, 1893.

O'Byrne, Michael Cyprian. *History of La Salle County Illinois*. Chicago: Lewis, 1924.

Ochoa, Rachel. "Vigilante Border Patrol Stays Active." *Hispanic* 13, no. 9 (2000): 16.

O'Neil, Bill. *War in East Texas: Regulators and Moderators.* Nacogdoches: East Texas Historical Association, n.d.

Paul, Almarin. "The Sixty Day Rule in San Francisco of the Vigilance Committee of 1856, by an Eye-Witness, Almarin Paul." North Baker Research Center, California Historical Society, San Francisco.

*Petaluna Argus,* January 14, 1856. Bancroft reference notes, BANC MSS 97/31 c, vol. 265, 8, Bancroft Library, University of California, Berkeley.

Pfeifer, Michael. *The Roots of Rough Justice: Origins of American Lynching.* Urbana: University of Illinois Press, 2011.

―――. *Rough Justice: Lynching and American Society 1874–1947.* Urbana: University of Illinois Press, 2004.

Prassel, Frank. *The Great American Outlaw: A Legacy of Fact and Fiction.* Norman: University of Oklahoma Press, 1993.

Richards, Leonard L. *Shays's Rebellion: The American Revolution's Final Battle.* Philadelphia: University of Pennsylvania, 2003.

Robert, Geoffrey, ed. *The History and Narrative Reader.* London: Routledge, 2001.

Robinson, Forrest G. "Mark Twain 1835–1910: A Brief Biography" In *Historical Guide to Mark Twain,* edited by Shelly Fisher Fishkin, 13–51. New York: Oxford University Press, 2002.

Rosenzweig, Roy, and David Thelen. *The Presence of the Past: Popular Uses of History of Lynching in the United States.* New York: Columbia University Press, 1998.

Russell, Sarah. "Ethnicity, Commerce, and Community on Lower Louisiana's Plantation Frontier, 1803–1828." *Louisiana History: The Journal of the Louisiana Historical Association* 40, no. 4 (1999): 389–405.

―――. "Intermarriage and Intermingling: Constructing the Planter Class in Louisiana's Sugar Parishes, 1803–1850." *Louisiana History: The Journal of the Louisiana Historical Association* 46, no. 4 (2005): 407–434.

San Francisco Committee of Vigilance of 1851 Papers, 1851–1852. BANC MSS C-A 77, Bancroft Library, University of California, Berkeley.

San Francisco Committee of Vigilance of 1856 Papers, 1856. BANC MSS C-A 78, Bancroft Library, University of California, Berkeley.

Sanders, Helen Fitzgerald. *X Beidler: Vigilante.* Norman: University of Oklahoma Press, 1957.

Sanders, Henry Fisk. "Early Judiciary of Montana." MC53, Box 5, folder 3, Montana Historical Society, Helena.

―――. "Organization of the Vigilance Committee." MC53, Box 5, folder 1, Montana Historical Society, Helena.

―――. "Trial and Execution of George Ives." MC53, Box 5, folder 2, Montana Historical Society, Helena.

Schwantes, Carlos. *In Mountain Shadows: A History of Idaho.* Lincoln: University of Nebraska Press, 1991.

Senkewicz, Robert M. *Vigilantes in Gold Rush San Francisco.* Palo Alto, CA: Stanford University Press, 1985.

Silver, Peter. *Our Savage Neighbors: How Indian War Transformed Early America.* New York: Norton and Co., 2008.

"A Sketch of the Panic of Eastern Texas, during the Month of April, 1836." Ragout Collection, Briscoe Center for American History, University of Texas, Austin.

Slaughter, Thomas. *The Whiskey Rebellion: Frontier Epilogue to the American Revolution.* Oxford: Oxford University Press, 1988.

Slotkin, Richard. *The Fatal Environment: The Myth of the Frontier in the Age of Industrialization, 1800–1890.* 1985. Reprint, Norman: University of Oklahoma Press, 1994.

———. *Gunfighter Nation: The Myth of the Frontier in the Twentieth-Century American.* Norman: University of Oklahoma Press, 1998.

———. *Regeneration through Violence: The Mythology of the American Frontier, 1600–1860.* Norman: University of Oklahoma Press, 2000.

Smith, Helena Huntington. *The War on the Power River: The History of an Insurrection.* Lincoln: University of Nebraska Press, 1966.

Smith, Tom. *Crescent City Lynchings: The Murder of Chief Hennessy, the New Orleans "Mafia" Trials, and the Parish Prison Mob.* New York: Lyons Press, 2007.

Smith-Rosenberg, Carroll. "Rebellious Dandies and Political Fictions." In *This Violent Empire: The Birth of an American National Identity*, 88–135. Chapel Hill: University of North Carolina Press, 2010.

Sonnichsen, C. L. *Ten Texas Feuds.* Albuquerque: University of New Mexico Press, 1957.

Sontag, Susan. *Regarding the Pain of Others.* New York: Picadour, 2003.

Spiegel, Gabrielle. "The Task of the Historian." Address delivered at the 123rd Annual Meeting of the American Historical Association, 2009, New York. Available at http://historians.org/info/AHA_History/spiegel.cfm.

Standish, John K. "Captain James Williams Was Fearless Leader of Montana Vigilantes; No Mention Made of Activities by Early Historians." Unpublished manuscript. Montana Historical Society, Helena.

*Strange Fruit.* VHS. Directed by Joel Katz. PBS/Independent Lens, 2002.

Streeby, Shelly. *American Sensations: Class, Empire, and the Production of Popular Culture.* Berkeley: University of California Press, 2002.

Summerfield, Charles. *Illustrated Lives of the Desperadoes of the New World: Containing an Account of the Different Modes of Lynching; the Cane Hill Murders; the Victims; the Execution; the Justification, etc. . . .* Philadelphia: T. B. Peterson, 1849.

———. *The Rangers and the Regulators of the Tenaha; or, Life among the Lawless: A Tale of the Republic of Texas.* New York: Robert M. De Witt, 1856.

Tell, David. "The 'Shocking Story' of Emmett Till and the Politics of Public Confession." *Quarterly Journal of Speech* 94, no. 2 (2008): 156–178.

Thomas, Benjamin. "The Historical Geography of Idaho Counties." *Oregon Historical Quarterly* 50, no. 3 (1949): 186.

Tolnay, Stewart, and E. M. Beck. *A Festival of Violence: An Analysis of Southern Lynchings, 1882–1930.* Urbana: University of Illinois Press, 1995.

Toole, Virginia. *Vigilante Women.* South Brunswick, NJ: A. S. Barnes, 1966.

Trouillot, Michel-Rolph. *Silencing the Past: Power and the Production of History.* Boston: Beacon, 1995.

Turner, Frederick Jackson. "The Significance of the Frontier in American History." In *The Frontier in American History*, 1–38. New York: Henry Holt, 1920.

Twain, Mark. "Letter to Hezekiah Hosmer, 15 September 1870." Hezekiah L. Hosmer Papers, SC 104, Montana Historical Society Archives, Helena.

———. *Roughing It.* 1872. Reprint, New York: Penguin Books, 1980.

———. *Roughing It.* Berkeley: University of California Press, 1993.

———. "The United States of Lyncherdom." In *Huck Finn; Pudd'nhead Wilson; No. 44; The Mysterious Stranger; and Other Writings*. New York: Penguin Putnam, 2000.

"Vigilantes Again—Two Men Hung." *Cheyenne Leader*, March 21, 1868.

Voorhies, Jacqueline. "The Attakapas Post: The First Acadian Settlement." *Louisiana History: The Journal of the Louisiana Historical Association* 17, no. 1 (1976): 91–96.

Wald, Patricia. *Constituting Americans: Cultural Anxiety and Narrative Form*. Durham, NC: Duke University Press, 1995.

Waldrep, Christopher. *Lynching in America: A History in Documents*. New York: New York University Press, 2006.

———. *The Many Faces of Judge Lynch: Extralegal Violence and Punishment in America*. New York: Palgrave, 2002.

Walton, Brian. "The Second Party System in Arkansas, 1836–1848." *Arkansas Historical Quarterly* 28, no. 2 (1969): 120–155.

Wells, Ida B. *Crusade for Justice: The Autobiography of Ida B. Wells*. Edited by Alfreda Duster. Chicago: University of Chicago Press, 1970.

———. "Lynching and the Excuse for It." *The Independent*, May 16, 1901.

———. *On Lynchings*. Manchester: Ayers, 1987.

———. *Southern Horrors and Other Writings: The Anti-Lynching Campaign of Ida B. Wells, 1892–1900*. Boston: Bedford/St. Martin's, 1997.

White, Hayden. *The Content of the Form: Narrative Discourse and Historical Imagination*. Baltimore: Johns Hopkins University Press, 1987.

———. *Figural Realism: Studies in the Mimesis Effect*. Baltimore: Johns Hopkins University Press, 1999.

———. *Metahistory: The Historical Imagination in Nineteenth-Century Europe*. Baltimore: Johns Hopkins University Press, 1973.

———. "The Question of Narrative in Contemporary Historical Theory." In *The Content of the Form: Narrative Discourse and Historical Representation*, 26–57. Baltimore: Johns Hopkins University Press, 1987.

———. *Tropics of Discourse: Essays in Cultural Criticism*. Baltimore: Johns Hopkins University Press, 1978.

White, Richard. "The Gold Rush: Consequences and Contingencies." *California History*, Spring 1998, 44.

Wiegman, Robyn. "The Anatomy of Lynching." In *American Anatomies: Theorizing Race and Gender*, 81–114. Durham, NC: Duke University Press, 1995.

Williams, Patricia. "Diary of a Mad Law Professor: Without Sanctuary." *The Nation*, February 14, 2000, 9.

Williams, Yohuru. "Anatomy of an Untruth: The Controversy of 'Picnic' and the True Cause of Lynching." *Black History Bulletin* 65/66, no. 4 (2002/2003): 1–4, 9–10.

———. "Permission to Hate: Delaware, Lynching, and the Culture of Violence in America." *Journal of Black Studies* 32, no. 1 (2001): 3–29.

Worley, Ted R. "The Story of Alfred W. Arrington." *Arkansas Historical Quarterly* 14, no. 1 (1955): 320–323.

# Index

**Lisa Arellano** is Assistant Professor of American Studies and Assistant Professor and Director of Women's, Gender and Sexuality Studies at Colby College.